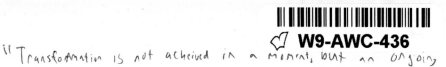
"Transformation is not acheived in a moment, but an ongoing relationship"

Taking It
to the Streets

p.62 ~ Spiritual Journey Model

A.R.T Model

64 ~ Possibilities & Limits of Arts

Taking It to the Streets

Using the Arts to Transform Your Community

J. Nathan Corbitt
and
Vivian Nix-Early

Baker Books

A Division of Baker Book House Co
Grand Rapids, Michigan 49516

Published by Baker Books
a division of Baker Book House Company
P.O. Box 6287, Grand Rapids, MI 49516-6287
www.bakerbooks.com

Printed in the United States of America

Library of Congress Cataloging-in-Publication Data
Corbitt, J. Nathan.
    Taking it to the streets : using the arts to transform your community / J. Nathan Corbitt and Vivian Nix-Early.
        p.   cm.
    Includes bibliographical references (p.   ).
    ISBN 0-8010-6422-8 (pbk.)
    1. City churches—United States. 2. Christianity and the arts—United States. I. Nix-Early, Vivian. II. Title.
BV637.C67 2003
246—dc21   2003010478

This book is dedicated to special members of our families:

To Nathan's mother, Gretchen E. Corbitt, associate pastor in the mountains of North Carolina before there was a debate about women in ministry, church organist and piano teacher, public school music teacher, children's community theater director, and international traveler, all while raising four children and being a pastor's wife. An agape and compassionate artist, she has been a spiritual mentor and professional encourager for fifty-two years. As incredible as it may seem, she has never spoken a negative word about anyone.

To Vivian's dad, Andrew W. Nix Jr., who has stuck it out in the hyperghetto, living and doing business incarnationally, leading his church and his community in fostering economic development and justice before it was popular to do so. He insisted on his children's involvement in the arts. He has shown her the way.

And to Dr. Verolga Nix, Vivian's aunt, who, with her genuine and loving heart and her own incredible musical talent, has uncovered and encouraged the musical gifts of so many young people in the public schools of Philadelphia. An agape artist of extraordinary standard, she has given hope, vision, confidence, and a future to those whom she has touched.

Contents

Structure

Vision

Practical Stories

Foreword

When I learned that a group of nuns in Haiti who had received a quarter-million-dollar grant would use the money to sponsor and develop a symphony orchestra in the capital city of Port au Prince, I was somewhat shocked. When I considered the incredible poverty of this poorest of all nations in the Western Hemisphere, and when I thought about the massive malnutrition that plagues the children of the capital, I instantaneously concluded that the money would have been better spent on things other than music. That was before I saw the symphony orchestra perform in an outdoors sports stadium.

The orchestra played before tens of thousands of the city's poorest of the poor. As I watched the impoverished populace react to the music, saw the ecstasy and pride in their faces, and saw the sense of dignity that the music generated among these people, I realized the nuns had done the right thing. When Jesus said "Man does not live on bread alone," he was reminding us that spiritual hunger can transcend physical hunger. And on that hot evening in that Caribbean island nation, I saw the poor people of Haiti receive food for their souls. Of course, they would be hungry in the morning, and their cries for economic justice would grow even louder, but the music of the previous evening had given some of them the nurturing they needed to press on in their struggle against the principalities and powers that challenged their right to aesthetic gratification as well as their right to economic well-being.

In his book *One-Dimensional Man,* Herbert Marcuse, the onetime neo-Marxist philosopher from the Frankfurt School and the University of San Diego, powerfully stated that art is revolutionary in its character: "It reminds us of what is not—and thus makes us discontent with what is."[1] Art lifts us out of the mundane and reminds us of the deeper longings of our hearts and souls that are left unfulfilled in the existential political order. Art stimulates our longing for the world we dream of but have not yet realized. It lifts our eyes and gives us a glimpse of the "heavenly city," where humanity is no longer alienated and intimate love is realized. In this sense, art helps us to carry out a prophetic ministry.

The best critiques of contemporary culture are to be found in the poetry and plays created by great artists, not in the statistical analysis of sociologists. That is why as a sociology professor I have always urged my students to take courses in drama and poetry. Plays such as *Death of a Salesman* by Arthur Miller and poems such as *The Wasteland* by T. S. Eliot expose the shallowness and emptiness of the lives of consumeristic, secularised Americans in ways that social scientists cannot. A careful study of Pablo Picasso's *Guernica* leads us into the subjective side of warfare and exposes the horrors, dislocations, and spiritual chaos of war in a way that historians can't begin to convey.

Works of art stir us to act and to change the way things are into the way things ought to be. Who can deny that the paintings of Diego Rivera provided major impulses for the Mexican Revolution, and who can question that the music of Bob Dylan, Joan Baez, and Tom Paxton provided the impulse for the powerful social movements of the 1960s?

This is not to say that the social sciences and the arts do not intersect. In reality, social scientists have often turned to the arts to gain insights for their sociological investigations. Perhaps no sociologist in the twentieth century exemplified this more than Pitcairn Sorokin, the onetime Harvard sociologist whose book *Social and Cultural Dynamics* paved the way for understanding how sociologists could use art to understand societal systems. Sorokin realized that while empirical analysis can provide an understanding of a society's values and practices, the arts can give us a taste of what is to come. The arts "feel out" the future and give expression to it long before objective analysis can provide any discernment.

Taking It to the Streets explores the prophetic dimension of the arts, especially as artists express themselves in the modern urban setting while fulfilling a special commitment to the poor and socially disinherited. The authors of this book show us how the arts can enable us to hear the cries of the oppressed as God would have us hear them, so that we might respond to these cries with works of justice.

The arts have long been a part of Christian worship. Even the most philistine of Christians recognize that. The sound of choirs, singing the great cantatas that generate awe and wonder in listeners, has been a part of Christendom since the Middle Ages. A sense of joyful transcendence has always found expression in hymns of praise. We all know that the psalmist of old called us to use musical instruments and dance to express our gratitude to God and to praise the holy name of the Creator of the universe. When Romans 8:26 tells us that there are groanings of the heart that we cannot put into words, there is a hint that the arts may be the closest thing to prayer, because the arts give expression to that which cannot be articulated in prosaic terms.

For a long time it was difficult for me to get into dance. But first with ballet and later with modern dance, I came to sense the glory of God being expressed in the rhythmic flows and movements of the human body. Dancing enables a spiritual energy to flow through the human body in movements that speak to the heart and soul of God. In artistic dance a rhythm—like the Tao of ancient

China—flows in and through all things, returning to the Divine in beautiful expressions that give us a taste of the aesthetic experiences that await us in a place beyond time and space.

I am prone to write off anything that I don't understand as not being art, and I ought to know better. For instance, I don't understand modern praise music. I have sarcastically said that if I get to heaven and I find they have an overhead projector with the words of hymns flashed on a screen, I'm checking out. In sermons I have jokingly contended that the difference between modern praise music and a machine gun is that a machine gun only has a hundred rounds. One of my friends has said that modern praise music has three notes, four words, and two hours. But such anecdotes say more about my own inability to grasp what's going on than about the value of the music.

At my own school, Eastern University, where the authors of this book serve as faculty members, we have a weekly chapel service at which attendance is voluntary. An overwhelming proportion of the student body shows up nevertheless, not so much to hear the speakers as to participate in singing praise music. Many of the students think I am somewhat of a spiritual person because I do not stand while they are standing during the singing time. Instead, I sit with my head in my hand, eyes closed. They think I'm praying. In reality, I'm trying to get the strength to endure the music. However, in those times that I have turned and looked over my shoulder, I have seen on the faces of the students all the signs of bliss that go along with a heavenly theophany. So many of them have their eyes closed and their hands lifted up toward heaven as they sing simple phrases such as "Shine, Jesus, Shine" over and over again. I don't get it, but Bob Dylan has rightfully said to old fogies like me, "Don't criticize what you don't understand!"

We must be reminded of what Jesus tried to tell us in his shortest parable, as set forth in the thirteenth chapter of Matthew. He claimed that the kingdom of God should be likened to a householder that takes out of his treasure chest "things new and old" (Matt. 13:52 KJV). In this parable Jesus told us that in the kingdom there must be room for the old forms of art (i.e., the old hymns—thank God for that!) and there must also be room for the new. We older folks must make room for the new art forms that we cannot quite grasp or understand, even as we ask the young people to leave room for the old art forms that we treasure and that still speak to us with awesome power. Thus, I pray that we—old and young alike—will make room for each other's art in our lives.

In this book the authors call us to be aware of and sensitive to the kinds of new art that are emerging among the urban poor and oppressed. The "street art" of the socially and economically disinherited is often ignored. Murals are appearing on the walls of old buildings. There are rap singers on the streets, and quartets harmonizing in new forms of jazz and rock are to be heard in subway tunnels. The authors call us to listen closely, that among these sounds, the sound of God might be heard.

Of course, this is not to say that all music is of God and that all sounds give expression to the divine Spirit. Indeed, at times music gives expression to evil spirits. We must enter into the arts with a certain amount of fear and trembling and must be able, by the enlightening power of the Holy Spirit, to discern which artistic expressions are of God.

The authors emphasize that love and intimacy can be extended to those around us through art. Through the arts, people can become affectionately connected. All of the lively arts have the potential for providing an empathetic community for those of us who feel isolated and alienated in our highly individualistic society. In short, the authors contend that the arts can build a sense of spiritual connectedness. I concur! I have seen this in the church, but I have also seen it elsewhere. Few things build camaraderie and a sense of unified purpose as the triumphant music of Christendom does. Charles de Gaulle once said, "The national anthem of France is worth at least a dozen divisions in battle."

Martin Buber, the Hasidic Hebraic philosopher-poet, talked about our need to transcend the "I-It" relationships we have with one another and ascend to the "I-Thou" relationships that are experienced in spiritual relationships. Buber says that in "I-It" relationships other people are simply objects, *things* that are part of the empirical world. He contends, however, that it is possible to enter into depth relationships in which we overcome our sense of separateness and feel a oneness that can only be expressed with the word *God!* We experience God's presence more powerfully through the intimacy of "I-Thou" relationships, Buber tells us, than through any theological tome or intellectual exercise. God is love, and those who love are born of God. So said the apostle John. So said the philosopher Martin Buber. Some of us have felt the joyful effervescence that comes when we interact in artistic expressions as a community. Thus, the arts can become a means for living out Jesus' commandment to love our neighbor as we love ourselves. Through the arts the Holy Spirit can give us a taste of that love wherein we know others even as we are known.

This book will go a long way in helping us all to foster the techniques that will make this kind of God experience a reality in our lives. Again, I emphasize that special attention will be given to how the arts can enable us to reach out to the poor and the oppressed, building relationships that will help to transform their lives and the communities in which they live. The apostle Paul tells us in the first chapter of 1 Corinthians that God has not chosen the wise, the powerful, and the rich to be the instruments for communicating his truth; he has chosen those whom the world calls "nothing." The authors believe this and thus call us away from the mentality that deems the arts to be the possession of a sophisticated elite. They call us to recognize the glorious expressions of truth and beauty that come not from the top down, but from the bottom up. Not from the aristocratic elite but from those who are at times referred to as "the wretched of the earth."

Commentators on the contemporary scene constantly talk of us having moved into a postmodern era. I cringe whenever the term postmodernism is used, because there is no exact meaning to the term. Hence it can be used by almost anybody to mean almost anything. In my opinion, and from what I have learned from others, postmodernism is simply the growing awareness that the logical positivism that has guided our comprehension of the world from the time of the Renaissance until recently has severe limitations. While modernism provided us with a mind-set that enabled us to explore the empirical world without the encumbrance of superstition and religious taboos, those who are into a postmodern mind-set contend that there are truths unattainable by the empirical, rational mind. Blaise Pascal, the philosopher-mathematician of a bygone century, once said, "The heart has reasons that reason can never know." He was saying that ultimate truth transcends the limitations of reason. The postmodernists agree and go on to say that the world and human nature refuse to fit into the neat categories of scientific frameworks. They concur with the words of Søren Kierkegaard: something infinitely transcendent about truth makes it "totally other" than what can be grasped by human intelligence. Postmodernists say there is a reality that computers cannot touch, even as computers become what some have called "spiritual machines."

Truth, argued Friedrich Nietzsche, cannot be apprehended through the *Apollonian* way, which is the way of the philosophers. He contended that truth can only be grasped through the *Dionysian* way, the way of passionate emotional surrender. It's not surprising that Nietzsche saw the pinnacle of the Greek era, not in the philosophers Socrates, Plato, and Aristotle, but rather in the great dramatists and poets such as Homer and Euripides. Nietzsche understood that it is in the abandonment that comes through the arts and in the emotions generated by them that one begins to taste the nectar of the gods. With such an approach to life, Nietzsche linked up with Richard Wagner and saw in the early Wagnerian opera the hope of translating the youth of Germany to a higher level of humanity than had hitherto been known. Nietzsche argued that even as it was the destiny of the ape to transcend itself and become man, so it was the destiny of man to transcend himself and become the superman. This transcendence, Nietzsche taught, could, in part, be achieved through the arts.

Nietzschean philosophy was distorted by his followers, who fostered an elitism that led to the Nazi mentality. What Nietzsche failed to see was that the Christ, against whom he was diametrically opposed, was the true aim of all art. If art carries us to truth, and truth is revealed in Jesus, then all great art should ultimately lead us to Jesus. If art does not lead us to Christ, it must be redeemed and sanctified and used to the glory of our Savior God. The authors of this book aim to help us do just that, and you would do well to read what they have to say.

Tony Campolo

Acknowledgments

This book would not have been possible without the following people for whom we are grateful and consider partners in ministry: James E. Lewis and the Louisville Institute, who funded our research; Chris Pack, who initiated contacts on the west coast; Laurie Williams, who served as a research assistant; Sandra Cruz; and Cynda Clyde. Nathan thanks his wife, Vickie, as always; Vivian thanks her dad, Andrew W. Nix Jr. We also thank our colleagues at the Campolo School for Social Change at Eastern University—faculty, staff, and students—who are always joyfully supportive.

We're grateful to Bob Hosack, Lynn Wilson, and the staff of Baker Books, who took a prophetic Christian publisher's risk with this book; Rhonda Forbes, who designed our cover on short notice; David Day, for the sculpture at Bethel Temple Church, which appears on the cover; and Janelle Junkin, who has been with us from the beginning.

We also thank a host of artists who gave us interviews from sixteen metropolitan centers in the United States. They are: Rosemarie Adcock, All Angels Church, Carlos Aquilar, Harriet Ball, Donna Barber, John Bjerklie, Sister Helen David Brancato, Phillip Brown, Rudy Carrasco, C. Ray Carlson, Carla Chapelle, Coz Crosscombe, Sister Carol Keck, Dan Curry, Mary Ann Degenhart, Grace and Bill Dyrness, Rev. Dr. Eric Elnes, Todd Farley, Ruth Naomi Floyd, Lisa Graham, Mark Hallen, Rev. Diana Holbert-Brown, Maxine Hull, Brian Joyce, Reggie Joyner, Janelle Junkin, Brian Kennedy, Rev. Tommy Kyllonen, Amanda Lower, Trayce Marino, Nan McNamara, Rev. Anthony Motley, Jennifer Moyer, Hans Nelson, Deborah Nicholson, Barbara Nicolosi, Ann Ostholthoff, Steve and Mary Park, Scott Parker, Minister Aaron Penton, Rev. Ralph M. Ross, Jackie Samuel, Mark Sandiford, David Schall, Russell and Cheryl

Sharman, Steve Smallman, Liz Spraggins, Tom Sullivan and John Russell, Pastor Joshua Swilley, Rev. Susan Teegan-Case, John Tiersma-Watson and Alberto Casteñeda, Sarah Thompson, Mary Lou Totten, Dana Velps-Marschaulk, Rev. Rebecca Verstraten-McSparran, Mara Wilson, Susan Tibbels, Rev. Duane Wilkins, and Stacey Williams.

Introduction

In 1989 Duane Wilkins, a professional dancer from south Philadelphia's tough Tasker Street neighborhood, approached his church about starting a dance group to enhance their worship. He was told that dancing was not an appropriate activity for young men. (The black community at that time perceived most male dancers as gay men who lived a decadent lifestyle.) Undaunted, and later encouraged by his Baptist pastor, Duane joined forces with his Catholic female dance partner and began Messiah Dance Works (MDW) in an empty community center building. For fourteen years Duane and Stacy have worked with the young people of the community to express the love of God through dance. These young people are mostly from single-parent households, have little hope for the future, exhibit a high dropout rate from high school, and have little connection to faith communities.

Today Messiah Dance Works is supported by both the Baptist and Catholic churches. All of the original students have now graduated from college, and the current troupe recently traveled to the Republic of Georgia to participate in a millennial Easter celebration. As in other effective faith-based arts organizations in Philadelphia and other major cities of the United States, art is the vehicle for opening the window of hope to young people and their families. Though dance is MDW's primary vehicle of ministry, it is integrated with teaching basic life skills and encouraging academic achievement, career motivation, and spiritual development.

Congregations and Artists

Church congregations often respond to the arts outside the four walls of the church with ignorance and resistance. They appear to be caught between praise and paranoia when considering the arts of contemporary culture that knock at their door. Some congregations display distaste and disdain for arts that are too radical or too aligned with social action. Other congregations are happy to enjoy the arts within the comfort of the sanctuary and thereby avoid the perils of the street literally just outside their doors.

There are several reasons congregations tend to limit their artistic expression to the confines of the church. Some artists in the church view art from a totally aesthetic perspective. "I am an artist, not a social worker!" one recent interviewee quipped. Others see the role of the arts as being exclusively for worship. But in general, the underlying lack of motivation for involvement in arts outside the sanctuary stems not only from a fear of engaging society but from a lack of knowing how to get involved. The result of such attitudes is that the influential and holistic role of the church is minimized in American society.

Increasingly, however, urban churches and people of faith are asking the following questions: What role can the arts play in calling *people* to personal responsibility and accountability and to lives of faithful hope? How can we use the arts to revitalize our *communities* and to provide a positive outlet for our children and youth? How can we use the arts to transform our *society* and impact our culture in a way that reflects the very best of values? How can we use the arts to transform our *houses of worship* into places of welcome and refuge for those living in need on the streets?

Likewise, Christian artists in urban areas are increasingly becoming involved in ministry outside the sanctuary. The urban context is one in which people and the communities and society in which they live are in need of change. Artists want to bring a life-transforming experience to the people in their communities, a life-transforming experience that comes only from the gospel, or the Good News.

We have observed that Christian communities bound to the sanctuary, as well as the artists within these communities, lack the following: a historical perspective and understanding of the cultural and transforming power of the arts, a theology for the arts of the street, a vocabulary for discussing those arts, and creative methods for bringing faith to action in the streets of society.

We hope this book will provide congregations and artists of faith both encouragement and concrete models for community mission and engagement.

Our Research

Over the past several years we have worked with many artists who, like Rev. Duane Wilkins, minister to their communities through the arts and who have led the way in artistic activity outside that of the traditional church, often in the face of opposition and lack of support on the part of the church. In a national research project, funded in part by the Louisville Institute, we visited, interviewed, and observed three distinct groups in order to discover the character-istics of a successful faith-based community arts program and how such a program can be replicated by Christians and churches who want to use the arts to transform people and communities outside the four walls of their buildings. These three groups were: (1) individual artists of the Christian faith who use their gifts to serve others, either in Christian churches and organizations or in secular society,[1] (2) churches or faith communities that seek to be relevant to those living in the marginalized urban communities, and (3) arts organizations, programs, and activities either within or outside the church.

The results of our research provided surprising and exciting insights. First, Christian artists were often working in isolation from other Christians involved in the same type of ministry within the same city.[2] It may be that working with a single community as intensely as these artists do does not afford them the time for a Christian ministry support or network group.

A second surprising observation was the type of person we found working within marginalized communities. These "urban prophets" and "agape artists," as we call them (and will define below), have strong personalities, tremendous personal drive, and a commitment to bringing about a New Jerusalem in the lives of those with whom they work and in the communities in which they live. They are not, however, angry street prophets ranting and pointing fingers in people's faces, as one might expect prophets to be. They are generous and gentle in their relationships with others and were happy to help us in our research. Almost without exception, these artists perceive their work as "giving back" to God, and they feel a strong calling to their work, a calling they need in order to endure the hardships they often face.

We were excited to find that these urban prophets are interculturally com-petent and acutely aware of cross-cultural issues in artistic development and learning styles. These artists are often bicultural, living cross-culturally, switch-ing language "codes" between cultures, and seeking to bridge the barriers of race and social class still prevalent in our country. Though they would not define themselves as such—and we might avoid the term because of its baggage to those outside of the traditional church—they are truly "missionaries" of the liberating gospel of Jesus Christ.

We also discovered a group of artists who know how to love people with and through the arts working in the marginalized communities of our cities. Working outside the comfort and support of the traditional church or work-ing in secular professions, these agape artists often live incarnationally among the poor. Using their artistic gifts to build relationships, these artists seek to empower and transform the poor and suffering of our cities. Agape artists are often unseen and unrecognized, but they exemplify the commandment to love our neighbor as ourselves. In the words of C. S. Lewis, they are "New People,"[3] or in our terms the "quiet ones of God," for in many cases they made no effort to bring attention to themselves or to their work. These quiet ones worked with calling, purpose, and humility to make the world a better place and to bring about the kingdom of God, or as we will call it, the NU JERUZ, a term borrowed from urban hip-hop culture.[4]

Many of the artists of the Christian faith that we found working within marginalized urban communities were professionally trained artists. Though most were unaware of the theories we describe in this book, all were developing and refining their methodologies and theologies for the arts in mission. Most saw their work as mission and ministry and used such phrases as "sculpting people into the image of God," "setting the picture right," "planting seeds," or "planting trees" to describe their work.

A few of these quiet ones of God identified with Jürgen Moltmann's *Theology of Play*. In 1972 Moltmann suggested that the Western world had lost the gift of joy and was bound to a work ethic of doing good, when we are really called *to be*. This *being* demonstrates a joy of existence and an awareness of God. Moltmann stated, "Only those who are capable of joy can feel pain at their own and other people's suffering." And, "Without the free play of imagination and songs of praise the new obedience deteriorates into legalism."[5] In an active and playful faith of free works, the quiet ones are called to be with others and to be there for others.

Some of the artists we interviewed identified with the John Perkins model of meeting the needs of the poor through holistic evangelism and social action. They have relocated to impoverished communities, are reconciling people to God and bringing them into a church fellowship, and are redistributing wealth and empowering the poor by finding "creative avenues to create jobs, schools, health centers, home ownership, and [creative activities]."[6]

Because of their experience with an institutional church that has made little room for the contemporary arts, especially the evangelical church, many of these artists are part of what we call *emerging faith communities*. Meeting in homes, alternative buildings, or informal gatherings, emerging faith communities often provide the artists with fellowship and support for their work in using their artistic gifts to serve others. Others remain committed to the traditional church but silently, and sometimes painfully, follow God's calling into the streets of society.

All of these artists believe we are called to be agents of transformation, to change *this* world—both the people and the societies in which they live—into what it should be. While those we interviewed did not always articulate this transformation with traditional theological language, they considered themselves part of what God is doing in the world in bringing about the NU JERUZ.

We were not surprised to hear of the suffering and rejection that some of these artists had experienced at the hands of their families, the institutional church, and individual Christians. Urban prophets often stand between the traditional church, which tends to be threatened by the ever-changing contemporary culture and offers little support to ministers of the street, and the often unbelieving people of the streets, where Christians are perceived to be more condemning than loving.

What this said to us is that the church needs a new paradigm and theology of the arts outside the sanctuary, one that provides for a horizontal theology that is complementary to the accepted vertical theology (described below). Christian artists should indeed "lift holy hands in praise of God" with their arts in the sanctuary and in their lives, but they should also be challenged and encouraged to give others "a cup of water" in Jesus' name and put a song in people's hearts through the arts in the streets outside the sanctuary. A horizontal arts theology requires radically different languages, approaches, and lifestyles than that to which most church artists are accustomed.

Changing the Paradigm of the Arts: A Horizontal Theology and Practice of the Arts

We are proposing a new paradigm, a different perspective, of the role of the arts and artists in Christian ministry and mission. Though not new for the many artists of the Christian faith who practice this theology outside the church tradition, it is new in that it is not taught in seminaries and Christian colleges and is little respected by church congregations. Until recently a horizontal theology of the arts was seldom encouraged by local churches, and it remains a peripheral avenue and focus for the arts of the church.

For the majority of the church throughout its history, and especially for church musicians and artists, the central theology and practice of the arts has seen the arts as being exclusively for the praise of God. This vertical theology of worship is often expressed in terms of "giving our highest art in praise for a high God." The vertical focus of this theology can be seen in phrases common in our churches, such as, "We *lift* holy hands in praise to God." Drawing this theology from Old Testament concepts of temple worship—most often expressed in the writings of Isaiah and the Psalms—church artists, pastors, and congregations center their vertical worship within the confines of church culture and the liturgy in the sanctuary. We refer to this practice of the arts as *celebrative art* and to those who practice it as *celebrative artists*. Celebrative arts play an important role in the church and will be discussed more fully later in the book. We respect this theology and practice and the lives and art of the many who are called to it. Yet it is only one aspect of church practice related to the arts, one in which the focus is often centered on the art and the artist as much as on the praise of God.

When Jesus was asked "What is the greatest commandment?" he replied, "'Love the Lord your God with all your heart and with all your soul and with all your strength and with all your mind'; and, 'Love your neighbor as yourself'" (Luke 10:27). The church is very familiar with the vertical act of loving the Lord our God with all our might and strength with the arts, yet many are not as aware or appreciative of the horizontal concept of loving our neighbors with and through the arts. We intend to encourage both aspects of this commandment, which are interrelated, but our primary focus will be on the latter. Excellent worship demands excellent love and forcefully propels this love out of the sanctuary and into the public square. The command to love our neighbors as ourselves directs us to a horizontal theology and practice of worship.

In this book we will discuss in detail three basic categories of artists who practice a horizontal theology of the arts. These include: *urban prophets,* who use the *prophetic arts* to speak for social justice and to call for repentance; *agape artists,* who use the *agape arts* to reach out to their neighbors, building transformational relationships of compassion and love; and *celebrative artists,* who use the *celebrative arts* (which in addition to being used in the vertical worship of the church also play an important role in a horizontal practice of the arts) to help people and communities celebrate transformation and renewal. While we seek to encourage a holistic life of worship through the arts that includes all three of these roles, we will focus primarily on the first two categories, as these roles have been given much less attention in literature.

The NU JERUZ

Throughout our discussions with artists and community arts workers, the phrase "a new heaven and a new earth" rang as a hopeful promise for a transformed community. It also served as a theological foundation for their work to realize the kingdom of God in the present. This vision of a world without pain and suffering and of structures and systems that are just and fair to the poor and marginalized motivates many artists of the Christian faith to live on meager incomes, live in "ghetto" communities, and risk their health and their lives to build loving relationships with the people living in the worst of communities. Yet in these so-called ghetto communities, the artists have found a NU JERUZ in the many rich and loving relationships they develop.

The prophetic arts and the agape arts are aesthetic expressions that are effective in conveying God's message within urban contexts. Artists who employ the prophetic and agape arts offer themselves in praise and service to God and to God's people who live in the margins of the society, "outside the city gates" of power and influence. Why?

Urban prophets and agape artists are people of faith. They believe that faith makes a difference; they believe that the world was set in motion by God, the Creator. The people of God's creation are headed on a journey of faith toward an end, the New Jerusalem, which will be the perfect culmination of God's interaction with the world he created, in spite of our personal shortcomings (sin) and the social evil that separate humanity from a just and right relationship with both the Creator and the created. In the present world God is at work to bring about love, peace, reconciliation, justice, and redemption. Urban prophets and agape artists work as a part of God's redemption plan. They act out of a strong calling and motivation to bring about the NU JERUZ, a foretaste of the New Jerusalem, by participating in what God is doing in the present.

The NU JERUZ is not so much a place, though we use the term to refer to the urban context, but a state of life in which people, communities, and societies are being transformed, a way of living in which all people are empowered to live lives that are full, free, and pleasing to the Creator in all aspects—artistically, economically, culturally, politically, spiritually, environmentally, and socially—until the journey of living faith is complete.

The NU JERUZ includes not only Christians, those who profess allegiance to the Creator through Jesus Christ, but also those who do not—those who are participating in what God is doing in the world because they have been influenced by the values of the NU JERUZ. Some of these people are on journeys in which they are encountering the Creator but have yet to openly declare an allegiance.

The NU JERUZ includes not only the institutional church but also institutions outside the church. Though we believe in communities of the faithful, in some cases churches appear to have been passed over by the Spirit because of their failure to seek the NU JERUZ outside the four walls of their sanctuaries while the communities around them suffer because of personal sin and social evil. Artists of the Christian faith often work in institutions outside the church—for example, government offices, art organizations, human service organizations—and seek to transform these institutions by integrating their faith in their art and relationships.

The NU JERUZ is a state of transformation and renewal. It includes people, communities, and societies who are on journeys of transformation. Lives and communities are being reformed, re-created, and renewed. In the NU JERUZ people move from a state of mere existence to a state of right relationship with God, themselves, and others. While the NU JERUZ (in our definition) is what God is doing in the world as a whole—urban, suburban, and rural—we will focus on the urban context, though we are well aware that all are interconnected.

In summary, the NU JERUZ is what God is doing in the world through people who are invited to join him in creating a place in which people, communities, and societies are transformed and are empowered—economically, socially, politically, and spiritually—to live in harmony with God, themselves, one another, and their environments.[7] For Christians, this of course includes a right relationship with God through Jesus Christ, but it is much more than that. It includes communities of faith who nurture believers and provide a friendly space and sanctuary for the seeker. Even more, it includes the whole of God's world in a journey toward redemption.

One might wonder what keeps us from experiencing the NU JERUZ. Evangelicals see personal sin as the primary barrier, while other Christians may see the broader evil that is present in social structures. In *Jesus Before Christianity*, Albert Nolan cited four basic barriers that are both personal and social (institutional). They are: the pursuit of wealth, status, in-group solidarity, and power.[8] These same four themes were at the core of Jesus' message to those who sought to bring the kingdom of God. Unless we as individuals and the cultural institutions we create can cross these barriers in both ideal and practice, we cannot experience the NU JERUZ.

Artists in the NU JERUZ

In our research we recognized multiple and important roles for artists in the NU JERUZ. We have touched on these roles already, and as we will discuss each group of artists and their work in the chapters to come, we offer here only a brief description of each group.

Urban Prophets

Urban prophets are artists who use their art to confront people, institutions, and society about wrongdoing and injustice as they bring people to a critical awareness of the need for change. They proclaim the Good News to people through their use of the arts. The art of the urban prophet focuses on the value of justice and is generally used as a communicative tool with a specific message.

Agape Artists

Agape artists are compassionate people who use the arts to dialogue with others and to assist them in finding solutions to personal and social problems. The work of the agape artist leads people and communities to renewal. Agape artists use their art to build relationships with others, and the relationship or outcome is often more important than the art. The agape artist focuses on the value of love and exemplifies the commandment to love our neighbor as ourselves.

Celebrative Artists

Celebrative artists play an important role in the NU JERUZ by leading the community in the celebration of each step toward transformation and renewal. They celebrate accomplishments with and for people. The celebrative artist represents the core values of the community, considers artistic tradition, and often strives for art that will most typify the standards of the community. The primary value of the celebrative artist is one of praise and aesthetics.

Arts in Redemptive Transformation: A Model

Our model of Arts in Redemptive Transformation (A.R.T.) (described in detail in chapter 3) offers a framework for how people, and artists in particular, can help to create a world in which people, communities, and societies are transformed through a journey toward redemption.

In recent years Christians, especially those involved in community development, have begun to use the word *transformation* to describe the positive changes brought about by their work and ministry in the world. In our model of transformation, we recognize three levels of social change or transformation: personal empowerment and responsibility, community revitalization, and societal transformation. Each of these levels of transformation is holistic and integrated. By holistic, we mean the transformation occurs within all aspects of personal and community life, including the psychological, physical, spiritual, economic, political, and sociocultural dimensions of life.

In the process of transformation, both people and communities move through three distinct stages. In stage 1, *Critical Awareness,* people attain critical awareness of a problem or issue. In stage 2, *Working Out,* they attempt to work out the problem through a variety of strategies until a solution is reached. In stage 3, *Celebration,* success or completion is celebrated as a way to publicly recognize and solidify the new state. Each new state then becomes the current state, and the process begins again in a progressive spiral of transformation.

The prophetic, agape, and celebrative arts play significant roles in the transformation process. In the critical awareness stage, the arts function in a prophetic role and confront people, institutions, and society about wrongdoing and injustice as they bring people to a critical awareness of the need for change. In the working out stage, the arts play a catalytic and synergistic role in the development of personal and social solutions that lead to renewal. In the celebration stage, the arts play an important role in leading the community in celebrating transformation and renewal.

We believe that all art—sacred and secular—is potentially redemptive. *Redemptive art,* from a Christian point of view, will always point people in a direction that (1) facilitates an external expression of an inner reality, which creates critical awareness that allows one to understand his or her place in the world; (2) raises one out of, or at least improves, an undesirable situation and leads to a better way of thinking, believing, feeling, and ultimately living; (3) provides an opportunity to experience a new way of life, to try it on, so to speak, as a rehearsal for change; (4) confronts both the consequences of personal sin and the evil in society that leads to social injustice; (5) instills a sense of wonder and awe of the Creator; and (6) ultimately leads to an understanding of God's redemptive plan in Jesus Christ through a personal relationship. For art to function with this level of a redemptive nature depends not solely on the art but also on the relationships established by the artists.

The Arts in Community and Social Development

Our model of transformation, which we describe in detail in chapter 3, is related to and draws upon several areas of study and practice within the community development field. Because churches and Christian artists often lack a historical perspective and theoretical background for community change processes, we present a brief overview of the work that has been done in this area as background information that will place our model in theoretical perspective.

Development Communication and the Arts

"Development communication has its origins in postwar international aid programs to countries in Latin America, Asia and Africa that were struggling with poverty, illiteracy, poor health and a lack of economic, political and social infrastructures."[9] Derived from theories of development and social change, development communication uses communication strategies to "raise the quality of life of populations, including income and well-being, eradicate social injustice, promote land reform and freedom of speech, and establish community centers for leisure and entertainment."[10] Development communication strategists employ a variety of concepts and theories to explain the human condition and to diagnose problems and develop communication to educate, change, and transform. This field is complex but can be simplified (and we are oversimplifying here) to two basic methods: diffusion models and participatory models.

Diffusion models of development communication rely on the diffusion or transmission of information, most often through the mass media. The goal is to create awareness and instill defined values.[11] The arts, particularly mediated arts, play a crucial role in reaching an audience with a particular message, with the intention of changing attitudes and behaviors. This model has been quite influential among evangelical Christians, who have used media-related strategies for evangelism in film, television, radio, and print. Two relevant methods used in diffusion communication are social marketing (SM) and entertainment education (EE).

Using concepts based on Western marketing and advertising strategies, *social marketing* seeks to understand an audience, plan and market relevant products, and change social behavior in a way that "improves personal welfare" and the community. In the United States you can easily recognize social marketing campaigns—television commercials, billboards, and print advertisements on the topics of smoking, seat-belt use, drug abuse, heart disease, and so on. SM is not without its critics, especially on issues related to social ethics. Critics see this approach as manipulative and as being too much like propaganda, in that it may not seek the support and involvement of the intended audience. SM also tends to focus on individual behaviors and ignores the broader sociopolitical forces that lead to the behaviors in the first place. Critics believe there is a role for SM as long as it is integrated with social action and community participation.

If you have ever watched *Sesame Street,* you understand the basic concept of *entertainment education:* Learning can be entertaining and fun. In this strategy, cartoons, music, drama, soap operas, and the like are used by "purposely designing and implementing a media message to both entertain and educate, in order to increase audience knowledge about an educational issue, create favorable attitudes, and change overt behavior."[12] Television, live performances, radio, and drama are used to educate people on a wide range of social issues. The success of this social transformation strategy varies depending on the credibility of the entertainer, cultural appropriateness, and audience. Churches have also used this strategy in recent decades to seek both behavioral change and spiritual development. One example of this strategy in a church context would be using a puppet ministry to teach spiritual concepts.

A criticism of diffusion models is that they rely heavily on theories related to behavior modification and are often individualistic and too consumer oriented in that they rely on information sharing.[13] They may lack an understanding of the social structures that contribute to the problem and fail to deal adequately with them. When used as part of a larger holistic strategy involving the community, however, they can be quite effective.

Participatory models of development communication, as found in the influential theory of Paulo Freire, use dialogical communication to find solutions to local problems within a community. This form of participatory communication uses small group and mediated art, such as drama (as used by Boal), popular music, and video to identify problems and seek solutions. Unlike the top-down approach used in diffusion models to create change, participatory models do not use professional change agents as the center of the social transformation process. The community, in horizontal communication, participates in their own process of change.

Another method within the participatory model is *social mobilization,* in which a larger group of stakeholders, communities, professionals, and government organizations work together to identify, plan, implement, and evaluate a program.

Participatory strategies also have critics. Communities may be isolated and may fail to use group media well. They may fail to translate their communication into programs that actually work or that address the identified problem. The participatory strategy might also fail to work in communities where there is strong division and conflict.

A more recent method used in development communication (promoted by the 1999 Carnegie Foundation report, *Communication for Social Change*) takes the "tool kit" approach of combining the above models in a broader planning and implementation process. Research is key in this approach, in that it stresses the need to define indicators of change and seeks to measure the impact of an intervention.

To summarize, in development communication the arts are treated as a communication media and are considered to have an important role in social transformation. This role is not central but one of support and communication within a broader, interdisciplinary transformation process.

Arts-Based Community Development (ABCD)

In 1977 a self-taught writer and musician named William Cleveland left college and found employment through the U.S. Department of Labor's Comprehensive Employment and Training Act. Along with many other artists, Cleveland was hired to work in hospitals, prisons, public housing, and other community programs that used the arts. Several years later, working with the Department of Corrections for the State of California in a program called Arts-in-Corrections, Cleveland found that "the arts could translate to the needs of communities and public institutions without losing power or integrity."[14] Along with his colleagues, Cleveland later established the Center for the Study of Art and Community, where he currently studies and writes about this relatively new and developing field of arts-based community development.

In 1992 William Cleveland published a groundbreaking book, *Art in Other Places,* which examined the unrecognized service of artists in community development within disenfranchised and marginalized groups in the United States. In this book Cleveland describes artists' relationships to their communities and the services that musicians, visual artists, dramatists, and dancers are performing with the physically and mentally disabled, the incarcerated, patients in hospitals, at-risk youth, and in the community in general.

Cleveland defines the new field of arts-based community development as "arts-centered activity that contributes to the sustained advancement of human dignity, health and/or productivity within a community."[15] This includes:

- Activities that EDUCATE and INFORM us about ourselves and the world
- Activities that INSPIRE and MOBILIZE individuals or groups
- Activities that NURTURE and HEAL people and/or communities
- Activities that BUILD and IMPROVE community capacity and/or infrastructure[16]

The diagram below, developed by Cleveland and the Center for the Study of Art and Community, maps four interconnecting "neighborhoods" of these art-centered activities and is a means to identify one's own activities within the field of arts-based community development. The diagram demonstrates the diversity of this field.

An Ecology of Arts-Based Community Development

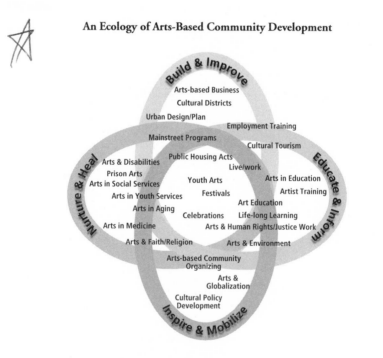

Cleveland's ecological arts model shows the interrelationship of all art forms, both formal and informal, within a community.

Since the publication of *Art in Other Places,* the growth of the ABCD field has been phenomenal. In addition to Cleveland's work, important work was done by the U.S. Congress and the president's office during the late 1990s. President Clinton appointed a task force to research what was actually being accomplished through the arts in the community. The study group produced a document called the *Coming-Up Taller Report.* Hundreds of people working in community arts programs were interviewed and community arts programs around the country were evaluated. (These interviews and evaluations can be found on the web site www.cominguptaller.org.) The Taller report, as it is commonly called, focuses on the impact of the arts on the social, emotional, and academic development and performance of students.

There is a growing movement within U.S. cities to include arts-based activities in strategies for community development. The collaborative strategies of comprehensive community initiatives (CCI), much like the social mobilization and toolkit methods mentioned above, include nonprofit organizations, churches, schools, government organizations, fund providers, and neighborhood organizations. Whereas the arts have previously been considered an "extra" that beautifies the community, they are increasingly being utilized as a central part of strategic revitalization.

What is noticeably absent from all of the models described above is the aspect of faith—except for a mention of arts and faith/religion in Cleveland's model. Do these methods and strategies contribute to the kingdom of God? Can churches and Christians utilize these strategies as they minister to others? Some Christians believe that these methods are not valid because faith is not mentioned; the models do not openly share the gospel of Jesus Christ and build the local church. Many local churches believe that partnering with community organizations compromises the leadership role of the church.

In spite of such reservations, for decades there have been many Christians—like Duane Wilkins—working in the community, outside the institutional church, using these methodologies and integrating their faith naturally.

Community Cultural Development (CCD)

Those of us who have worked in missions overseas or in nongovernmental organizations around the world are well aware of the use of the arts in a variety of community activities. In a report for the Rockefeller Foundation, researchers Don Adams and Arlene Goldbard point out, "The community cultural development (CCD) field is global, with a decades-long history of practice, discourse, learning and impact."[17] Since before the 1970s the arts have been used in economic development, health education, and community development. Though Christian missionaries have never used the term "community cultural development," they have for decades utilized the visual, musical, and dramatic arts in their holistic missionary work. But as Adams and Goldbard state, "The United States' active community cultural development field is nearly invisible as a phenomenon."[18] Until recently there has been little infrastructure, education and training, or support for these activities.

Adams and Goldbard provide definitions for each part of the term *community cultural development:*

- *Community* is that which emphasizes collaborations and participation between artists and other community members. This is a distinction from the "one-to-many arts activity," as in the performing arts;
- *Cultural* is the generous concept of culture (rather than, more narrowly, art) and includes the broad range of tools and forms in use in the field, from aspects of traditional visual and performing arts practice, to oral-history approaches usually associated with historical research and social studies, to the use of high-tech communications media, to elements of activism and community organizing more commonly seen as part of non-arts social-change campaigns; and
- *Development* is the dynamic nature of cultural action, with its ambitions of conscientization [critical awareness] and empowerment that link to other community development practices, especially those incorporating principles of self-development rather than development imposed from above.[19]

In their book *Creative Community: The Art of Cultural Development,* Adams and Goldbard provide seven basic principles for the field of CCD:

1. Active participation in cultural life is an essential goal of community cultural development.
2. All cultures are essentially equal, and society should not promote any one as superior to others.
3. Diversity is a social asset, part of the cultural commonwealth, requiring protection and nourishment.
4. Culture is an effective crucible for social transformation, one that can be less polarizing and create deeper connections than other social change arenas.
5. Cultural expression is a means of emancipation, not the primary end itself; the process is as important as the product.
6. Culture is a dynamic, protean whole, and there is no value in creating artificial boundaries within it.
7. Artists have roles as agents of transformation that are more socially valuable than mainstream art world roles and certainly equal in legitimacy.[20]

Again, we affirm these definitions and principles. But as in the other models of social transformation that we have mentioned, faith is not part of this perspective. It is, however, congruent with the Christian worldview, with the noticeable difference of allegiance. We believe that faith is a driving force for which there is no parallel, and it is integral to our model of transformation.

Artists of the Christian faith have for the past century lived out their faith in a culture characterized by a sacred/secular dichotomy, often working as professionals outside the traditional roles expected of artists within the church context. It is our hope that by sharing what we have learned from our research we might help to recover a fuller perspective for the many Christians and churches who have not yet seen the validity or the urgency of ministry that integrates faith in all aspects of life, including the arts.

A History of Faith-Integrated Arts Programs

Though using the arts in personal and community transformation may be a new concept to many Christians, it is by no means new to the many artists of the Christian faith who work outside the four walls of the church.

The use of community arts programs in America has its roots in the late nineteenth-century settlement house movement. Settlement houses were centers that offered recreation, education, and community services in the poor neighborhoods of European immigrants.[21] Exposing immigrants to dominant cultural forms was seen as a way to "acculturate" or assimilate them into mainstream, or "common," culture.

In the mid-1930s artists were called on to lay aside their criticism of and alienation from mainstream culture and become part of the Popular Front movement as a way to show a solid American front and to contribute, along with other activists, to the fight against the growing fascism in Europe.

Following the Great Depression of the 1930s, art initiatives were part of President Roosevelt's New Deal programs to put people back to work. The Public Works of Art project commissioned murals for schools, orphanages, libraries, museums, and other public buildings, broadening the vision that arts had great social value and could be used for social change.[22]

But in the McCarthy era of the 1950s, the prophetic role of artists was pushed farther underground. It wasn't until the 1970s that the role of arts and artists in community service was revived permanently, with the Comprehensive Employment and Training Act (CETA) programs during the Nixon-Ford years.[23] These efforts had been spurred on by the strong role that the arts played in community identity during the civil rights movement of the 1960s. During this time international support and influence for the activist community artist role also came through the writings of Frantz Fanon on the process of psychological liberation expressed through culture, Augusto Boal on theater pedagogy, and Paulo Freire on the "critical consciousness" approach to education.

The history of faith-integrated arts programs parallels that of secular community arts programs and had its beginnings mostly in traditional evangelical missions and social action and the social justice movement of Catholics.

In 1865 William Booth, a Methodist minister in England, began preaching in London's East End. Concerned about the poverty and decadence of the city, Booth used many means to reach the poor and unchurched, including marching in the streets with musical instruments. Not only did he preach in the streets but, with the help of his wife, began to feed and house the poor. The Booths combined the arts and social ministry.

At first the Anglican Church was hostile toward Booth's methods. The church did, however, begin to respond to the degrading and debilitating effects of the Industrial Revolution on the urban poor. In 1884 Samuel Barnett, an Anglican clergyman, invited his university students to live in the slums "as an outpost of education and culture." This resulted in the first settlement house, through which Barnett's students ministered to the poor. The settlement house movement was soon introduced into the United States, by both Christians and non-Christians, to meet the needs of immigrants, the poor, and the unemployed in U.S. cities. Related to the so-called social gospel, the emphasis of this movement was not so much on saving souls but on meeting the social needs of the suffering poor. Drawing from this movement, pastor and settlement house worker Charles Sheldon wrote *In His Steps* in 1896. With over 60 million copies in print, this influential novel called on Christians to become socially active in the world and was the impetus of the popular Christian expression "What Would Jesus Do?"

Those familiar with the modern missionary movement of the nineteenth and twentieth centuries recognize that while evangelism, or "winning the lost," was the primary focus for many groups, those who lived with the poor recognized the need to develop education, health care, and economic prosperity—in other words, to minister or work with the whole person. Their response to this need resulted in the growth of the many indigenous Christian art forms within communities whose artists became Christians and responded to their context.

The decades between the 1930s and the 1970s brought tumultuous and radical changes in our society and in the life of the church as well. In the various social movements of this time, the arts and artists had a prophetic role. The civil rights movement challenged the very fabric of our nation as well as the traditional church, which supported the status quo, and confronted the evil of the racism and segregation that had plagued our country since the inception of slavery. Art was often at the forefront of this movement, prophetically speaking out in drama, dance, visual arts, and music.

In the 1960s Vatican II released the worship of the Catholic Church from Latin into the vernacular of local people. This, coupled with the writings of

Karl Marx, caused Latin-American theologians to reevaluate the meaning of the gospel for people who were being oppressed by foreign powers from without and corrupt leaders from within. Liberation theology was born and made a tremendous impact by pointing out that the traditional methods of the Western church were too closely aligned with oppression itself and often unintentionally worked to keep the poor, poor.

The influence of Vatican II and the movements of the early twentieth century also caused the church to be more concerned about the contextualization of the gospel. New efforts were made to present the gospel, including Scripture, within the context of those who hear it, by relating it to the language, customs, and worldview of each culture. The arts have begun to play an increasingly important role in evangelism and the world mission of the church. Why? The arts, if nothing else, are the face of a culture. But even more important, they carry the very core of the Christian worldview and belief system.

The church's focus on the arts has been primarily within the sanctuary or for specific types of direct evangelism. The local church has until recently been derelict in using its resources for the betterment of the community in which it resides. Churches are struggling in the urban context to become relevant to a commercial, media-driven culture and to address the needs of the increasingly diverse population that has been brought to the doorstep of the church through the mass migration of peoples caused by the U.S. urban-suburban-rural shift and by the global shifts in populations due to war, famine, and acts of injustice. The Western church has followed Western cultural artistic values and has been prone to spectate when it comes to the arts rather than participate in presenting a relevant gospel through the arts.

Faith Integration

We would like to include a note about the nomenclature "faith-integrated," which we use as opposed to the more commonly used "faith-based." When we began our own nonprofit arts education organization, BuildaBridge International, we registered as a "faith-based" organization. While we still use this term, we have begun more frequently to drop it from our materials. In the streets of society beyond the four walls of the church, few people have a grasp of faith and religion and the language used to describe them. In our view, "faith-integrated" is a more appropriate descriptor for programs such as ours, in that it denotes activities infused with the values of the Christian faith, peace, love, justice, reconciliation, and redemption.

Our mission is not to overtly proselytize or teach about religion but to be the gospel presence in the tough places of the world and in the margins of our society. In our work at BuildaBridge, we express our evangelistic goals through a continual invitation to those in our midst to join in what God is doing in the world. We work with churches and individuals who do evangelize and share their faith openly, and we are supportive of their ability and call to do this. We have observed a marked difference in the focus of arts programs between those centered within the church (church-based) and those that seek to serve the broader community (faith-integrated). The following chart summarizes the major distinctions as we see them. Readers may discover additional differences in the broader national discussion of faith-based programs.[24]

Faith/Church-Based Community Arts	Faith-Integrated Community Arts
Focuses on religion or is dependent on a formal religious institution	Is not dependent on a formal religious institution
Religious institution provides services to community	Those involved live a life of service to others in religious or other contexts
Programs are centered in a religious building or space	Programs and ministries serve the broader community outside the church, whether centered in a church building or not
Often seeks to increase the influence or size of the religious institution	Seeks to build the NU JERUZ, which includes but is not limited to the religious institution
Affiliation is key	Relationships are key
Motivated to increase the church	Motivated to serve the community as an extension of the church
Often seeks a reconciling relationship through Jesus Christ through diffusion	Seeks a reconciling relationship through Jesus Christ through incarnation
Often separates the religious from the secular aspects of life	Values of the faith are inherently present in all one thinks, says, and does

Why We Write

We all come from different backgrounds and experiences that invite us to find our unique role in transformation from different perspectives. We have sought to integrate our faith and our professional lives as university educators with a practical ministry that fulfills our calling in the world in which God has placed us. Telling our more recent stories and those of several artists involved in the streets is a backdrop for understanding the place of the NU JERUZ and thus the place where we begin our narrative.

Art has power: the power to translate the emotions and intellect into form, the power to express personal and community beliefs and values through concrete symbols, and the power to transform—to change one's life and the circumstances in which one lives. Made in the image of God, a creator God, all people are gifted for creative work. Some, laboring for years in the inner city, have demonstrated the power of the arts to transform children and youth, bring communities into just relationships, and to improve the economic and social lives of their ministry audience.

Additional Resources

One of the benefits of technology, especially Web-based technology, is the ability it gives individuals and groups to provide information that would be economically prohibitive to publish. We have created a web site, which we will refer to in the text of the book. Visit www.urbanprophets.org for profiles, pictures, and diagrams regarding this book and the artists mentioned. In addition, you may purchase from us an interactive CD containing excerpts from many of the artists we interviewed during our research for this book.

We invite you to visit our ministry web site at www.buildabridge.org. This site provides an opportunity for the reader to become directly involved in a community arts ministry. The site also contains news articles, training opportunities, and ministry related to arts in service to communities.

It may prove helpful to read a prequel to this book, *The Sound of the Harvest* by J. Nathan Corbitt (Baker, 1998).

Part 1

The Arts in Redemptive Transformation

1

Taking the Gospel to the Streets
Current Context for the NU JERUZ

In this chapter we provide a view of the city as a context for ushering in the kingdom of God in the present. Cities have problems that are created by both personal sin and social evil. Poverty, violence, inadequate housing, poor health care, and lack of education are prevalent in every major city around the world. The result is that a majority of the world's poor live in squalid conditions in which even the basic human needs are not met, resulting in a life of hopelessness and fear. It is a situation in which personal sin and social evil combine with population growth to perpetuate social injustice and to exasperate the human capacity: our ability to solve the problems we create. The city is, on the other hand, also a vibrant, convivial, diverse, exciting, and creative place. Rather than view the city as a place divided between good and evil, we believe there is a secular city in which many people stand between the city of God and the city of Satan, undecided yet informed and influenced by both. These people are awaiting a message of hope, reconciliation, and compassion, and many of them work for the common good through common grace. It is in the secular streets outside the sanctuary that we find a place of hope and a call for the prophet.

As you read this chapter, ask yourself the following questions:

1. Are Christians working in the places of greatest need, even among the least of our neighbors?
2. Are we "called" to work in these places of need over the long term?
3. Do we have a vision for redemptive transformation that is shared by a community?
4. Have we relocated for incarnational ministry among the poor, or can we sustain a relationship with those in need beyond our brief periods of volunteerism and our special offerings?

Should I not be concerned about that great city?

Jonah 4:16

Nathan: From the Suburbs to the Ghetto

"Pow-pow-pow-pow" thudded a rapid-fire noise around me. I lay frozen, searching for my place in the world amidst the night darkness. Awakened from a deep sleep, my eyes were still tightly closed; I wasn't sure where I was and hoped it had only been a dream. I searched my senses for smells in the air and felt the heat of the room. *Was it Uganda?* I wondered. There I had once slept through what I believed to be an onslaught of Milton Obote's forces as they moved on Kampala. Distant barrages of mortar fire had disturbed my sleep, and I awoke to discover it was only the coming thunder of rain.

I opened my eyes. A flashing blue light passed by the bedroom window as I heard running footsteps and muffled voices. This was not Uganda. And this was no storm; it was pistol fire. I was awake.

Earlier on this snowy January night the roads to my home in the suburbs had become impassable, and a friend from north Philadelphia had insisted I stay over until the weather cleared the next morning. It was the safe thing to do. *Safe?* I began to chuckle to myself. *Sure, I could have been stuck in the warmth and safety of my pickup on the Schuylkill Expressway. There were even nice hotels all along the way.* Lying motionless, I listened from my bed. It grew quiet and I drifted back to sleep.

"Yep, that's what it sounds like," my host clarified when I shared my experience at breakfast. "I must have slept through it. I'm used to it after thirty years here. That's how it is in the ghetto. Just don't get up and go look out the window. You might catch a stray bullet." He joked, but he was serious.

By noon the roads had cleared, and I drove my usual shortcut through north Philadelphia to Valley Forge. I had been taking this shortcut for two years now. This morning I looked more closely. In this section of the city, Philadelphia seemed more like a war zone than the City of Brotherly Love. Little change had come to the ghetto in the past decade. "Ghetto is a misnomer," anthropologist Russell Sharman had once corrected me on a visit to East Harlem. "The people in these neighborhoods are the *working poor,* living on less than $20,000 a year." And Elijah Anderson, in *Code of the Street,* reminded me that decent and moral people far outnumber street people in the inner city, but they all must live by a code of respect: "In order to live and function in the community, they must adapt to a street reality that is often dominated by people who at best are suffering severely in some way and who are apt to resort quickly to violence to settle disputes."[1]

Driving home, I could feel the oppression and suffering of the people living in this poverty. Block after block in north Philadelphia consists of burned-out houses and empty lots. It was drab and ugly, and at times noisy and congested. I was conflicted over the comfort of the cul-de-sac townhouse to which I returned and the call to serve my neighbors of the streets—a conflict resolved by a decision to move to the city.

Vivian: From the Hill to the Hyperghetto

I had a nervous vision of the gunshots just before the sounds sent me running out of the room. Dad showed me the hole in his window. Had he been sitting on the couch, he would have been hit squarely in the back. We looked out the window and saw the parking lot through which the drug dealers regularly run and shoot.

It was only nine o'clock on a Saturday morning—my only day to sleep reasonably late. So why must I wake up to blaring rap music? With an angry frown, I stumble over to peer out of my second-floor window. I see a man lying asleep in the front seat of a car parked below the window. "How can he sleep with all that noise!" I mutter to myself.

No one is in the driver's seat. The driver has left the car running and the radio blasting, bass on level nine, while he runs in somewhere to do who knows what. As my eyes search the corners and side streets visible from my window, I see him return to the car and screech off, leaving a vapor trail of irritating sound behind him. The hyperghetto—Elijah Anderson's term for the worst of the ghettos—is full of inconsiderate arrogance.

No one recycles here. I wonder why. There is little visible beauty, mostly asphalt and ugly decay. The murals that dot the neighborhood only color the asphalt and often add to the clutter, especially when trash is thrown about the street beneath them.

I do find God here, though. An occasional porch on a well-maintained house sports the bright colors of impatiens and pansies: an oasis, a reminder of God's presence. Such oases are usually the homes of longtime residents who are retired or who now have middle-class incomes. They don't move because of ties to the church, to family and friends, and to the community and because there is no house note to pay. They would not recoup the value of their houses if they decided to sell and move out of the neighborhood.

There is pride here. Today my small side street is blocked off for its annual painting. The residents all contribute what they can for the supplies, and the younger folks paint the curbs bright white, the hydrants yellow, and the appropriate color lines for no-parking zones and curb cuts for wheelchairs. The hopscotch grid is painted permanently in the middle of the small street. The residents take responsibility for their streets. But why do they have to? There is no street painting and public cleaning on the Hill.[2]

The streets in the hyperghetto are full of people from morning till night. The morning finds the regular work and school crowds but also hair braiders plaiting the tresses of their first customers, who sit in kitchen chairs on the sidewalk. The ride home from work finds the stoops full of men, women, and children; corners full of young boys; kids riding bikes, swerving between the parked and moving cars (one must drive five miles per hour in order not to hit one of these little ones); imitation Weber grills, card tables, and chairs out on the sidewalks. There are no air conditioners in the windows of the row after row of poorly maintained houses.

But who are these people I see? To find my compassion for them, I have only to look earnestly into the eyes and faces of the children. I speak and discover their politeness and their pleasantness. I wave from the car, and they become people rather than objects. Were I to really minister here, I would need to visit each of them as neighbors. Go into the stores in the daytime. Learn their names. Then my fear would diminish. I would become one of them and not a visitor.

A Common Cause

The experiences we describe here have led us to understand the realities of the city. The poor seem to be warehoused in ghettos, while those in the suburbs live in a virtual heaven, seemingly realizing their kingdom in the present, while so many others suffer in a living hell. Consider the evidence of the plight of children who live in these poor communities and the effects such conditions must have on them.

In Philadelphia, for example, a recent mayoral study graded the schools in these communities with a C-/D+. The state has taken over the schools. We frequently talk with teachers who are quitting because of overcrowding, violence, and the lack of resources.

The fewer available jobs and changing family-life patterns in these communities are greatly affecting these children. Many young people spend 40 percent of their time without adult supervision or companionship. Many more are alienated from the communities right outside their doors. Among tenth graders, less than one-third attend religious activities once a week, while only 20 percent participate in youth groups or recreational or arts activities outside of school. Only one in fourteen volunteers or is involved in community service.

Almost 14 million children in the United States live in poverty, with living conditions worse than those of poor children in fifteen of the eighteen Western industrialized countries. These children are the most likely to go to inadequate schools and face danger in their neighborhoods and the least likely to have access to recreation and support services.

Almost 4 million children in the United States are growing up in severely distressed neighborhoods that have high levels of at least four of the major risk factors: poverty, unemployment, dropout rates, female-headed families, and family reliance on welfare. In the United States one child dies from gunshot wounds every two hours; three million children each year are reported to be abused or neglected. Teen suicide, youth violent crime arrest rates, and unmarried teen birth rates are all rising. According to the U.S. Department of Health and Human Services, only 45 percent of fifteen-year-olds are risk free.

As we will see later, one should avoid thinking that the inner cities are void of good. Most young people in the inner cities graduate from school; they just have fewer opportunities. And many families seek to raise their children with traditional family values; they just have fewer resources.

What about the churches in these communities? Several years ago we took a walk on a Wednesday afternoon through block after block of one neighborhood, looking for a potential church that might partner with our community arts program, which assists churches to develop after-school arts education. With kids running in the streets, unattended and unstimulated by a positive and structured experience, we passed church after church that had locked doors.

Out of our experiences and realities, very diverse realities, we began to ask ourselves the following questions: How do we as Christians, artists, and academicians respond to the obvious needs around us? What is an appropriate way for artists to participate in what God is doing in the world to bring about his kingdom in the city? Over the next several years, as we began to work together, and as a result of our opportunity to research the work of artists of the Christian faith in the United States, we began to see God at work, firsthand.

Since writing this manuscript, we have seen God at work in Philadelphia through those who may or may not recognize him. Philadelphia has distinguished itself as a city that partners with faith-based organizations to bring about positive community transformation. Mayor John Street's Neighborhood Transformation Initiative, announced in February 2003, though controversial for some, will nonetheless bring significant redevelopment to some of the most blighted areas of the city by using mixed-class, low-density, and other contemporary housing theories and practices. The city's departments regularly invite faith-based organizations to assist in public work, including BuildaBridge International, which provides direct service (using the arts) to a number of transitional homes in partnership with private industry and the city's department of human services. Recognizing the importance of schools to the social, moral, and economic rebirth of cities, Philadelphia's new CEO of the public schools, Paul Vallas, is rolling out an aggressive plan for a transformed educational system that includes the involvement of organizations and institutions of faith. At the time of writing this book, none of these plans have come to fruition, and we await results amidst a slowing economy, war, and federal, state, and city budget cuts.

A Gospel to, from, and for the Urban Context

A Gospel to the Streets (Go Ye! Hit and Run)

"Ding, ding, dingy ding!" a cowbell rang in the distance. It was a warm July evening along Miami's Bay Front Park. Thunderclouds hung beneath an evening sun as distant music moved in waves with the growing sea breeze. A familiar giant guitar rising above the palm trees announced the Hard Rock Café and an open performance area, where a small audience pulsated to the Cuban salsa band within. Rows of outdoor cafés hosted young lovers sipping drinks while gazing into each other's eyes, groups of tourists admiring the beauty of the ocean, and locals enjoying a choice *churasso* steak by the bay.

A local charismatic church that used the arts to reach the unsaved and unchurched had invited us to attend a national conference focused on urban youth evangelism. It was pure unadulterated street evangelism. Superb gospel choirs singing black and Latin gospel music drew a large and enthusiastic crowd. Two hundred young people—some eager and others more timid—approached passersby with a friendly smile, an invitation to a church drama later in the week, and gospel tracts. A director hawked CDs of the gospel choirs between sets. It was an interesting mixture of gospel and commerce but one that seemed well suited to the carnival-like atmosphere of the experience.

Bay Front Park in Miami provided a perfect venue for this taking of the gospel to the streets by visiting youth from around the country. Bay Front Park offers patrolled sidewalks and a safe public thoroughfare where local businesspeople, Miami residents, and tourists can meet and converge in a common space. In American culture and history, it is in the public square of free speech that ideas can compete on an equal basis. Bay Front Park's public performance pavilion allows free and safe access for "preaching" a variety of gospels (good news) to an audience who eagerly awaits the entertainment in the almost mall-like commercial atmosphere. Music is the hook, pulling people into a space where they can choose to listen to a simple message of soul salvation. Today it is the gospel of Jesus Christ; tomorrow it is the gospel of urban culture provided by local rock bands. Just as one selects a meal from a menu, browses through the racks of clothes and curios, one can select a message that appeals to the eyes and ears.

The scene we are witnessing is the kind of image that most people, especially Christian evangelicals, see in their minds when they hear the phrase "taking the gospel to the streets." It is a traditional message and method with which the evangelical church (Baptists, Pentecostals, and others) utilizes the arts in evangelizing the world, at home and abroad. To "individualistic evangelicals," as Ron Sider refers to them in *Good News and Good Works,* evangelism is taking (going out into the street) and presenting the message that "Jesus saves" and inviting one to give their soul and life to Jesus.[3]

One cannot deny the results of this kind of evangelism. The "hit and run" ministry (as the local minister refers to it) of Trinity Church in Miami employs this method through their music and youth department and is producing numeric growth. The church campus that sits between I–95 and other major roads dotted with trailer dealerships and commercial sites is virtually spilling out of the one-acre lot and into the streets. The church sanctuary, or Praise Dome, is a huge prefab bubble. Trinity is a diverse church, with many ethnic groups and nationalities, in a Christian world that has often been accused (and proven) to harbor racism. The campus has a counseling center and a youth center complete with billiard tables. Trinity's message is simple: "Accept Jesus Christ and be saved. Receive eternal life and salvation from an eternal hell."

One has to admire the commitment of these musicians to prepare the music, transport equipment, and plan and deliver an outdoor concert. They show true courage in sharing their beliefs in the public space of a major city. And we observed a number of passersby accept the tracts and discuss their content with interest. It was a "soft sell" in a friendly atmosphere.

Just blocks away, however, in a regentrified section of the downtown area, homeless men sleep on the sidewalk, prostitutes walk the streets, and at-risk youth have trouble finding recreation amidst boarded-up youth centers and locked church doors and often end up resorting to drugs and violence. One doesn't see these people at Bay Front. And one wonders if they were to receive an invitation to the drama later in the week, whether they would or could find transportation. One also wonders what would happen if the concert were to be held in their neighborhood, among the poor and marginalized. How would their lives be changed?

A Gospel from the Streets (Upon This Rock 'n Roll, Hip-Hop, and Jazz)

"Agh! Agh! Chi-agh agh!" The street was in the church, if one would call it a church. Many pastors wouldn't, and several complained on a monthly basis. But one could not mistake the symbols of hip-hop culture as turntables turned, rappers rapped, and B-boys break-danced in a "sanctuary" that seemed more like a ghetto street club on Saturday night than like a Thursday night youth church service in northern Tampa. But make no mistake about it: Pastor Tommy Kyllonen, a.k.a. Urban D, is serious about reaching a multicultural youth culture addicted to hip-hop, marginalized by the traditional church, and in need of a relationship with Christ. The sign for Crossover (the name of the church) is a colorful graffiti painting of the name, which is amplified by a parked van bearing another graffiti rendering of "Jesus saves."

"I want these young people to have a relationship with Christ," the lean and youthful Pastor Tommy shared with conviction. "I want to reach people who would not attend other churches or who might not be accepted. I want to do it in the language of the culture, the hip-hop culture."

And it is working. The church has grown from just a few young people to several hundred. Pastor Tommy has served this small church nestled in a lazy residential section of Tampa, bringing youth from all over the city into a community that nurtures, loves, and encourages them in a community of believers, providing a haven of the kingdom for those lost in an urban world of drugs, violence, and dysfunctional families. The church has recently begun to confront the social issues raised by the youth: AIDS, child molestation, and abortion.

Not concerned about hair color, ethnicity (Tommy himself is a Philadelphia Greek married to a New York Puerto Rican), social class, or denomination, Crossover shares the concerns of a growing number of Christians in the United States: how to reach those the church has neglected, society has marginalized, and Satan has trampled. Highly specialized for a specific audience, avoiding a clear relationship to the traditional church, utilizing contemporary culture, and taking names that resemble designer stores in a shopping mall, these communities of faith provide a haven for those who live in the margins of society outside the city gates of economic and political power.

Tribe, Scum of the Earth (our favorite name), and Crossover represent a new era for emerging Christian faith communities; for not only have they shed the names of a traditional church that has lost power and credibility amidst moral failings, but they are using the arts in a creative way to make the gospel relevant to our media- and technology-driven culture. Decidedly multicultural, charismatic, and contemporary, these gospel-taking groups are "bringing in the sheaves" and "rescuing the perishing" as the old evangelical hymns exhort. The church, or the emerging faith community, is the center and lifeline for new converts and joining faithful alike.

Appealing and safe from the evils of the outside world, these faith communities and the pastors who lead them focus on building a kingdom community that is the shining light on the hill above the trash heaps of society, a safe haven and refuge for the weary and worn. Both of the examples we have given—the old-fashioned street evangelism in Miami and the innovative emerging faith community in Tampa—have one thing in common: their focus is primarily on winning souls and building a local church. While one may take their language to the street and the other from the street, both churches' interaction with the street is limited to traditional activities of worship, evangelism, and personal discipleship—all of which are focused on the edification of the institutional church, however unorthodox its structure.

Both of these examples are traditional approaches to taking the gospel to the street. They reflect individualistic evangelicalism and church-centered mission, which are the approaches associated with most of the churches within the United States. These approaches play an important role in sharing the gospel, the Good News of Jesus, and offer a clear message of redemption, salvation, and personal transformation. They are clear in their message and in their methods. Yet in our cities a quiet but growing movement of artists of the Christian faith are developing a new approach. Because of profession and concern for taking a holistic gospel to the poor and marginalized, these artists are incarnating the gospel outside the walls of the sanctuary in dramatic ways—ways that are often uncomfortable for many people in the traditional church but ways that must be admired and studied.

A Gospel for the Streets (Suffering outside the City Gates)

"Boom, boom, shaboom, boom." North of the city, 10 P.M. You can feel the sidewalk vibrate rhythmically underneath your feet as you walk to the corner on Frankford Avenue. People spill out onto the street and into the small courtyard of a gutted building. Cigarette smoke and jasmine incense comingle in the air with the sounds of the heavy rock music pulsating from the doorway. You push your way through a small group of wine-sipping middle-aged adults dressed in designer casual wear and engaged in polite conversation. Men with shoulder-length hair and punk-looking young adults gulp beer and laugh loudly in order to be heard over the deafening music of the live band playing in the corner of the gutted room. The ceiling above has cracks so large you can see the room on the second floor, and exposed wood shows the wear of a hundred years or more.

"Hi!" the friendly voice of a bubbly and bouncing-to-the-music Sarah Thompson greets you. "I'm so glad you could make it. This is the building I was telling you about. The CDC (community development corporation) I work for helped a group of artists buy this building. They're going to turn it into a coffeehouse and art showroom, with thirteen studio spaces for working artists upstairs. Isn't it wonderful?"

It is wonderful. Sarah Thompson is a young, committed Christian and a graduate of Eastern University's Urban Economic Development Program. She is working with local artists to bring about real social transformation in the once mean streets of this part of north Philadelphia. But where is the church in this scenario? Several blocks away stands a beautiful stone church building. It was built by a mainline denomination almost a century ago. When industries in the area began to close due to the changing urban economy that resulted from internationalization, the neighborhood transitioned from its background of predominantly working-class Irish Catholics, who went looking for jobs elsewhere, to an ethnic mixture including Vietnamese, African-American, and Latino populations. Property values fell, the church sold out to a Christian group of which little is known by those in the area, racial conflict erupted, and drugs moved in.

Now we are in the middle of a very diverse group of people who are trying to revitalize the area—artists. (Experience has shown, by the way, that artists work well in this situation because they are some of the first people willing to take the risk by buying lower-cost housing and improving the neighborhoods. On a cautionary note, however, it doesn't take long for others to follow, property values begin to rise, and the potential for "gentrification" occurs as lower-income folks who do not own houses must move to other "low-income" areas.) If the church is present, it is not there as an institution. But as you look around, you can feel its influence in subtle yet strongly connected ways. God is at work here.

You look around the room. A DJ is cuing his records in the center of the room. His T-shirt reads "Jesus is Lord." The drummer, drenched in sweat, waves at you amidst his drumming patter. It is Julius Rivera! Julius is the son of Pastor Vega, a street preacher who operates a mobile Sunday school van for community kids in the tough Kensington communities. An excellent musician, Julius is a member of the Circle of Hope Church located in Philadelphia. Circle of Hope has taken a unique strategy of reaching out to the people of the city who may not attend traditional churches. And there is Sarah Thompson, networked with friends from a number of churches and Christian organizations.

Whether these Christian young adults realize it or not, they are participating in what Jung Young Lee calls a theology of marginality.[4] This theological position, which has roots in liberation theology and is similar to the evangelical work described in Orlando Costas's *Christ Outside the Gates,* encourages people to move both in and beyond the centers of cultural and political power and to live and minister in the margins of our society. It is a position of mission in which the person of faith lives, not in the comfort of the sanctuary but in the diversity of the street.

Unlike the first two examples, these artists of the Christian faith have chosen to incarnate—to live, work, and serve as members of marginalized communities—*in the streets,* where long-term results are achieved by a gospel of social involvement and action. They have chosen to work in the secular world, where their roles and the rules of engagement may be dictated by others and where their message of hope and redemption must be lived on a daily basis.

What do these three stories have in common? In each of these examples, a young artist and those they work with are seeking to bring about transformation—in the lives of people around them and in the cities in which they live. These artists want people to have an abundant life—a good life, as we will define it later—and pray that through that life society would be a better place to live. They pray, hope, and work for the kingdom of God to reign in people and in the cities in which they work. Another commonality is that each of these artists is working within the urban environment—an environment that can be tough and unrelenting to those who choose to live there and to those who are called to serve there. While we applaud the efforts described in each of these examples, our focus will be on artists who are living incarnationally in the marginalized communities within our cities.

Before moving to the next chapter, consider these questions: What should renewed communities look like? What is the vision for our cities? Scripture and our artist interviewees both give us specific visions for this new community, the NU JERUZ.

We find several passages in Scripture that lead us to a vision of the NU JERUZ. Isaiah indicates a *reversal in the fortunes* of God's people when salvation comes. Cities in ruin are rebuilt; joy, freedom, beauty, and praise replace mourning, bondage, ashes, and depression. Confusion gives way to satisfaction; the people, their relatives, and descendants enjoy places of respect and honor among their peers.

Nicodemus's conversation with Jesus (see John 3:3) reminds us that *new attitudes* are a necessary part of the NU JERUZ. Kingdom characteristics are also described in Romans:

> For the kingdom of God is . . . righteousness, peace and joy in the Holy Spirit. . . . Let us therefore make every effort to do what leads to peace and to mutual edification. . . . It is wrong for a man to eat anything that causes someone else to stumble . . . or to do anything else that will cause your brother to fall.
>
> Romans 14:17, 19–21

The emphasis here is that we should have unselfish consideration for others, building them up, supporting them, and helping to resolve conflict in pursuit of harmony.

From Galatians 5, we learn that *new behaviors* are important. We know that "adultery, fornication, uncleanness, lewdness, idolatry, sorcery, hatred, contentions, jealousies, outbursts of wrath, selfish ambitions, dissensions, heresies, envy, murders, drunkenness, revelries, and the like" (vv. 19–21 NKJV) will not be practices present in the kingdom of God. On the contrary, life in the kingdom will be characterized by "love, joy, peace, longsuffering, kindness, goodness, faithfulness, gentleness, self-control" (vv. 22–23 NKJV).

God's provision is for all. The prophet Joel extends God's spirit of provision, safety, healing, restoration, and personal fulfillment to all, regardless of race, gender, or social class.

> I am sending you grain, new wine and oil, enough to satisfy you fully; never again will I make you an object of scorn to the nations. I will drive the northern army far from you. . . . I will pour out my Spirit on all people. Your sons and daughters will prophesy, your old men will dream dreams, your young men will see visions. Even on my servants, both men and women, I will pour out my Spirit in those days.
>
> Joel 2:19–20, 28–29

This provision is a *message of hope*. A characteristic of any legitimate prophet is the delivery of a message of hope. Amos adds his vision of restoration: restoration through everlasting relationship and friendship, restoration with a redemptive purpose—hope for the future, a second chance.

> "In that day I will restore David's fallen tent. I will repair its broken places, restore its ruins, and build it as it used to be. . . . New wine will drip from the mountains and flow from all the hills. I will bring back my exiled people Israel; they will rebuild the ruined cities and live in them. They will plant vineyards and drink their wine; they will make gardens and eat their fruit. I will place Israel in their own land, never again to be uprooted from the land I have given them," says the LORD your God.
>
> Amos 9:11, 13–15

Christians have a goal and an eternal destination. This changes the way we behave in the present. The description of the New Jerusalem in Revelation (21:9–21) summarizes the hope for the NU JERUZ. John described the New Jerusalem as a great and holy city, lit with the glory of God and restored to splendor and beauty with the best and most precious of building materials: gold, jasper, sapphire, chalcedony, emerald, sardonyx, carnelian, chrysolite, beryl, topaz, chrysoprase, jacinth, amethyst, pearls. It was secure (great and high walls), dignified (angels as gatekeepers), and included the universal church (the inscribed names of the twelve tribes of Israel of the Old Testament and the names of the twelve apostles of the New Testament). It possessed trees that bore fruit continuously, an unpolluted, crystal clear, pure river of life-giving water, and the natural medicine of the trees' leaves for perpetual healing.

The NU JERUZ is for the "least of these" (Matt. 25:40). This, along with the descriptions from Revelation, is evidence of God's promise of a continuing restorative process on earth to lift up the downtrodden. The reversal mentioned in Isaiah, then, can also be anticipated in the renewal of God's kingdom on earth. Of all the poor, the urban homeless population is one of the most destitute. But we can expect that in the NU JERUZ they will be raised up with great visibility to positions of honor as testimony to the power of grace, mercy, and love: God's as well as ours toward our fellow humans. The Isaiah passage also reveals the process by which transformation comes: through those of us who take up the call to a positive ministry of proclamation, healing, and love.

The NU JERUZ is more than a biblical image. It is a practical, concrete reality that is brought about by the way people live their lives. The following characteristics of the NU JERUZ embody all of the Scripture passages mentioned above.

- Planting of new vineyards (urban gardens and rooftop vegetable gardens)
- New and rebuilt ruins: houses, schools, community centers
- New community fabric: new attitudes and a spirit of unity
- Pride in the gifts, talents, and accomplishments of those dwelling in the community
- Long-term friendships, relationships, and commitments
- Fellowship, reconciliation, and celebration across race, class, and gender lines
- Rebirth of the church (praise and worship) outside its conventional walls
- Renewed aspirations and career dreams
- Academic success and creativity
- Economic and small business growth and a viable consumer base
- Holistic health care provision
- Renewal and celebration of the community's culture, history, and people

2

The Language of the NU JERUZ

In this short chapter we want to clarify certain terms and concepts that will be used throughout the remainder of the book. As with any language, it is difficult to carry on a conversation unless one has fluency in the basic vocabulary. We recognize that the terms we are using in this book may have different meanings. Our primary concern—whether one agrees with our concepts or not—is that we are speaking the same language for the purpose of our discussion.

As you read, this chapter should answer the following questions:

1. What is meant by the terms *community* and *transformation?*
2. What are the three levels of transformation, and what are the goals of each level?
3. What is meant by the terms *streets, gospel,* and *taking,* in the phrase "taking the gospel to the streets"?
4. What difference does a faith perspective make in our lives?

A *community* is any group of people who, by circumstance or design, are working toward a common goal and are using all of the members' gifts to accomplish this goal.

Transformation is the intentional process of bringing about change in the world—a change in which people, communities, and their systems are economically, socially, politically, and spiritually renewed, given new vision and power of capacity to live a life in harmony with God, themselves, one another, and their environment.

One cannot deny the radical changes in our society in the past decades. We have seen ethnic cleansing in Bosnia, genocide in Rwanda, continuing crisis in the Middle East, major corporations falling under the weight of greed, and terrorism that proposes to gain justice through premeditated acts of violence. We have seen the liberation of people held under authoritarian and theocratic governments, as well as new freedoms for gender, race, class, sexual orientation, and ability. Many have benefited from scientific and technological advancements; we are now able to communicate instantaneously with people all over the world and to obtain news at a moments notice—including "live war," which has made a difference in how we view war, its consequences, and our role in it. The world watches in wonder and anger as the genetic engineering that can heal a broken body and produce more food threatens to create a world copyright on life—a copyright that would be in the hands of a few who benefit financially and who would destroy the mystery of life. Not all of these changes are welcome, and many are loathed. And we watch, wait, and wonder at the future of life on this planet. Many repeat the old saying of our grandmothers: "We are going to hell in a handbasket. Can this world be saved?"

Social change refers to the evolution of culture and society and their institutions over time. Social change is ubiquitous and is both intentional and unintentional. And because some changes matter more than others, social change seldom occurs without controversy. Planned social change, in which people band together to bring about change, has brought and continues to bring about revolutionary, reformative, and redemptive social movements. In recent years Christians, especially those involved in community development, have begun to use the word *transformation* to describe the positive change and impact of their work and ministry in the world. Placed within a biblical worldview, this transformation involves God's work in the world from the beginning of time, a journey that is to culminate with a new heaven and a new earth at the end of time. This transformation includes bringing people into a right relationship with God through Jesus Christ, incorporating believers into supportive communities of faith, and bringing about the kingdom of God on earth in the present, as was established by Jesus during his incarnational life.

In this book we refer to three levels of social change or transformation: personal empowerment and responsibility, community revitalization, and societal transformation. Each of these levels of transformation is holistic and integrated. By *holistic*, we mean the transformation occurs within all aspects of personal and community life, including psychological, physical, spiritual, economic, political, and sociocultural dimensions of life.

In the first level of social change, *personal empowerment and responsibility*, the ultimate goal is for a person to change in attitude and behavior. The transformation of individuals reveals itself as people transcend their circumstances through renewed minds and deepening spirits. They have new vision, and thus new meaning, for their lives accompanied by a greater awareness of God's presence. That awareness is related to an individual's new vision—having hope, showing love for one's neighbor (putting others first), and understanding one's relation to others and to the community. Ultimately, people (individuals and communities) take responsibility for their actions and seek to change their circumstances.

In the second level, *community revitalization,* the goal is to develop strong and healthy communities. Vital communities include whole, functioning families and the presence of effective cultural, religious, financial, educational, and commercial institutions that participate in the community and provide sources of work, income, housing, and cultural expression.

In the third level, *societal transformation,* the objective is to renew social systems so that they are just, to reform policies to bring about fair and equitable treatment of all citizens, and to realize a better quality of life within the society. Societal transformation involves the political, economic, technological, and social systems created by people for the governance of a society.

These three levels of transformation and the various aspects of life are interrelated in an ecology of transformation. That is, by changing one level, all levels are changed to different degrees. For example, the innovation of rap, which began as a prophetic artistic expression (personal) that drew from black preaching and political rhetoric, led to hip-hop culture in urban communities (community) and eventually impacted American and international culture (societal) through new styles of dress, language, and music and by changing or reinforcing the values of today's youth. Rap music has grown into a $1 billion industry, though many now consider it to be far from its origins, in both message and values.

Taking the Gospel to the Streets

To provide a concrete definition of what we mean by "taking the gospel to the streets," we begin by briefly defining each word of the phrase, in reverse order, before moving on to examine each term in more detail. By *the streets,* we mean the urban world, but we are referring to something more than a geographical entity; we mean the whole of urban culture and the streets as the places in the city that are often outside the gates of city power, the places in the city where one finds marginalized communities and cultures.

We define the *gospel* as the Good News of Jesus Christ in a holistic, living faith that includes not only salvation but also good news for the poor, the alienated, the imprisoned, and the suffering. Christians are mandated to tell the

Good News, and in *taking* the gospel to others, we propose an incarnational model of "being" that is rooted in the theology of Jürgen Moltmann and draws from relational cultures.

The Streets

We assume a Christian worldview of the city, a view that is drawn from the visions of Isaiah and Revelation and from the teachings of Jesus. We appreciate the many positive aspects of cities, and we recognize that over 50 percent of the world's population live in cities. We also recognize the spirit or soul of the city related to biblical and theological principalities and powers of the spiritual world.[1] While the worldview of the secular sociologist would explain this as personal problems and structural dysfunction, the Christian worldview sees it clearly as being a result of personal sin and social evil.

So what is so great about a city? Talk to the residents and they will tell you that in spite of the stereotypical view that one usually sees portrayed on television or in film, the city is a vibrant, convivial, diverse, exciting, and creative place. Historically, cities have sprung up at seaports and inland crossroads as centers of commerce and trade. They are places infused with the myths of fortune seekers, immigrants escaping religious and political persecution, and idealists searching for freedom of mind and heart. One can trace the history of a city through its social structures. The edifices of political power rise and fall within the structures of church, industry, commerce, and finance. Many people are drawn to the city because of the attractive and possibly rewarding economic opportunities to be found there.

Worlds meet in the city, in the diversity of its people and in the diversity of their worldviews. Unlike those who live in cohesive and cloistered suburban and rural communities, urban residents are often freed of the constraints of a single worldview. In the streets of the city, people are free not only to express themselves but to try on the varied belief systems found in urban culture, as if they were in a secondhand clothing store. Every idea has been tested, worn, and shared. This creates an unusually trying challenge for the Christian worldview, and especially for the church. Several years ago a group of Eastern University youth ministry majors wanted to test the suburban/urban perceptions of the church by videotaping people's responses to a word-association game. Going out to the main street of suburban Wayne, Pennsylvania, near Eastern's campus, the students asked a number of people for their initial response to the words "Christian" and "church." The responses were very positive: safe, good, cool, nice. Then the students took their camera to Philadelphia's South Street, a very popular tourist street that was gentrified in the 1970s. It is an urban street, filled with shops, stores, restaurants, and every imaginable belief and culture. You might not be surprised how people on this street responded to the words "Christian" and "church": stupid, lame, fake.[2]

Artists create in the city. The freedom and encouragement afforded artists in the city, by virtue of its openness, diversity, and history, produces some of the world's greatest art—art that represents the heart of civilizations, the aspirations and dreams of a society.

Diversity connects in the city. *Urban* refers to the culture of the city. Cities are legal and geographic spatial entities. For example, Philadelphia has a charter issued by the state of Pennsylvania and has city boundaries. These boundaries are important to the legal and economic systems of the city and are used to produce revenue through taxes and to define the basis for services. Yet cities also provide the place and space for the connectivity and diversity of urban life and culture. Cities and their urban life and culture are not monoliths, however, and there is a constant flow of goods, services, ideas, and problems from rural communities, suburbs, and other cities and places around the world. Cities are both microcosms of the world and conduits through which the people of the world pass.

As we saw in the previous chapter, cities have problems that are created by social evil and overpopulation. However, one should avoid stereotyping the city as a negative place and the poor as hopeless individuals; most people of the city, poor and rich alike, find hope in a God of grace and in his daily provision and work to transform themselves and their communities into a just and godly society. In this geographical and cultural arena, art becomes a tool of prophetic word and transforming work.

So when we use the term *the streets,* we mean the public environment of the communities outside the direct influence of the institutional church, even though the church may be located in the same community. We mean the marketplace of society, where diverse ideas compete on an equal footing. In short, we mean "the world."

The Good News (Gospel) for a Good Life

Throughout the ages people have asked a basic philosophical and theological question: What is the good life and how can I attain it? Nearly every television commercial asks and answers this basic question in thirty seconds. Movies and plays do the same in the form of stories. Our educational systems teach the values of our culture, in which is embedded the core of our belief about the good life and how to attain it. Major political ideologies and religions do the same. Those who give allegiance to God and call themselves Christians have a spiritual worldview that answers the three basic questions about the good life: What is the good life? What keeps me from attaining it? What is the way to salvation or redemption?

In the past year we have talked at length to over sixty artists of the Christian faith about the arts and the kingdom of God. And while they expressed a variety of views and theologies—all based upon the concept of salvation—we have chosen a very simple definition of the good life that encompasses the beliefs and expressions of those interviewed. While this definition may be too general for some and too narrow for others, we use this definition within the context of the book.

The good life is being reconciled to God and to our fellow human beings—a reconciled relationship with God and humanity. The primary barriers to that reconciliation are both personal and social and involve the pursuit—for personal and political gain—of money (greed), status, in-group solidarity, and power. The way to reconciliation (often referred to as salvation) is through an intimate and personal relationship with God through the person of Jesus, that is, living as he lived—accepting one's responsibility to live a life that brings about the ultimate realm of God in the world. The gospel's message of the forgiveness of sin and the ability to begin life anew gives hope to many people.

The gospel in our view is clearly holistic. In what Ron Sider calls "A DISTURBING KINGDOM COMMUNITY," because of many evangelicals' emphasis on personal salvation at the expense of social action, he gives a litany of principles for his view of a whole gospel:

If the gospel is not just forgiveness of sins, but the Good News of the kingdom of God . . .

- We cannot separate a reconciled relationship with God and a reconciled relationship with brothers and sisters in Christ's body.
- We understand that reconciled social and economic relationships in the body of Christ are one part of salvation.
- We understand more clearly that ministering to both the physical and spiritual needs of people is not some optional possibility, but essential to the gospel.
- We see more vividly that the Christian community, if it is faithful, will always challenge what is wrong with the status quo.
- That any sharing of the gospel that does not include a significant concern for the poor is unbiblical.
- We cannot share the gospel adequately just by preaching. We have to live it too. Words and deeds must go together.[3]

Faith makes a difference. If we have an awareness of eternity, we have a sense of purpose, a goal beyond the present, a future orientation that engenders hope. Our truth is one that disbelieves coincidence and embraces providence, which leads to optimism. We view each person as a child of God, made in his image and therefore worthy of love, respect, and a right to a quality life. Good and evil are the urging and outcome of forces greater than ourselves.

Steve Turner, in his book *Imagine: A Vision for Christians in the Arts,* speaks to the faith factor: "Reality as viewed by a Christian is different from reality seen through secular eyes. The fact that we are aware of an eternity ahead and spiritual realms around us alters our perspective on everything else. We have a different view of good and evil. We have a different truth. We have a different view of the person."[4]

Taking It to the Streets

We believe that people are to be agents of transformation, to change *this* world—both the people of this world and the societies in which they live—into what it ought to be. To bring about this change, one must not only call individuals to live a responsible life through a spiritual relationship with God but also have a loving and mature relationship with one's neighbors and the systems in which they live.

This kind of transformational work is an integrated part of one's life, a natural expression of who one is in relation to others. It causes one to respond to others based on common ground, meeting others as fellow human beings, not from an egocentric or ethnocentric viewpoint. Transformation is not achieved in a single moment but through an ongoing relationship.

Dr. John Perkins believes that "more Christians are discovering the simple truth that people empowered by God are the most effective solution for the spiritual and economic development of the poor, and that the very physical presence of God's people is the surest way to begin tackling the problems of our poorest communities."[5] His theory can be simply stated in three words: *relocation, reconciliation, and redistribution*. Through holistic evangelism and social action, he calls on committed Christians and their families to *relocate* to communities of need, become a part of the community, work alongside the community, model healthy lifestyles, and raise up Christian leaders.

Perkins further believes and advocates that *reconciliation* not only includes reconciliation to God through Jesus Christ and nurture in the church but also reconciliation to others through the true love of Jesus Christ that breaks down every racial, ethnic, or economic barrier as all Christians come together to solve the problems of the community—"the entire body of Christ, black, white, brown, and yellow, rich and poor, urban and suburban."[6]

When Christians relocate and reconcile, the result is *redistribution*. As God's people live in a community of need, they apply their knowledge and skills as members of the community and help to find "creative avenues to create jobs, schools, health centers, home ownership, and other enterprises of long-term development."[7]

We have observed many cases of a disease we call *ecclesiosclerosis*—a hardening of the local church toward the problems of the world and an irrelevance to the culture of contemporary society. Through our research we discovered a new kind of faith community, Christians of another generation who find their "church" in noninstitutional faith communities—Bible studies, informal gatherings, and groups serving in urban communities—that serve the same purpose of nurture and discipleship as that of the traditional church.

Artists, cultural organizations, and churches are part of a broader community. Rather than take a unidimensional approach to the issue of transformation, individual artists and local churches must work in collaboration with individuals, associations, and institutions that reside in the same community.

Major Principles

1. Sharing the gospel is a collaborative concern for the whole person.
2. Transformation is an intentional process that leads to renewal, a new vision, and empowerment and affects all aspects of life for the person, the community, and society at large.
3. The Good News gives people, communities, and societies hope for a good life as they conform to the kingdom of God.
4. A faith perspective provides an unparalleled sense of purpose, motivation, and compassion for the world that results in action.
5. The arts are part of the kingdom of God and, as such, have a role to play in the transformation process as we work to bring about the NU JERUZ.

3

The Arts in Redemptive Transformation
A Model for Change

The Spirit of the Sovereign LORD is upon me, because the LORD has anointed me to preach good news to the poor. He has sent me to bind up the brokenhearted, to proclaim freedom for the captives and release from darkness for the prisoners, to proclaim the year of the LORD's favor and the day of vengeance of our God, to comfort all who mourn, and provide for those who grieve in Zion—to bestow on them a crown of beauty instead of ashes, the oil of gladness instead of mourning and a garment of praise instead of a spirit of despair. They will be called oaks of righteousness, a planting of the LORD for the display of his splendor. They will rebuild the ancient ruins and restore the places long devastated; they will renew the ruined cities that have been devastated for generations.

Isaiah 61:1–4

As you go, preach this message: "The kingdom of heaven is near." Heal the sick, raise the dead, cleanse those who have leprosy, drive out demons. Freely you have received, freely give. Do not take along any gold or silver or copper in your belts; take no bag for the journey, or extra tunic, or sandals or a staff; for the worker is worth his keep.

Matthew 10:7–10

Then I saw a new heaven and a new earth, for the first heaven and the first earth had passed away, and there was no longer any sea. I saw the Holy City, the new Jerusalem, coming down out of heaven from God, prepared as a bride beautifully dressed for her husband. And I heard a loud voice from the throne saying, "Now the dwelling of God is with men, and he will live with them. They will be his people, and God himself will be with them and be their God. He will wipe away every tear from their eyes. There will be no more death or mourning or crying or pain, for the old order of things has passed away."

Revelation 21:1–4

Who, having read these famous prophetic passages, has not been moved at the depth and breadth of their vision? One can feel the hurt of the world and at the same time dream of a time when there will be no pain or hurt in the world. These passages provide the passion and the vision for what the world can and will be in the end of times (Revelation), a call to be involved in transforming the world in the present (Isaiah), and the way for bringing about the transformation (Matthew).

In this chapter we will describe our model, called Arts in Redemptive Transformation (A.R.T.), for how artists can be involved in bringing about the NU JERUZ. This transformation process is a journey of faith for people, communities, and societies. In our transformation model, drawn from a variety of disciplines, we discuss how change occurs and how the arts (1) are a catalyst for transformation by confronting social injustice and personal sin and creating *critical awareness* of the need for change, (2) serve a mediating function in *working out* transformation as it begins to take place, and (3) are significant in the *celebration* of renewed people, communities, and societies.

This model of transformation lays the groundwork for succeeding chapters. As you read, this chapter should answer the following question: What distinguishes the three stages and the eight steps of the A.R.T. model?

HEAVEN: A place where I can walk safely—[where] the name-calling, bigotry, and ignorance would end.[1]

From the play Standing Out in a Drive-by World

Good art, whatever its form, helps us both individually and corporately to perceive reality in a new way, and by so doing, it opens up possibilities of transformation.[2]

John de Gruchy

Life as a Spiritual Journey

Dr. Lee Spitzer, a Baptist pastor, draws on his Jewish heritage and the Bible to describe life as a spiritual journey that helps us to interpret our place and purpose in the world. Spitzer delineates two levels of goal-oriented spiritual journeys. He describes the Redemptive-level spiritual journey as one that "embrace[s] goals related to personal or corporate wholeness and spiritual growth" and the Mission-level spiritual journey as "not centered on oneself, but on ministering to other people for the sake of the Kingdom of God."[3] The ministering to others leads to a greater definition and clarity of one's life story. These stories and their understanding help life to be meaningful and to express their identity and vision of the world.[4]

It is Spitzer's belief that people pass through five distinct phases in their spiritual journey. Phase 1, the Unconscious Journey (preparation), is a phase in which God prepares people for a spiritual task to which they feel called. Phase 2, the Encounter with Revelation (discovery), is the discovery of a task-specific goal or purpose for our journey and leads to a response. It is both our call and our response to the call. Phase 3, the Conscious Journey (cooperation), "denotes the Christian's conscious experience of God and His People working together toward a common task-specific spiritual journey goal." The Conscious Journey is empowered through God's Spirit in the miracle and appearance of the gifts of the Spirit and in bringing about truth and justice. Phase 4, Reaching the Goal (arrival), signifies an end to only one phase of the journey and is marked by reflection and worship. Spitzer calls this phase a sort of "death experience" in which a person has an opportunity to "identify with Jesus' passage from life, through death, to resurrection." Phase 5, Resurrection and New Life (renewal), replaces the letdown experienced in the arrival phase with "a new sense of vitality and purpose." The person and community have now reached a new stage of maturity. The process then starts again in a spiral of journeys toward fullness and maturity.[5] While our transformation model (A.R.T.) draws on all of the models presented in the Introduction, it agrees with Spitzer's ideas in that life is understood to be a redemptive eternal journey.

Summary of the A.R.T. Model

The Process of Transformation

In the process of social transformation, both people and communities move through three distinct stages. In stage 1, *Critical Awareness,* people attain critical awareness of a problem or issue. In stage 2, *Working Out,* the person, community, or society attempts to work out the problem through a variety of strategies until a solution is reached. In stage 3, *Celebration,* success or completion is celebrated as a way to publicly recognize and solidify the new state. Each new state then becomes the current state, and the process begins again in an upward spiral of growth.[6]

NU JERUZ: Arts in Redemptive Transformation Model

People and communities are propelled from each stage to the next by a *connector*. The connector from critical awareness to the working out stage is a commitment of will, or *allegiance*. The connector from the working out stage to celebration is the attainment of the goal, or *completion*. The connector from celebration to renewal is *assessment*.

The Role of the Arts in the Transformation Process

The arts play an important role in our transformation model. There are three basic art typologies in A.R.T.: prophetic arts, agape arts, and celebrative arts. In the critical awareness stage, the arts function in a prophetic role and confront people, institutions, and society about their current state, wrongdoing, or injustice as they bring people to critical awareness of the need for change. The art of the urban prophet is generally used as a communicative tool with a specific message. The primary value of the prophetic arts is justice.

In the working out stage, the arts may play a catalytic and synergistic role in the development of personal and social solutions that lead to renewal. The art of the agape artist is developed in relationship to the needs of others, and the relationship or outcome is often more important than the art. The primary value of the agape arts is compassion.

In the celebration stage, the arts play an important role in leading the community in celebrating transformation and renewal. They celebrate accomplishments with and for people. The celebrative artist represents the core values of the community, considers artistic tradition, and often strives for art that will most typify the standards of the community. The primary value of the celebrative arts is praise.

Possibilities and Limitations of Art

Though we will discuss the specific power of art in the next chapter, we present here the basic possibilities and limitations of art within our transformation model for the purposes of our discussion. Artistic expression in the various art forms of dance, drama, visual arts, and music is uniquely bound to the context in which it is produced. Understanding culture and how culture drives events is important in planning and interpreting change. In other words, the "vocabulary" and "rules" in any art form must be learned before there can be a common understanding of the language of the art form, which will allow it to have the greatest impact.

While artistic expression reflects culture and informs experience, it also constructs reality in concrete forms. Art is created from the beliefs and motivational goals of the artist(s). This construction of reality opens up the imaginative possibilities for participants, who may not have "seen" the artist's reality previously, and provides a vision for the future.[7]

Artistic expression has action potential that may lead people to act in ways that they had already been considering, albeit perhaps subconsciously. Art becomes a voice for the unspoken. In this way art acts as a catalyst, sparking the imagination and bringing new realities and behaviors to life.

Artistic activities create an environment in which relationships can be built and change can take place or be worked out. Much like a petri dish in a laboratory, artistic activities provide a potentially formative and friendly environment where people can grow personally and in relationship to others. This occurs because the created environment is conducive to experimentation, exploration, and a sense of play, outside the boundaries of the immediate culture. The creation of such an environment is highly dependent on a relationship of trust between the members of the group and between the group and its leader/teacher.

The greatest limitation of art in social transformation has more to do with relationships than with art. Art created in relationship with others bridges barriers, provides an open and trusting environment, and potentially builds the spirit of community.

Art in redemptive transformation is not a panacea or stand-alone activity. Art is often the missing link in the transformation process and will greatly enhance personal or social change when used in collaboration with other disciplines or fields. In other words, art has no meaning without people. Art alone will not bring about transformation, just as bringing economic development to a community without considering the aesthetic experience of the residents cannot alone improve the quality of life—which is one manifestation of transformation.

Finally, artistic expression is not a neat or exact science. It is intuitive, emotionally expressive, playful, fun, and creative. To suggest that art and artists will bring about redemptive transformation alone overestimates the power of art and the role of the artist. But one should never underestimate the power of the arts and the role of artists who bring the ability to think and act "outside the box," to imagine possibilities, explore options, and rehearse change in collaboration with other elements of community.

The A.R.T. Model in Detail

The Arts in Redemptive Transformation model has eight basic steps. A person, community, or society may enter the process at any time, but the sequence of the steps is important in bringing about transformation. As a word of caution, the actual transformation process is not as neat as the model presented here, and the process can be sidetracked by a change in the context or by an influential leader. We will first present the model in its entirety and then provide several examples from our experience.

Stage 1: Critical Awareness

Art has the potential to change both our personal and corporate consciousness and perception, challenging perceived reality and enabling us to remember what was best in the past even as it evokes fresh images that serve transformation in the process.[8]

John de Gruchy

STEP 1: CURRENT STATE

This is the place, time, context, and circumstances in which a person, community, or society finds itself. While people may not know the reasons for their circumstances or understand how to change them, they often feel the emotions of both joy and pain. They may not, and usually do not, even have an awareness of the possibility of a different life. They need to be awakened to a different reality in order to change.

STEP 2: CRITICAL AWARENESS

One of our favorite expressions is, "If you don't know where you are, you don't know who you are." Critical awareness means being aware of one's circumstances, how the circumstances came about, and what role one can play in changing them. Paulo Freire calls this "critical consciousness," when "men and women develop their power [of capacity] to perceive critically the way they exist in the world with which and in which they find themselves; they come to see the world not as a static reality but as a reality in the process of transformation."[9]

STEP 3: NEW COVENANT, OR ALLEGIANCE

Once one has a new perspective and capacity to change, he or she must first make a personal decision and then enter into a new covenant or new allegiance within a community context. A barrier to change is lacking the will to change, including admitting the need and desire for change. As a biblical example, Jesus asked the man who had been lying by the Bethesda pool for thirty-eight years a very important question: "Do you want to be made well?" (John 5:6 NKJV). In other words, do you care enough about your problem to do something about it, even if it requires some action, effort, sacrifice, or suffering on your part?

Some people don't want to change. Like the Bethesda man, they answer with self-pity. Or when God sends someone to help, they play the martyr or victim ("Nobody loves me!"). Allegiance means getting up and committing to action. It is the connector between being aware of a desirable change and making the commitment to bring it about. But as Freire has also pointed out, many of the oppressed are in a system that needs changing. The oppressor must also commit to change.

In the Christian worldview, Christ himself is our mediator (Heb. 8:6–13), a legal term for one who arbitrates between two parties. Christ mediates between God and mankind. He established the new covenant. Its establishment on "better promises" makes the new covenant better than the old. The new covenant provides forgiveness of sins (v. 12). It involves an inward and personal relationship with God (v. 10). Consequently, there is no longer any place for the old covenant, which was faulty, "obsolete," "growing old," and "ready to vanish away" (vv. 7, 13 NKJV).

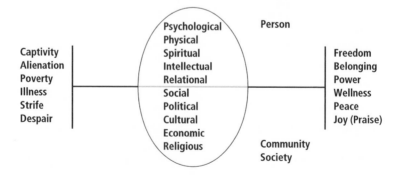

The new covenant, or new allegiance, is a commitment to learn new skills and to collaborate and cooperate with others for positive transformation. In this, however, the poor in wealth, health, and spirit might not yet have the *power of capacity*—the "skills and resources that enable critical choice and successful action to change their situation."[10]

Stage 2: Working Out

Therefore, my dear friends, as you have always obeyed—not in my presence, but now much more in my absence—continue to work out your salvation with fear and trembling, for it is God who works in you to will and to act according to his good purpose.

Philippians 2:12–13

STEP 4: DELIBERATION, OR WORKING OUT THE NEW COVENANT

In step 4 the person or community enters a stage of working out the desired transformation. Commitment and deliberation are a continual and interrelated process until a solution has been reached and action begins. The working out requires a process of dialogue, planning, goal setting, strategizing, collaboration, organizing, implementing, and evaluating. This may be a formal process. For instance, art therapists often design a working plan with a client, and community organizations often write strategic plans.

Once the solution(s) has been reached, there is what Mark Mattern refers to as a pragmatic phase "for discovering and creating commonalties and acting on them."[11] Coming to common agreement and working out a problem can place the person or community in conflict with external communities. The solution(s) being worked out may, and often does, create conflict with external forces, and the community of the new covenant must then work out, often in the face of confrontation, the resulting barriers to transformation.

How does one decide what goals and objectives are important and necessary in the working out stage? The goal of transformation is to bring people into a right relationship with God, each other, and their environment. It is to seek peace, justice, well-being, and redemption in the spiritual, social, economic, emotional, physical, and political lives of people, communities, and societies. The following graph illustrates the holistic goal of transformation. Alienation, for example, is more than an emotional problem of feeling alienated. In order to transform alienation, the person and the whole community must be involved in changing the emotional attitudes, psychological beliefs, relational behaviors, and spiritual conditions of all concerned to create belonging. It also involves broader economic, cultural, political, and environmental concerns.

The transformation process is complex, involves an "ecology" of change, and is only one journey of faith among a progression of journeys in the lives and communities of people. Practically, artists working with a community collaborate with other disciplines in order to have a holistic plan of action. The transformation process can be quite messy, and it takes a lot of work. For example, in recent years BuildaBridge International has sought to fulfill its mission of "crossing cultural boundaries and bringing faith to life through the arts in the tough places of the world" by working with at-risk children in Philadelphia and abroad. We collaborate in this work with organizations that are already working with street kids and homeless children through education, psychological counseling, technological training, and spiritual development. Our role is often to provide opportunities for improving self-esteem, developing arts activities that utilize positive creative energies, improving drab environments through murals, and enhancing what is already taking place. Our role may also include improving education by integrating the arts for more effective learning. We had an opportunity to provide collaborative arts service recently when we partnered with the city of Philadelphia to assist in transitional homes. In two of the seventeen shelters there are over three hundred homeless children. In our pilot project in one of these shelters, we found that there were no arts activities for the kids, and the environment was drab and unstimulating. As of this writing, we are developing an ongoing arts program as part of a more comprehensive shelter revitalization in partnership with the city, local businesses, and the shelter's staff, parents, and children.

STEP 5: GOAL COMPLETION

The connector between working out and celebration is the attainment of the goal, or completion. Reaching small goals is important in the transformation process. Therapists assist the client in setting many small goals while working toward a larger life goal. Long-term community projects plan for stages of completion. Achieving small goals provides encouragement as the community sees progress toward their transformation.

Stage 3: Celebration

STEP 6: CELEBRATION

Once a person or community has worked out a solution, they reach a new and different level of success. Celebration recognizes the success, acknowledges the heroes of the project, and provides an event for expressing joy. This is often done through special events in which the positive changes of transformation are incorporated into the "official" life of the community. For example, in the Community Bridge project that took five years and involved nearly 130,000 neighbors, small celebrations along the way were needed to keep people involved and motivated.[12] These were in addition to a large celebration at the completion of the project. The arts have always played an important role in celebration. For through artistic expression, we are able to play and celebrate with the highest of our creativity and emotions.

STEP 7: ASSESSMENT AND NEW AWARENESS

Sometimes by formal evaluation—but more often by an informal and new awareness of context, roles, and worldview—the person or community reenters the process of transformation. They move into another cycle of change, with new problems to solve. But they have moved one level closer to the NU JERUZ.

How does one know there has been movement toward the NU JERUZ? What are the signs or indicators? Indicators of transformation are drawn from a vision of the goal of transformation. Indicators are important in assessing the movement toward a redeemed nature. These signs are measurable and could include such things as: clean streets (physical), presence of self-esteem (psychological), recognition of God (spiritual), and so on. In a well-designed development or strategic plan for community development, arts therapy, or education, such indicators are called "outcomes." They are the visible changes that have been accomplished from among the broader goals of the desired transformation. These indicators and outcomes provide the person or community with concrete realities to assess their progress and to begin another transforming journey.

STEP 8: NEW CURRENT STATE, OR RENEWAL

At this stage the person or community find themselves in a new current state. They have reached a new level in the never-ending journey of transformation. The new current state of renewal corresponds in the cycle with stage 1, in that there is now an opportunity for further renewal.

Gotta Dance! Personal and Group Transformation

One of the outcomes of cross-cultural learning is the development of flexibility. Flexibility is the ability to adjust one's cultural behaviors to a new context. Developing flexibility is a basic goal when one desires to live and work across cultural boundaries. The expressive arts are vital characteristics of culture, and our emotional attachment to them and cultural beliefs about them can often become barriers to cross-cultural competence and flexibility. It is therefore not unusual for the arts to be major obstacles in removing the barrier of in-group solidarity.

In 1999 we led fifty-nine people to Egypt on one of our Educational Safaris. The purpose of these safaris is to cross cultural boundaries and to learn about other cultures and their faith expressions. Among the group on this safari were the Angels of Harmony, Eastern University's gospel choir. They are a lively group of gospel singers, and their concerts are filled with joy, passion, rhythm, and dance. They express the heart of the African-American music culture and are used to receiving standing ovations and many "hallelujahs" wherever they sing. But not on this trip.

Early in the safari, the Angels were invited to sing in a Presbyterian church, the largest in the country. The church was packed with people of all ages and from all walks of life. Not more than three minutes through the first number, just as they were beginning to break a sweat with their singing and dance, worshipers began to leave the sanctuary.

As in most church conflicts, the members of the congregation complained to the minister, and word reached us via our host. "We don't like disco in our church. God requires reverence." We were about to become *critically aware* of a major difference in our worship cultures. In Egyptian culture many people are reflective in their worship style. Prayer, hymn singing, and worship rituals are carried out with formality and reserve. The Angels had breached that culture.

We knew we had to *work out* this problem, or our concerts would likely offend others and we would miss the opportunity to build bridges between cultures and develop relationships. Part of our working out was to call the group together and explain the situation. We needed a *commitment* on their part to come to a solution. Some of them grew very intense: "This is our culture, we shouldn't have to change that; they need to learn about us." True enough; we wanted to expose Egyptian Christian culture to the joy and expressiveness found in gospel music. But if we offended people, we might find ourselves without an audience.

As directors we set a rule that in future concerts there would be no movement. The singers would have to dance in their hearts, not an easy thing for them. While we had *verbal allegiance* to the idea, we weren't sure their hearts were in it. Throughout the week we continued to work it out. We visited a mosque and learned about Islam, toured the country, and learned about Egyptian culture. During the week we were invited to an Orthodox church, where their choir performed ancient songs accompanied by strings and cymbals. At the end of the service, our group was invited to sing a gospel song. Then we had an opportunity to meet each other, talk about our different worship expressions, and build relationships. It was a wonderful time of fellowship. Our cultures began to learn about each other. At the Angels' final concert at CEOSS (the Coptic Evangelical Organization for Social Services, the largest community development organization in the Middle East), our new Orthodox musician friends came to hear us. There was no dancing, and we had *reached one of our goals.* We were able to *celebrate* with our new friends when they asked for an encore and stayed following the service for more conversation.

Had we met our goal? Had we helped our choir to become cross-culturally competent? One of the indicators would be to see a change in attitude on the part of the group after they had returned from the trip. Here is what one student wrote:

> As a young woman who is highly involved in the ministry of dance, I have come to a greater appreciation of the Arab culture. I must admit that I was one of the Angels who were very offended that we were being told not to move when we sang. Now I realize that you have to reach people where they are—and you cannot do that if you have offended them.[13]

The ultimate question we have to ask ourselves is: Are we bringing about the NU JERUZ? And we would say yes, in a small way. We are removing barriers of in-group Christian solidarity in that we are learning to accommodate the views and needs of others. Doing this on a regular basis, however, requires much more work, as we will see in chapter 12 when we discuss renewal.

In this example we have seen how an art experience provided the environment for transformation to take place. In the following example we will see how a piece of art helped bring about societal transformation in a small but significant way.

Black Jesus: Societal Transformation

In his excellent book, *Christianity, Art and Transformation,* South African John de Gruchy tells the story of the remarkable journey of a painting.[14] During the apartheid years of South Africa, many Americans were oblivious to the struggle for racial equality in South Africa. Those in South Africa knew that having America's support could be instrumental in changing power and bringing about justice and equality.

While the artist's intention may never have been to attract international attention but simply to paint the crucifixion for his context, he would impact the outcome of apartheid. In 1962, at the time of the famous Rivonia Trial when Nelson Mandela was convicted of treason and sentenced to Robbins Island, Cape Town artist Ronald Harold painted a black Christ being crucified. The painting was first hung in St. Luke's Anglican Church in Salt River. What made this picture interesting, and offensive to some, was that the black Christ was the image of Chief Albert Lutuli, and the soldier piercing his side was Prime Minister Verwoerd.

When the Dutch Reformed Church became *aware* of the painting, they lodged an official complaint with the government censorship board because it "offended religious convictions." Soon the painting was shown on CBS in the United States, which not only raised *critical awareness* in the States but even more so for the South African government. While the government tried to confiscate the painting, it was secretly smuggled to London, where it was sold to raise money for the opposition movement, a strategy that supported the *working out* of political transformation. Years later, after apartheid ended, a special celebration was planned in Cape Town featuring "Art and Apartheid." Though Harrison didn't have the painting at the time, he located the painting in London and returned it to South Africa, where it now *celebrates* significance at the national gallery and provides a memory of the past.

While the goal of Harrison may not have been to help transform his society but merely to comment on it, his painting became a part of the movement and the working out of South Africa's political transformation. An important part of justice and equality in a society is for the aesthetic expressions of all cultures to be valued and recognized by the government. A key indicator of this goal is the increased space and recognition given to art of all cultures in public places. Has redemptive transformation occurred? Is South Africa moving toward the NU JERUZ? Certainly this is one indication that it is.

Spitzer's model of transformation, summarized earlier, is based on what is now called *narrative theology*, meaning that our lives are progressing stories rather than static realities. One can easily see the correspondence between the A.R.T. model and goal-oriented transformation models like Spitzer's Spiritual Journey. The spiritual nature of the A.R.T. model recognizes that God is at work in us and in our world as we become partners with God and with others in working out what God is doing in the world.

Finding One's *Eschaton*

What are artists to do in redemptive transformation? Where and how do they become involved? At a recent series of lectures at a center-city church, we presented our transformation model as a way of challenging artists to become more involved in transforming the world through their art. Many artists see their art as a very personal and creative endeavor. Others live professional lives and have very little time for community activities, especially those artists who have growing families. The church too has sometimes been more concerned with the end times than with the present times, which allows us to be relieved of the social consequences of our "time" while feeling safe that we have been "saved."

God is speaking to us in our time, today. The question we have to ask is, What is my place in the journey of redemptive transformation, and what gift has God given me to bring about his kingdom in the present? As Albert Nolan suggests, the event that defines the present—our time in the NU JERUZ—is our *eschaton*.[15] Our *eschaton* is a time of choice, either/or, when we are compelled to choose to act. It is the purpose, the calling, the decision, the act of involving ourselves and our art in redemptive transformation.

Artists have a unique opportunity to explore and enact a ministry that can impact the world—a world that is at our doorstep, on our street, and in our community. It is an opportunity to live the gospel by sharing our art in compassionate ways that bring critical awareness of the need for change and by celebration of the victories of life as people and communities enter into the NU JERUZ. We as artists need to answer the call of our *eschaton* through A.R.T.

> Let us weep until our tears turn into indignation, our indignation into determination, our determination into action, and our action into a better society where our children and generations to come can enjoy life, liberty, and the pursuit of happiness. And the Tupac Shakurs need rebel no more and can turn their genius to things that are beautiful, lovely, and good—to the love and celebration of life: black and white, male and female, young and old.
>
> Herbert Daughtry

4

The Transforming Power of Art
God at Play in the World

In this chapter we will take a look at the transforming nature of the arts and the theology of play that serves as its backdrop. We will differentiate five powers of the arts—creative or catalytic, cultural, political, spiritual, and redemptive—and within these categories offer a quick literature review of their impact in education and in social, personal, community, economic, and spiritual development. Throughout this discussion we apply the arts as a source of power to illustrate how the arts have action potential within the transforming process. Finally, we will explore both the benefits and the limitations of the arts in personal and social transformation.

As you read, this chapter should answer the following questions:

1. Do the arts actually have power?
2. If so, what kind(s) of power?
3. How do we know the arts have power? How is the power manifested?
4. In what ways do the arts act as a catalyst for transformation, bring about critical awareness, assist in the working out of solutions, and celebrate change?
5. What is an appropriate faith perspective of transformational art in the NU JERUZ?
6. What is unique about certain art forms that allows them to be effective in bringing about transformation?

The main work of the creative person—and the main reward of a creative arts program—is to be able to look at the world with wonder and awe, to be able to direct attention to the richest, most significant parts of the world, to ask the penetrating questions, to design the most effective strategies for accomplishing goals, and to create the most significant symbols to represent the experience.[1]

Peter London

The theater is a weapon. A very efficient weapon. For this reason one must fight for it. For this reason the ruling classes strive to take permanent hold of the theater and utilize it as a tool for domination. In so doing, they change the very concept of what "theater" is. But the theater can also be a weapon for liberation. For that, it is necessary to create appropriate theatrical forms. Change is imperative.[2]

Augusto Boal

Now the Spirit of the LORD had departed from Saul, and an evil sprit from the LORD tormented him. Saul's attendants said to him, "See, an evil spirit from God is tormenting you. Let our lord command his servants here to search for someone who can play the harp. He will play when the evil spirit from God comes upon you, and you will feel better." So Saul said to his attendants, "Find someone who plays well and bring him to me."

1 Samuel 16:14–17

The Power of the Arts

The theater is a weapon, and it is the people who should wield it.[3]

Augusto Boal

Art has power and can be an important part of the transformation process. Art has power to translate emotions and intellect into form. Art has power to express personal and community beliefs and values through concrete symbols. Art has power to transform—to change one's vision for life, quality of life, and life circumstances.

Recent studies from governmental and nongovernmental agencies and from research centers in the United States and abroad suggest that the arts have the power to impact individuals, communities, and society at large. Because the arts are so pervasive in our society, however, we often fail to recognize their presence and their impact and to calculate accurately the important role they play in our lives. Imagine our culture without museums, parades, advertising, films, television, community theaters, parks, gardens, music of all varieties, dance companies, music in worship, arts and crafts, summer park concerts, and so on. If for no other reason, the expressive arts are necessary in society to improve our quality of life.

In 2000 the Chicago Center for Arts Policy published a qualitative research project that examined the impact of the informal arts in Chicago. Examining twelve different case studies, the researchers discovered that the arts bridge differences of class, race, and ethnicity. The informal arts (as opposed to the professional arts) build capacity by providing important "opportunities for adult expression and creativity" while building "individual and community assets" important for "civic renewal." The study found that the informal arts create a tolerance of difference, trust and consensus building, collaborative work habits, creativity in solving problems, and the ability to imagine change. The informal arts strengthen the entire arts sector through intellectual, creative, and economic exchange.[4]

According to Professor Roger Graef in his report on the arts in prisons, "The Impact of the Arts in Criminal Justice Settings," the arts provide a liberating opportunity that is the antithesis of imprisonment, where conformity is mandatory and real life is suspended. The arts counter imprisonment by "encouraging people to make choices, decisions and personal statements, to be open to stimuli, assimilate influences, have enthusiasm, take risks and take responsibility."[5]

Aesthetic art philosophers and critics find value in art itself and believe there is power in the very existence of art. Yet artistic expression is also highly functional. Art fulfills important roles in society by teaching values and ideas, healing emotional hurts, building relationships, and providing employment. In part 2 of this book we will offer specific examples of these outcomes. Anthropologists study art because of its ability to reflect the worldview of the cultures that produce it. But the greatest power wielded by art and given to all of us by God is the outlet it provides for our natural instinct to play and create.

A Theology of Play

Amy Scheer, a professional theater director and drama teacher now living in Iowa, has written a faith-integrated curriculum for developing children's community theater for BuildaBridge International. In her opening chapter, "Changing the Culture through Drama," Scheer notes the following:

> A child approaches his world with a sense of wonder. He wakes each morning full of possibility for the new day. But this playfulness is often all but snuffed out, as children in today's world carry heavier responsibilities and knowledge of the worries of the world than their little shoulders can carry. We must make it our mission to preserve the sanctity of children and childhood; remember that Jesus made clear that becoming like children is a necessary prerequisite to experiencing heaven (Matthew 18:1–5). How wonderful it is to provide young people with a safe place to play, to express

themselves creatively, through drama. The older the child, the more he may need to be reminded of the importance of play and how little is needed to facilitate it.[6]

Children love to play, and good teachers know how to play with them. In *The Theology of Play* Jürgen Moltmann dialogues with three other theologians and suggests that the church and society in the middle to latter part of the twentieth century had forgotten how to play as a demonstration of their freedom in Christ. The work ethic had infected every aspect of the church's life, from social ministry to worship.

Play is an authentic human expression. It is a way to rejoice in the glory of God and to enjoy the pleasures of creation. Yet Moltmann cautions that "if on earth everything turns into play, nothing will be play, it becomes impossible to distinguish between good play and bad play. . . . Play should liberate, not tranquilize, awaken, and not anesthetize. Liberating play is protest against the evil plays of the oppressor and the exploiter. Thus play seriously and fight joyously."[7] This inner spiritual play, to use our imagination, has many outward manifestations. We are to "be there for others" in responding to the needs we see around us. But we are also "to be there with others" in relationships that are enjoyable, even playful.

Learning how to play is difficult for many Christians in our society. Driven by a purpose and working to save the world, many Christians are so serious about the world's problems that they get lost in their work and the methods for going about it, and a sense of joy in the Creator is consumed in the game of work. Joyful play must be experienced not only as an inner spiritual play with God but in relationship with others.

In his recent study, *The Rise of the Creative Class*, Richard Florida states that over 30 percent of the U.S. workforce is now employed in a creative sector. Artists, scientists, and other creative types comprise a new and influential affluent social class with lifestyles that exhibit openness, diversity, individuality, and meritocracy. Their work is not bound to a particular place, and they often choose to reside in cities that are open to their values. They are, according to Florida, a major force in developing human capital and economic growth. He cautions, however, that this class may tend to live in isolation. If these creative people are to make a difference in the world, they must be connected to the diverse community. "We cannot hope to sustain a strong Creative Economy in a fractured and incoherent society."[8] Playing alone, playing without concern for or connection to those around us, does not lead to redemptive ends.

Moltmann suggests a theology of play in which we are to do more than *be there* for others. The motives for serving others are not to *do for*, or to *do* in order to fulfill our own need to do; we are to *be*. We can learn a lesson in *being* from relational cultures that do more than be there *for* others (working at a distance to help), but who strive to be there *with* others (incarnational living) in pain, suffering, joy, and dance.

There are three basic lessons in Moltmann's theology of play. First, those who are concerned for the plight of the poor and marginalized will have a difficult, and often short, career or ministry if they do not have the ability to find the inner "dance with God" that is manifested in a life of joy amidst the drudgery and messiness of ministry. Second, the expressive arts are a way to "try God on" and to find the inner joy of the Creator—to find him in the creative moment and in the unbounded joy of dancing, singing, acting, drawing, and creating. This does not mean that there are not restrictions of good taste. You can dance and have a good time without being on the floor dirty dancing.

Finally, Moltmann says the church itself has a chance to embrace its "value of being . . . by demonstrating human freedom in its [the church's] own life and by manifesting its rejoicing in that freedom."[9] Thus, the creative arts are the expressions of joy, the playrooms and playtimes that allow us to praise God in joy, as well as in pain, and to "try on" salvation and liberation in preparation for life in community with others.

Scheer reports the story of Jane Avery, artistic director of Our Town Theatre in Oakland, Maryland, who has a heart for kids and a gift of reaching them through theater. One of her students, Tom (not his real name), who had been physically and emotionally abused, was liberated through his drama class. He wrote in his Declaration of Independence:

> I, Tom, do hereby declare myself independent from unhappiness. . . . To rid myself of these memories and the baggage I carry around because of them, . . . I need to develop roles on stage so that I can understand the thoughts and hearts of others, . . . releasing all of my dreadful memories through energy and creativity in performance and giving others happiness who watch and listen.[10]

There is power in play.

Five Artistic Powers

The following five types of power are important in understanding the role of the arts in redemptive transformation: creative or catalytic power, cultural power, political power, spiritual power, and redemptive power.

Creative or Catalytic Power: In the Image of God

Art is a form of knowledge: the artist, therefore, has the obligation of interpreting reality, making it understandable. But if instead of interpreting, he limits himself to reproducing it, he will be failing to comprehend it or to make it comprehensible. And the more reality and art tend to be identical, the more useless will be the latter.[11]

Augusto Boal

The word *create* was introduced into the English language, from the Latin *creatus,* in the fourteenth century. It literally means "to bring into existence." Today this word permeates our culture and speaks of innovation, intelligence, and influence.

For Christians, the word *create* is held in high esteem, in relation to the power of God ("God created the heavens and the earth" [Gen. 1:1]), and is therefore at the root of the conflict regarding the arts in the church. In a conservative Reformed view, the word *create* is reserved for the creative acts of God.[12] Humans do not actually create; they "tend the garden" by taking existing materials and developing God's creation with wisdom and responsibility. In this view there is often a mistrust of art that imposes limits on artistic expression. In the extreme, some Christians take the commandment "Thou shalt have no graven images" as a commandment to remove artistic forms from worship. In an opposing view, art and the artist are "small *c*" creators. Made in the image of God and living as a new creation (Gen. 1:26; 2 Cor. 5:17), humans have been given the power to create and are gifted with the spirit to bring into being what they have imagined. Art, as an expression of God's creativity, is a way to experience the very nature of God.

It is our view that art and artistic expressions are gifts of God. Because artistic expression is part of all human existence, it is a part of common grace and is evidence of God's creation. It is God's gift for our polluted lives, broken spirits, and places without hope, a gift for celebrating the victories of life.

Amy Scheer says, "God is a creator. Making theater is an act of creation. We partake of this quality of God when we help to create a thing of beauty, of excellence. It is inevitable that students who participate in this creation will sense, on some level, the holiness of God; even a work of excellence without the mention of God can lead a person toward him. And if faith is hope in things not seen, then nurturing the imagination could be considered Faith Training!"[13]

People are gifted with the power to express inner thoughts, interpretations, feelings, and emotions in the form of concrete external behaviors through visual arts, music, drama, and a variety of artistic expressions. Artistic expressions and the artists who "create" them are catalysts, agents that "provoke or speed significant expression, change or action."[14] The catalytic power of the arts provides an opportunity and tool to contribute to the transformation of people, communities, and society. Based on the recent research we and others have done, we now list ways in which the arts have been found to impact the transformation of people and communities within different disciplines. Some of these points will be taken up more fully in part 2.

In community development, artistic expression can:

- Provide neighborhoods with hope and a sense of identity
- Beautify public places
- Rekindle the spirit and connect us to the power of God and to one another

In education, artistic expression can:

- Offer an experiential approach that incorporates and accommodates a diversity of learning needs and styles
- Engage people and assist them to make sense of difficult, complex, vital, and universally human experiences
- Play a role in the development of higher-order thinking skills, problem solving ability, and motivation to learn
- Assist the development of metaphoric language, vocabulary, observation, and critical thinking
- Clarify the idea of process (movement)
- Improve academic performance and standardized test scores
- Increase school attendance and decrease dropout rates
- Deepen development of creativity and imagination
- Increase memory retention of facts and concepts (especially songs and poetry)
- Teach about other cultures and worldviews
- Improve attitudes toward school and community
- Reignite the will of teachers to teach

In personal development, artistic expression can:

- Encourage people to make choices, decisions, and personal statements
- Open individuals and enable them to assimilate influences, have enthusiasm, take risks, and take responsibility
- Allow the emergence of new values
- Improve social skills
- Improve dexterity and fine motor coordination (drawing)
- Provide an expressive outlet and vehicle of cohesion for teens struggling with issues of identity, body image, and role experimentation
- Stimulate dreams and options for the future
- Assist people in coming to grips with personal problems and habits

- Teach discipline and teamwork
- Decrease the likelihood of antisocial behaviors
- Provide public affirmation

In economic development, artistic expression can:

- Enhance the economic status of individuals and communities
- Increase the capacity of individuals to acquire employment
- Create an environment for economic growth

In faith and spiritual development, artistic expression can:

- Rekindle the human spirit that embodies the Spirit of God
- Increase awareness of God and the holy
- Strengthen ties to a community of believers
- Teach values and biblical knowledge

Cultural Power: The Power of Symbols

Symbols are the language of the arts. The arts and artistic expression have cultural power by their ability to be and to provide concrete symbols of a culture. These symbols become banners of a culture. Related to culture, the arts have social power by informing and influencing the social mores of a society. They provide identity and cohesiveness but also act as barriers to cross-ethnic collaboration. For example, as illustrated in the last chapter, the distinctive worship and faith music of African-Americans made it difficult for Egyptian and African-American Christians to participate in each other's worship expressions.

Symbols are powerful in representing and communicating beliefs and values. This is seen most clearly in the visual arts, where even a single symbol can have tremendous power. On the 5600 block of Chestnut Street in West Philadelphia, elderly community member Grace Lindsay, age seventy-eight, was staring at a mural near her neighborhood shop. Nineteen-year-old Kenny Green walked up, and Mrs. Lindsay took his photograph by the mural as they exchanged words. According to an article in the *Philadelphia Inquirer,* this encounter set Kenny's life in a new direction. Mrs. Lindsay was admiring the change that had been made to the mural since it had first been painted by artist Ras Malik in 1979. Malik had initially painted a young African-American boy of twelve playing basketball with an expression of joy on his face. Mrs. Lindsay was concerned each time she looked at the mural. "That's all you can be? It *has* to be more than that. You can still be *that,* but you have to get your education." A community activist, Mrs. Lindsay encouraged the Cobbs Creek Neighborhood Advisory Council to send a polite letter to the mural arts program. The council responded by reenlisting Malik to transform the young boy from a basketball player to a graduate with cap and gown. It was this image that greatly impacted Kenny. "It just gave me hope—like just 'Go! Go! Go!' . . . It puts you right in the middle of life and it lets you know that life is serious, like, get real—head to the future."[15]

This mural is one of over three thousand murals now to be found in virtually every neighborhood in Philadelphia, all painted by local and professional artists. The mural arts program of Philadelphia is one of the most successful in the United States. Started by Jane Golden during the Wilson Goode mayoral administration in the 1980s, murals were effective in cleaning up graffiti blight in many neighborhoods by providing opportunities for many artists in the 'hood to express themselves in constructive, community friendly ways. The murals provide many messages about values, honor neighborhood heroes, and denote cultural identity, territory, and history.

Symbols have the power to mediate and negotiate conflict. Dressed in his usual purple robe, black socks, and sandals, Baptist bishop Malkhaz Songulashvili has systematically set about reforming the non-Orthodox Baptist church in the Republic of Georgia using the arts. A biblical translator, theologian, and archaeologist, Bishop Malkhaz has studied the icons and art of the historical Georgian Orthodox tradition. While exploring an ancient cave, he came across an icon of a cross that he later adapted for use as a symbol for the Georgian Baptists. This is where the conflict began. Very few buildings were allocated for non-Orthodox worship during the days of the Soviet Union. So today the Georgian Baptists share a building with Russian Baptists and German Baptists, each group holding their own worship services at different times and in their own language.

"I will not worship in a garage!" the bishop quipped with a smile, explaining his reasoning for including visual art in the "sanctuary." The Russian Baptists, however, do not believe in images and icons, especially not crosses. They hold to the conservative thought that there should be no graven images in the house of God. But there is another reason for their belief as well. In late-nineteenth-century Russia, Orthodox believers would beat Baptist believers with wooden crosses in an attempt to get them to convert to the Orthodox church. The beatings only stiffened the Russian Baptists' resolve against icons and intensified their collective memory. So when Malkhaz had a large painting of the cross mounted on the wall behind the pulpit, the Russians complained forcefully. Malkhaz worked out a compromise. During the Georgian service the cross is visible. During the Russian service a large cloth is draped over the cross. And in a wonderful irony, the Russians mount over the cross a huge painting of an open Bible.

Economic Power: Gainful Employment and Productive Places

The arts have a certain amount of economic power. The music industry alone is worth $40 billion worldwide. Cities are using the arts and art districts as part of their inner-city revitalization strategies. As we stated earlier in our brief description of Richard Florida's book *The Rise of the Creative Class,* creativity has become a major driving force in our culture. As we will see in our chapter on the economic power of the arts (chapter 9), the arts provide opportunities for building human capacity in employment and for the revitalization of attractive and creative places that attract businesses and creative people.

We must be cautious with this power, however. As we have noted, one of the major barriers to the NU JERUZ is the pursuit of wealth. While the arts are an attractive strategy for development and an attractive goal for many who desire the wealth created by entertainment stars and recording artists, the pursuit of wealth through the arts can be a seductive goal, whereas gaining opportunities through artistic gifts in a right relationship of personal and community responsibility can be a redemptive goal.

Political Power: Creating Capacity

Men and women develop their power to perceive critically the way they exist in the world with which and in which they find themselves; they come to see the world not as a static reality but as a reality in the process of transformation.[16]

Paulo Freire

In 1970 Paulo Freire published one of the most influential books in education and community development of the twentieth century. In *Pedagogy of the Oppressed,* Freire introduced the concept of "participatory dialogue," which states that people learn more effectively through dialogue than through being fed information, especially in the education of the poor, oppressed, and marginalized. Freire believes that the poor are dehumanized by oppressors of class, and "only power that springs from the weakness of the oppressed will be sufficiently strong to free both." The oppressor, "who is himself dehumanized because he dehumanizes others, is unable to lead the struggle."[17] Based on his education work with the poor in Brazil, Freire believes that through dialogue the poor can come to a critical awareness by "learning to perceive social, political and economic contradictions, and to take action against the oppressive elements of reality."[18]

Four years later another Brazilian, Augusto Boal, published *Theater of the Oppressed,* in which he applied the concept of theater as participatory dialogue. As "poetics of the oppressed," theater was a language for a "rehearsal of revolution," or social transformation.[19] Participants are asked to become a part of theater, rather than mere spectators, by actually creating the drama as it occurs and are thus empowered to rehearse the reality of social change. We will demonstrate this later in the text.

In his book *Acting in Concert,* Mark Mattern provides a model for understanding the power of the arts in the political process. Mattern uses the term "acting in concert" as a metaphor for community-based political action through music. His concept of power, or acting in concert, "entails a conception of power as a capacity for critically formulating (democratic) goals and carrying them into action using available and appropriate means that produce the desired results."[20]

Using popular music as an example (though Mattern's ideas could apply to all popular arts), Mattern defines three basic ways in which music plays an important role in the political process as a communicative forum. First, in the *deliberative* form of acting in concert, music (or any art form) is a way of debating and articulating differences. This was illustrated in the story of Bishop Malkhaz and the cross. Second, in the *pragmatic* form of acting in concert, music can create community by promoting unity and recognizing commonalties, including common problems. The Philadelphia Unity Day celebration was initiated in response to the problem of ethnic prejudice and intentionally includes the music and arts of a variety of cultures. Third, the *confrontation* form of acting in concert "marshall[s] the energies of one community against another."[21] In reality, artists and communities use all three of these forms of power to negotiate community concerns. The political power of the arts is an "alternative communication forum" for participating in the political process.

Spiritual Power: The Battle of Good and Evil

Reality as viewed by a Christian is different from reality seen through secular eyes. The fact that we are aware of an eternity ahead and spiritual realms around us alters our perspective on everything else. We have a different view of good and evil. We have a different view of truth. We have a different view of the person.[22]

Steve Turner

Anthropologist Eloise Meneses believes, as do many Christians and non-Christians alike, that art has spiritual power. Starting with a very high value of the arts, Meneses believes that art pervades our lives and is the finest expression of the human spirit. She also believes that art has the power to express evil just as easily as it expresses good, just like the human heart.[23] If, as many Christians believe, art is the embodiment of God's creative power, it is also possible for art to embody evil. If the arts have catalytic power for positive transformation, it follows that the arts can have the same power for negative transformation.[24] Art can be the sign of a sick society, according to Meneses. Examples include pornographic art, films that promote gratuitous violence, and music lyrics that degrade women.

Part of the problem in recognizing the spiritual power of the arts has to do with the scientific worldview of Western society that either does not recognize the spiritual world (a mechanistic worldview) or separates the physical from the spiritual (a dualistic worldview). In his book *Imagine: A Vision for Christians in the Arts*, Steve Turner discusses the difference between religious art and Christian-informed art: "I believe that Christians should be writing poetry with godly perception rather than poetry about religion."[25] For many Christians, unless art is specifically Christian, it is secular and potentially evil. This belief severely limits the potential for both good and evil that exists in art and the power of capacity it can bring in the kingdom of God. In an age when people thirst for spiritual renewal, and society has already been impacted by the influence of Christian values, we believe that Christians would do well to find those values that are in congruence with their worldview and work cooperatively for the betterment of society. This can only occur when the Christian artist is mature enough in his or her faith to apply spiritual wisdom and critical judgment in his or her art and to analyze the meanings in the art of others. They will then have an opportunity to bring the real message of faith, the source of the values. According to Turner, all art that "dignifies human life and introduces a sense of awe"; art that "carries the imprint of clear Bible teaching" and calls for peace, love, and forgiveness and reconciliation; or art that "has themes of original sin, human moral freedom and the spiritual realm" can form a "useful bridge between the believing community and the unbelieving audience."[26] This means that if the arts do indeed have potential for good and evil, it behooves Christians to take art seriously and to engage in its expression in society as a spiritual source of power.

Redemptive Art: Contributing to a Better World

In chapter 2 we noted that while all creative work is transformative in some way, not all transformative work is redemptive. Redemptive work brings people and communities into a right relationship with God and with each other. Truly transformative work, as we've defined it, must be redemptive in nature. It is possible for nonredeemed people to create transformative work that is redemptive, just as it is possible for redeemed people to create transformative work that is nonredemptive.

Think of art as a story and the artist as the storyteller. Dance tells stories in movement, visual arts in symbols, music in emotion and word, and theater (film, music videos) in a combination as a reenactment of life. As we mentioned in chapter 2, the story told by art answers three basic questions regarding culture: What is the good life? What keeps me from attaining it? What is the way to salvation or redemption? Not all art forms tell explicit stories, and these stories must be studied for their implied meaning. The meaning is determined by culture and worldview, as well as by the intention of the creator.

Some art is very difficult to "read." There is, then, another level that must be considered. That level is the context and the motive or intention of the artist. A violent movie can be redemptive if it is placed within a context of education, where it can be discussed and alternatives can be given. It can also be seen in relation to the motive of the artist who produces it. If the movie is produced as a way to bring attention to a specific problem, and if the intended outcome is achieved and the movie motivates people into action for a better way, we would consider it redemptive. If on the other hand, the movie only angers people, encourages violent actions, or is produced merely to provide the cathartic effect of vicarious acts of violence, we would consider it nonredemptive.

The problem in discerning the redemptive or nonredemptive nature of art is that it requires a knowledge of art, tolerance and openness for dialogue and difference, the ability to understand the language of the art form, and the ability to protect one's views in the midst of conflict. An extreme example of this can be seen in the controversy that surrounded a 1989 photograph titled *Piss Christ*. This photograph, indirectly funded by the U.S. government through the National Endowment for the Arts (NEA) and the National Endowment for the Humanities (NEH), was of a crucifix submerged in a vat of urine. There was an outcry of disgust from politicians and Christians alike. As a result, the NEA and the NEH were allowed no budget increase in the years 1995–2002 because the Republican-controlled Congress objected to the "obscene and inappropriate projects" being funded.

If this photograph had not been highlighted by the media, it would have gone unnoticed. In an age of media sound bites, no in-depth analysis of this work was reported. The artist, Andres Serrano, was reported to have publicly stated that he was a devout Christian and was simply trying to illustrate the suffering and degradation of the passion of Christ.[27] If this indeed was Serrano's intent, it was lost on a society and religious culture that does not take the time to dialogue about art or that lacks the language to do so.

In review of our concept of redemptive art, we suggest that the movement toward the NU JERUZ must always be kept in focus.

1. Redemptive art brings an external expression of an inner reality, creating a critical awareness that allows people to understand their place in the world. An example of this comes from a trip we made to Rwanda

several years ago, following the genocide. In a workshop with young children who had never spoken of their experience, we asked them to draw pictures of their memories. They drew pictures of homelessness, death, and the devastation of war. They also drew pictures that revealed worry, anxiety, and thoughts of suicide. It was through this externalization of feelings that had yet to be expressed that emotional, physical, and spiritual intervention could be made.

2. Redemptive art raises one out of, or at least improves, a situation in which people find themselves and leads them to a better way of thinking, believing, feeling, and ultimately, living. Many artists who use the arts of the street as a way to develop pride and community spirit believe that merely using the art of the street brings about a better community. Certainly we encourage local art forms as a method of developing pride and community spirit. It is not, however, the presence of the art form that provides a better way of thinking, believing, feeling, and living. The salient aspect of redemptive art is the striving for excellence in creation and presentation as well as in the content. Poorly done ghetto art does little to transform but merely confirms and reinforces an already bad situation. We have seen this principle beautifully demonstrated by Duane Wilkins, the minister of dance we mentioned in the introduction. Duane has traveled with BuildaBridge all around the world as a resident artist ministering to homeless children and to church congregations. The children's first response is to want to dance the dances they already do at home or see on TV. "No!" Duane says, "First we will learn the basics and then we can do the shake-shake." Then for several days he hones the group in the basic moves of praise dance, which he and Stacy have adapted from ballet, lovingly disciplining the often rowdy groups into refined dancers. Then they do the "shake-shake," with flare and professionalism, just for fun. Without realizing it until the end, the children have reached a new level of artistry and praise.

3. Redemptive art provides an opportunity to experience a new way of life, to try it on as a rehearsal for change, as we saw in Amy Scheer's example story about Tom. Through the power of drama, a young boy was lifted out of the emotional trauma of abuse. He not only learned to think more positively but relied on drama to allow him to practice new roles and ways of loving others.

4. Redemptive art confronts both the evil in society and the consequences of personal sin. As offensive as the language and lifestyles of hip-hop and rap artists have been, one cannot deny their directness in confronting a society that is divided by race and social class. One often has to wade through obscenities to hear the message—for some, a major barrier to hearing the message—but these artists are not denied an audience among the young and among their own ethnic groups.

5. Redemptive art instills a sense of wonder and awe of the Creator. The aesthetic nature of the created beauty of dance, music, drama, and visual arts brings people into the power of the Creator. Whether we openly acknowledge the source of the creativity or not, this sense of wonder and awe piques the spiritual curiosity within both the artist and the observer.

6. As Steve Turner points out, redemptive art ultimately leads to an understanding of God's redemptive plan in Jesus Christ through a personal relationship. This happens on two levels. First, as people become more aware of God's plan, they are increasingly exposed to the language and meaning of the cross. The arts at the center of the faith provide didactic teaching and emotional expression within the context of a loving Christian community of faith. It is here that overtly Christian terms, symbols, and beliefs can be interpreted in formative evangelism. On a second level, as much as the art itself, it is the art and the person in relationship and the power of the Spirit that ultimately leads to an understanding of the redemptive plan.

The Unique Assets and Limitations of the Arts

Each art form has unique assets and limitations that contribute to its effectiveness or ineffectiveness in the transformation process. While it is beyond the scope of this book to deal practically with each form and its assets and limitations in redemptive transformation—though we have given many examples throughout the book—we provide here a general list of the kinds of arts that are used in A.R.T.

By the expressive arts, we mean all forms of expressive and aesthetic culture used within both formal contexts (concerts, worship services, museums, and galleries—often called the fine arts) and informal contexts (street, home, community—often called the community arts).

Assets	Limitations
Visual Arts: Sight	
Painting, sculpture, cartoons, murals, banners, textiles, fabrics, photography, comic books	
• Provides concrete symbols of identity • Provides for the creation of new symbols • Provides an alternate to speech as a form of communication • Creates lasting impression through images • Are excellent in celebration by visualizing accomplishments	• Requires common understanding • Carries cultural meaning and may create barriers • Abstract art requires more interpretation than representational forms • Requires more one-on-one mentoring • Requires space and supplies that can be expensive

Assets	Limitations
Dance: Movement	
Classical, folk, urban (step dancing and break-dancing), mime, karate, yoga	
• Creates a language of action that is not dependent on verbal ability • Uses the full body • Creates physical awareness of self and others	• Often requires interpretation and explanation • Requires the development of a body language • May have negative connotations for many Christians and requires a refinement of language for the church context
Music: Sound and Word	
Instrumental, choral, popular, videos	
• Deals in emotional and symbolic sound • Facilitates unlimited kinds of messages for any discipline/knowledge area • When used with words communicates both a direct and an allegorical message • Has strong emotional impact	• Impact is often individualistic but can create community • Emotional language is learned and highly dependent on the context • Requires significant training to reach fluency • A competent and trained leader or performer is critical
Drama: Story	
Theater, storytelling, film, puppetry, creative writing, comic books	
• Creates and reinforces the myths of culture • Rehearses reality • Assists in the discovery of self and situation • Preserves and reviews history (personal, academic, and communal) • Envisions the future and encourages "future" thinking • Supports imaginative thinking • Allows trying out multiple solutions to problems and situations	• Requires a language of theater • Can reinforce the status of the elite (true of all the arts) • Can tend toward a professionalism that is exclusive (true of all the arts) • Requires props and stage space, which may be expensive
Technology: Energy	
Web design, graphics, art production (music recording and film)	
• Global in nature; allows geographical boundaries to be crossed instantaneously • Allows for convenient in-home access • Permeates and transcends cultural boundaries	• May be expensive; access often depends on finances • Requires technical skills and knowledge of computers and software • Is generally an individualistic endeavor

Summary

Just as God created man and woman for the purpose of a relationship with him, so creation and redemptive creative acts should foster and reconcile relationships. Works of art are created for us to enjoy and for others to be in relationship with those who create. Art allows us to participate in a process of re-creating, of communicating, of learning truth, and motivates us to reach out to others.

And now, the rest of the story. Remember Kenny Green and Grace Lindsay in the story of the mural? While the story in the *Inquirer* gave credit to the mural for a change in the direction of Kenny's life, the relationship established by Mrs. Lindsay when she cared to interact with someone on the street, and the action taken by Mrs. Lindsay and the neighborhood association, were the real catalysts for the change. The mural set dialogue and action ino motion.

The greatest power of art may be the building of relationships through the art-making process as we work to bring about the NU JERUZ. We summarize the principles of this chapter as a reminder of this process.

- A.R.T. recognizes that art is a reflection of God's creative and life-giving Spirit.
- A.R.T. is the vehicle, the platform, and the event for relationship building. Art itself does not save.
- A.R.T. provides the emotional moment for uncovering truth.
- A.R.T. has the power to transform people through healing, community through identity and relationship, and society through value clarification.
- A.R.T. calls for artists to be catalytic agents of change by identifying with the poor and using the arts in acts of love. Artists can provide a message of hope to impoverished, marginalized, and disenfranchised people and to the communities in which they live. Artists can be instrumental in redeeming cityscapes, community spaces, and people's lives.
- A.R.T. is more than window dressing and must be done in collaboration with other disciplines.
- A.R.T. is God's gift for our polluted lives, broken spirits, and places without hope.
- A.R.T. is the response ability of people of faith, the ability to express concrete emotional responses to the spirit of God.
- A.R.T. provides neighborhoods with hope and a sense of identity and creates beauty in places that are noisy, ugly, and smelly.

- A.R.T. provides people with beauty.
- A.R.T. rekindles the spirit and connects us to the power of God.
- A.R.T. is the sign that God lives and empowers people with his creative will and gives us hope for redemption and renewal.

5

The Artists of Redemptive Transformation

In the introduction we briefly defined a typology for the arts in redemptive transformation, with three basic roles for the arts: *prophetic arts, agape arts,* and *celebrative arts*. In this chapter we will look more closely at how the arts and artists of the Christian faith function within these three roles in bringing about the NU JERUZ.

NU JERUZ: Arts in Redemptive Transformation Model

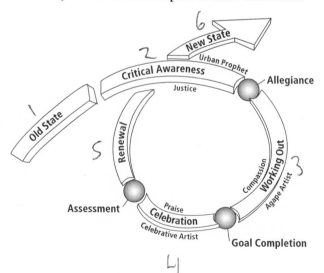

To illustrate our typology, we will focus on the lives and ministries of a number of artists we have met through our research and also on the lives of biblical personalities that are the ancient antecedents of modern-day prophets.

Our hope is that this typology will give artists an identity and a clear role in bringing about the NU JERUZ. Ideally, an artist is a whole and complete minister possessing the gifting and ability to be a prophet for justice, a compassionate lover of people, *and* a leader of celebration.

As you read, this chapter should answer the following questions:

1. What are the three basic roles for the arts and artists in the redemptive transformation process?
2. What are the primary values, purposes, and areas of activity related to each role?

Prophets in Unlikely Places

The heat and humidity were so bad in January that the local people often said "It will cook your brain." Each noon in the middle of the street in front of the central post office, a preacher in full-length garb shouted at passersby in Arabic, sweat pouring from his body and drenching his garment until it was sopping wet. He seemed to preach only in the noonday sun, proving his loyalty and suffering for the message. People couldn't understand him and no one even seemed to listen. They appeared to be a bit afraid of this man and quickly crossed to the other side of the street. One rarely sees a prophet these days, at least not in the United States. The idea of radical devotion to one's faith being displayed in the streets of society brings images of religious fanatics—not unlike this scene in Mombasa, Kenya. We found ourselves wondering what a prophet might look like in an American city.

We drove into the heart of Atlanta, found our way into the razor-wire-protected parking lot of Safe House Ministries, where we waited for Mark Sandiford (a.k.a. Mark Y Rage). We were hoping for a glimpse of a fire-breathing, straight-shooting, gospel-preaching, raging-against-society prophet. As a homeless man walked into the lot of Safe House Ministries, we were greeted by several conservatively dressed and clean-cut interns from the Midwest. "Mark is on his way," they told us as they got into their cars and left.

Within minutes, a mop-headed black man wearing purple sunglasses drove through the gate in a well-worn jeep. Dressed in jeans and wrapped in a white scarf edged in Ethiopian colors, he walked toward us. We were about to meet the reggae musician we hoped would be our "Prophet." And he was, but not in the way we expected.

"I've read the Bible carefully," reggae singer Mark Y Rage says with earnest devotion. His impeccable English covers all but a trace of his Caribbean accent. His dreadlocks fall about his face, and sunglasses cover his "morning eyes," the result of an all-night club event the night before. It is two in the afternoon. "I've looked closely," he continues, "and I cannot find myself there. I read about pastors, teachers, administrators, but where do you find musicians in the New Testament?" Then he boldly proclaims, "I am an urban prophet. I am a Levite who leads people into the praise of God. Instead of the temple sanctuary, I do it in the streets!"

Who are the artists of God who grow from the environments and contexts of injustice, racism, poverty, violence, addiction, homelessness, and joblessness; the artists who begin to root out causes, call the people of God to task, and work for the elimination of these injustices? As we discovered over the past year of traveling to meet these artists, they are often unknown—the silent ones, suffering and placing themselves at risk both within their environment and within the traditional church in order to deliver truth. But they are definitely called and committed to transforming people and communities. They are our modern-day Hosea, Amos, Nehemiah, Isaiah, Jonah, and other Old Testament prophets; they are the voice of Jesus and carry the liberating cross of Christ outside the comfort of the sanctuary into the streets of the urban world.

In nearly all the interviews we conducted around the country, there was an underlying sense of a spiritual identity crisis among artists working outside the walls of the sanctuary. Like Mark Y Rage, the dancers, visual artists, musicians, thespians, and other creative artists we interviewed are comfortable with themselves as people and are confident in their artistic abilities. However, in the face of criticism from the traditional church, where orthodoxy demands they work within the boundaries of acceptable behavior for "Christian artists," these artists stand between the world to which they are called and the church from which they come—a church they love, but one that, in their view, does not love them; a church that has lost a vision of the NU JERUZ and that "wrestles with its own demons."

Within the secular or nonchurch environment, artists who call themselves Christian face another problem. Calling oneself a Christian can repel the very people with whom the artist seeks to build a relationship. Aligning oneself with the church also places an immediate barrier between the artist and a professional world that has a very low view of "church art." It is therefore not uncommon in the professional world to find what we might call "closet Christians," artists who may hide their Christian label. In other words, being a "Christian" is seldom an asset. To be a loving representative of Jesus always is.

Consequently, artists working in the same city may know each other professionally and yet not know that the other is a "believer" or "follower" of Christ.

And the artist who is a believer or follower of Jesus may not fellowship with a church because of a failure in love on the part on the traditional church. Yet we found most artists to be quite devout church supporters, and some were theologically trained.

Faith-Centered Artists

They come in different shapes and sizes, genders and ethnicities, denominations and geographical locations, but faith-centered artists begin from the recognition of and allegiance to a Creator God. They believe in and recognize the creative power of God—the same creative ability given to God's creation. They believe God created the heavens and the earth and cares for them and the world in which they live. Not all of them would call themselves "born again," avoiding either the label or its implications, but their actions and conversations express an allegiance, power, warmth, and love of a Creator God. It is this love and their faith that distinguishes these faith-centered artists and that gives them their unparalleled motivation, commitment, discernment, and impact.

Motivation

It is an *agape love* and the example of Jesus that motivates these artists to serve others and to work to bring about the kingdom of God. All of them did this through their art forms, whether drama, visual arts, dance, music, or technology. Most of them are deeply involved in the lives of others on a daily basis as ministers of the healing and redemptive power of the gospel, acting as mother, father, brother, or sister to those in need of a friend, mentor, or family guide.

Commitment

The faith-centered artists' love was driven by a powerful desire to "give back" as they became involved in ministry to God, to God's community, and to others. This giving back was often at great sacrifice, though we heard little complaining. "For every three units of suffering, I get back three hundred units of joy," community developer Rudy Carrasco told us. Dana Velps-Marschalk, a community dance director in Atlanta, left her affluent home to follow her call and was living on less than $4,000 per year at one point, well below the U.S. poverty level. Scott Parker is working several jobs to make ends meet. All of these artists do what they do out of a calling and commitment.

Discernment

Faith-centered artists see the Spirit in the process of their work, from the inner voice of creativity to the guiding of their work that has no guarantees. Their faith in a sustaining and creative God strongly influences their choices on a daily basis, not only in how they live their lives but also in how they create and use their art. The most notable choice was the subjects of their art. While many musicians would readily sing of their relationship to Christ, others might not mention Jesus but would instead sing about his concern for the poor and marginalized. A number of dance instructors focused more on the inclusive justice of dance. They encouraged and included those who did not fit the physical model of a professional dancer, focusing instead on the message of justice this inclusion would send to the audience. If, as Albert Nolan suggested, the barriers to the kingdom are a pursuit of wealth, status, in-group solidarity, and power, the artists we witnessed have leaped the barriers to the kingdom and have found their *eschaton* in acts of faith and compassion.

Impact

And what about the results or impact of these artists' work? One can see it in the smiles on the faces of the children with whom they work, in the relationships they have formed in their communities, and in the intensity of those who perform, dance, draw, and sing. For most of the artists, this seems to be enough. Their lives are so harried dealing with daily living, relational problems, shootings on the street, property maintenance, city taxes and services, that spending time in formal evaluations seems an expensive and time-consuming proposition—commodities that are in short supply when one is about God's work. Many of the artists rely on God for the outcome, without a care for themselves. With the growing need for financing and funds, however, the artists all seem to be thinking of ways to show the fruits of their labor. They also openly wish for the support of the church faithful who could be sharing more of their wealth with the poor. (We will address this issue in chapter 9.)

Citizen Artists

Bill Cleveland, whom you met in the introduction, believes that artists should be "citizen artists."[1] Though not a Christian, Bill expresses the voice of the many people working in arts-based community development who are motivated to create a better society. He understands the important spiritual role of the arts: "There is a spiritual reality in the world. One can't do this work without the creation sounds. Artists are agents of the community. Where we come from, where we are going, are important questions—transcendental questions. The arts are important for exploring these places in a respectful way and with depth."[2]

We were curious what perspective Bill might have about Christians who work in the field. He has worked with Christian artists throughout his life. Bill says that "in the prison system especially there is a significant presence. There are many faith-based volunteers who lead Bible studies and who bring companionship and normalcy." He believes, however, that there can be a conflict when coupling the (overt) faith message and the artist's work in the public environment. Community work is often government connected, in the fields of health care, education, and so on. Public art must adjust to the requirements of these institutions. The mixing of missions and sharing personal views are often inappropriate and may complicate different situations. People may not trust the Christian artist.

But Bill goes on to say, "Some of the most effective artists have been Christians. I have known them a long time and get to know them. They appropriately understand that their faith is a part of them. Faith guides the way they work: their motivation, patience, sense of dedication, and commitment to their work."

We can understand Bill's view that religious discussions can complicate an artist's work in the public environment. But Bill's comments lead us to believe that faith integration is important to many artists working in the public sphere. As we will see in the following example of Donna Barber, artists can be a presence of blessing anywhere and can be silent witnesses of the love of Jesus. The point we want to make here is that artists of the Christian faith have a role in the public square—as artists, as citizens in the broader society, and as Christians.

The Typology

To review, in the *critical awareness* stage of the A.R.T. model (see diagram on p. 92), the artists and their arts function in a prophetic role by confronting people, institutions, and society about wrongdoing and injustice and bringing them to critical awareness of the need for change. In the *working out* stage, the arts may play a catalytic and synergistic role by healing and nurturing people and help them to develop personal and social solutions that lead to renewal. In the *celebration* stage, the arts play an important role in leading the community in celebrating renewal.

Though the artists we interviewed used various names to refer to themselves and their work as artists, their gifting for ministry falls within three distinct categories: prophetic artists, agape artists, or celebrative artists. Artists in all three categories share a distinctive call to faith-centered art. The proposed arts typology (see below) signifies both a place of artistic expression (street, community center, sanctuary) and the purpose for the creative endeavors. These are not stand-alone categories. Combinations may be found within a single context, and single artists may be involved in all three places and/or purposes. While some artists and their art may fall within only one category, other artists may fulfill the roles of all three categories.

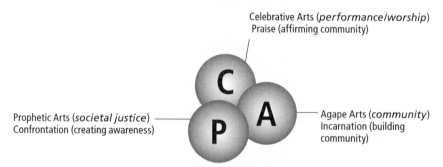

Celebrative Arts (*performance/worship*)
Praise (affirming community)

Prophetic Arts (*societal justice*)
Confrontation (creating awareness)

Agape Arts (*community*)
Incarnation (building community)

The important idea of this chapter is that artists are called to a particular *eschaton,* one's calling and the role one is to play in bringing about the kingdom of God in the lives of people, communities, and society. At certain moments it may be to speak a prophetic word, at other moments to participate in community development, to praise and give thanks for an important milestone in the community, or to praise God in the sanctuary. As we go on to describe the specifics of the three basic roles artists play in redemptive transformation, we want to note that we believe all artists should be involved in seeking social justice, compassionate community ministry, and celebrating or praising the Creator God for life's victories.

Urban Prophets

Prophetic artists, or urban prophets, and the prophetic arts are those that confront the injustices of racism, bigotry, and economic and social inequities. Using drama, visual arts, and music with words, their role in the transformation process is to create critical awareness of the need for change. Urban prophets and the prophetic arts confront injustice both within the church and in society at large.

CONFRONTING INJUSTICE WITHIN RELIGIOUS STRUCTURES

A student recently commented on this principle by saying, "It's fine for an artist to rail against the three big ones—fornication, alcohol, and gossip—in a worship service. But I don't know of an artist that would ever be invited back who began to sing about the sins of the church as a whole or about the lives of its leaders." And it's true; often this kind of confrontation is done from outside the church, directed in.

The early 1990s presented many racial issues in the United States. In 1991 a bystander videotaped Rodney King being beaten in public by the police, and in 1992 race riots broke out in Los Angeles. It was prior to and amidst this tension that hip-hop became an outspoken and political voice. Controversial, bitter, and angry artists like Ice Cube, Ice-T, and Dr. Dre (who subsequently have found their way into the established film industry) typified the modern-day urban prophet lashing out at social injustice.

One rap group, however, seemed to project a positive and proud African-American culture while still extolling a social revolution. Drawing on the group's resilient culture and spiritual faith (though not a Christian group), Arrested Development produced raps that presented the strength, pride, and positive nature of their culture with insightfulness and humor. Part of the American societal problem to Arrested Development was the unempowering of the Christian faith as seen in Baptist church worship. If nothing else, this rap group typifies the voice of a generation dissatisfied with formal and institutional Christianity, which they believe has failed to deal with the real and present issues of the poor and marginalized. In Arrested Development's song "Fishin' 4 Religion," they professed that the church "makes me fall asleep" and that the church congregation praised a God who did not want the members to take action but preferred to watch them "weep."

CONFRONTING INJUSTICE IN SOCIETY

The prophetic arts are not new to our society, though we have often failed to value their role. But at unusual times and in the face of much opposition, God seems to call them forth, Christians and non-Christians alike, to bring a spiritual awareness of an evil reality.

Billie Holiday was born in Philadelphia in 1915. A song stylist, Billie is remembered for her haunting voice as well as her renditions of popular songs with big bands. Her childhood was fraught with problems of truancy, and she even did a stint in a Catholic home for wayward girls. She experienced the racial injustices that plagued many black artists of the era, as portrayed in the recent film *Dorothy Dandridge*. In 1939, at the Café Society in New York—one of the first integrated nightclubs—Billie sang "Strange Fruit," a song about a lynching. Still prevalent in the South at the time, the lynching of blacks was a gross and inhumane practice that needed the attention of a country yet to come to grips with its racism. Radio stations at the time refused to play the song, and producers refused to include it on albums. Whether the song directly influenced a transformation in our society or not, it was an early and public voice for social justice. "Strange Fruit" describes a lynching in graphic terms with the analogy of the bleeding dead (fruit), swinging from poplar trees in the South.

TRUTH IN ADVERTISING: ADBUSTERS

In many people's minds the prevalent consumerism of Americans is a destructive force for individuals, families, our society, and those who live in need outside the United States. Americans currently consume a majority of the world's resources. As early as 1977 Ron Sider confronted evangelical Christians in his book *Rich Christians in an Age of Hunger*. Driven by desire, targeted by the media, and unaltered by lack of awareness and the desire for change, people spend and consume in the "pursuit of happiness," which they see as their inalienable right. While many Christians are still silent and inactive on this issue, it has not gone unnoticed or unvoiced by the media generation.

Adbusters Media Foundation, based in Vancouver, British Columbia, is a nonprofit organization committed to "advance the new social activist movement of the information age."[3] Their frightening political aim, if taken at face value in an age of terrorism, is to "topple existing power structures and forge a major shift in the way we live in the 21st century." With a readership of eighty-five thousand and a network of artists, activists, writers, pranksters, students, and educators, they use a magazine, a web site, and an advocacy advertising agency to "coax people from spectator to participant in the quest for a world in which the economy and the ecology resonate in balance." Their antiadvertising art often parodies TV commercials and magazine ads. While some people may have an aversion to the foundation's message, one cannot help but be drawn into the discussion with the entertaining, often stinging *adbusters* that get at the truth of much advertising.

Consumerism is just the tip of a global iceberg of injustice, whose many layers include the giving of diseased blankets to the Native Americans, grocery-store chains charging more for their meats in lower-class neighborhoods than in well-to-do areas, banks charging outrageous interest rates to folks of color, white slave trade and the selling of young Asian women into prostitution, toxic dumping in low-income neighborhoods, the systematic killing of Afghani women professionals, the blackmail of African countries who owe debt but need medicine from Western pharmaceutical companies, adoption agencies that charge more for the adoption of a black baby than for a white baby, the disproportionate number of black males on death row, and children and families who get sick and die because they lack health insurance or access to health care.

Grave injustices are often headlined, with organized offensives launched by visible organizations. But what of all the small, everyday, almost invisible injustices that continue beneath the radar screens?—the institutional *isms* yet to come to someone's attention?

In March 2002 ABC aired a twenty-minute piece on how art therapy was being used to heal the pain and grief of children in New York who had lost a parent in the September 11 tragedy. Being in the midst of research for this book, and Vivian being a music therapist, we were eager to hear what had been discovered about the power of the arts to bring healing. It was a positive report, consistent with the experience of many who use the visual arts for healing: while the art therapy does not solve the person's problem, the art allows one to express, externalize, interpret, and understand their feelings and emotions, which allows for more realistic coping. The reporter announced that while the therapist began working with only a handful of children, word had spread and she received requests from the families of forty more children. We sadly observed, however, that all of the children featured were white and looked to be from families who could afford the therapist's fees. What about all the children whose families cannot afford private therapy fees, children who would also benefit from such therapy?

God is no less concerned about the redemption of our systems than he is about the redemption of individuals; we are held to personal responsibility for both. In his book *Christ Outside the Gate,* Orlando Costas reminds us that "sin is structural [or corporate] as well as personal. . . . Institutions disobey God, act unjustly, and set themselves up as gods. . . . Just as personal sin affects the community, social [corporate or community] sin affects the individual."[4] Our modern-day urban prophets, like their biblical forerunners, are often more likely to rail against and call our attention to the unjust "sin" of our institutions and our governmental, financial, and judicial systems than to individual sin. As Costas notes, however, the two are inextricably tied, making prophetic intervention at both the individual and corporate levels necessary.

Not all TV evangelists are insincere; not all megachurch pastors are motivated by greed. But they are suspect because of the many who have been exposed as rip-off artists using the name of Christ; so too are the pastors and evangelists and boards of trustees and congregations in city and suburban churches—your church and my church. If the collections, tithes, and offerings are sitting in a bank account mounting up interest, we are serving only ourselves. If our benevolent fund offerings go only to sick members of our congregation, we are serving only ourselves. If our sanctuaries and buildings grow larger and more plentiful to serve only our membership, we are serving only ourselves. If our ministries reach no farther than the doors of our buildings, we are serving only ourselves.

On our first trip to interview some artists for this book, we had the awesome pleasure of visiting the church of one of the artists. There was no question that this artist's work was sacrificial, loving, healing, and focused on those in need. The environment of his church, however, said something different. The church, located in one of the wealthiest sections of the city, has spent millions of dollars on unbelievable technology, facilities for every age group, need, and whim, including simulated teen nightclub atmospheres in the name of making Christ relevant. After retaining their kids, will they, and do they, reach out to help the poor?

Jesus was and is angered at the exploitation and injustice perpetrated upon those who genuinely seek him. His language that day at the temple was strong, his actions violent. The huckstering was immediately replaced by acts of healing and comfort and the praise singing and dancing of children.

The prophetic arts, those that speak against the sin and injustices committed by individuals and society, are often informed by religious and faith values, not in contradiction to them. The prophetic arts speak to the empowerment of people and communities, liberation of the oppressed, and righting the wrongs of society.

LIMITATIONS OF THE PROPHETIC ARTS

In the view of some, the limitations of the prophetic arts are the radical language and the seemingly unloving directness with which they present themselves. Ever susceptible to commercialization (especially music), once the prophetic art "buys into" the system, it can become corrupt and thus lose its power and voice. A second limitation is the tendency to alienate potential partners in the fight for social justice by blanket condemnation or criticism of those within a system who may be quietly trying to change it from within. For example, our first impression of the suburban church of the artist we visited may have been correct, yet it was the church of an agape artist who gave his life to others. Were there many more such artists there? Finally, because prophetic art may be produced by those outside the religious system, it may not be taken seriously or may not even be heard by those to whom it speaks. It may even be downright rejected.

BIBLICAL BASIS FOR THE PROPHETIC ARTS

The primary theological impetus and focus of the prophetic arts is most often drawn from the Old Testament prophets, the teachings of Jesus calling for the kingdom of God in the present, and the passages in Revelation calling for a New Jerusalem. The most common themes in the prophetic arts are the alleviation of poverty, the liberation of the oppressed, the care of prisoners, and the healing of the sick.

Amos, the prophet of justice and a member of the working class, prophesied around the same time as Hosea, when Israel was under the rule of King Jeroboam II. Israel was at peace with the border countries and there were few military threats. The GNP was up and the stock market was bullish. This was the golden age of peace and prosperity in Israel. Consequently, there were two classes of people: the wealthy and the poor. Israel controlled crucial trade routes, so merchants piled up big profits. Imports of stone, furniture inlaid with ivory, top-grade meat and fine wine, the finest body lotions, and Egyptian perfumes were all readily available. In this prosperous, capitalistic environment the Israelites slipped into insincere worship at best, and idolatry, gross mistreatment of the poor, and unethical business practices at worst.

Like Jesus in his confrontation of the religious leaders of his day, Amos neither bit his tongue nor spared the feelings of or respected the positions of the government officials, military leaders, businessmen and women, or the wealthy leisure class who lived at the expense of the poor. Using the blunt, scornful, often sarcastic vernacular of a southern farmer, and using the art forms of pictures (the visions), storytelling (chapter 4; 5:18–20), drama (8:5–6), preaching, satire (4:4–5), and poetry (Oracles to the Nations and Oracles of Woe), Amos did what all true prophets do: he indicted people for their crimes, warned them of impending punishment, gave opportunity for a plea bargain based on confession and repentance (5:4–15), consistently suggested the remedy ("Seek the LORD and live"), intervened through prayer for God's mercy on those charged, and painted a vision of hope and future restoration (9:11–15).

Amos brought a piercing indictment against the women of Israel who, while not directly oppressing the poor, nevertheless required their husbands to keep them in the luxurious lifestyle to which they had become accustomed. He knew that their insensitive attitudes would eventually lead to a humiliating enslavement. "Hear this word, you cows of Bashan, who are on the mountain of Samaria, who oppress the poor, who crush the needy, who say to your husbands, 'Bring wine, let us drink!'" (4:1–3 NKJV). Amos was not shy.

Amos told the corrupt elders and judges who conducted official legal business at the "gate" that they would never enjoy their nice houses and gardens or the rewards of their labor because they were "afflicting the just and taking bribes; diverting the poor from justice at the gate" (5:10–13 NKJV).

The people of Israel and their neighboring countries were guilty of brutal and inhumane treatment not unlike that of our twenty-first-century world: they sold bad wheat weighed with loaded scales, sold people into slavery, took bribes, killed people with iron-toothed sledges, allowed their anger to rage unchecked, butchered pregnant women, plundered, looted, and in general trampled the weak and remained oblivious to those in need.

Amos was not confronting pagans. He was confronting God's people, persistently pleading, preaching, and praying for their transformation. He gave up his job, his home, and his family to move to unfamiliar territory, where he was rejected, belittled, called a traitor, and told to get out of town—not by the pagans but by, of all people, the priest.

Where are the Christian artists today who are preaching this message of justice? We will meet some of them in chapter 6, "Arts as a Voice of Justice." We did not, however, at least not in our surveys, discover any prophets with the force of language exhibited by Amos. The urban prophets we will highlight are more gentle, refined, and politically savvy. Their messages are more often lived out rather than preached in the streets. Being offensive, obstinate, and abrasive would repel their audience, an audience that has one hundred cable channel options. Pushing a button is easy compared to dealing with a screaming prophet at your front door who refuses to go away. Our culture is different from the culture of ancient Israel, and our prophets have adapted their styles to fit our culture.

"Amos" prophets do exist in our society, but fortunately or unfortunately, their messages may never be heard because of their style. They are the gangsta rappers and hip-hoppers who, while having a heritage of Christian faith, are the victims of injustice in our society.[5] They call for a revolution, a violent one, and in the thought of some sociologists, unless the injustices are dealt with, the United States could see severe ethnic and social conflicts in our own country. Some artists' messages have been quickly corrupted by a recording industry that knows how to market to a restless youthful generation more concerned for style than substance, who may be unconsciously "hearing" and learning nevertheless.

In this present-day kingdom of God, social evil is present in political, economic, religious, and social structures that oppress the poor. D. J. Haynes believes that artistic prophets

- Discern and analyze critically what is happening in society in relation to the past
- Identify with the plight of society's victims
- Unmask hypocrisy
- Evoke hope that results in action[6]

As we will see in the next chapter, urban prophets

- Exhibit a strong calling, as in the compelling case of Jonah, who could not escape his role as God's voice, despite running in the opposite direction of his target audience
- "Preach" a specific message out of a vision for justice and personal redemption
- Often use the language of the streets but live a life of compassion

The role of the modern urban prophet continues that of the Old Testament prophets, the apostles, and Jesus. Their message to "seek good and not evil, that you may live" (Amos 5:14 NKJV) is as critical today to the reclaiming of God's people and the building of his kingdom on earth as it was twenty-seven hundred years ago when Amos walked the streets of Israel.

Agape Artists

And this commandment we have from Him: that he who loves God must love his brother also.

1 John 4:21 NKJV

Agape artists use their artistic gifts for mission and ministry (broadly defined) outside the four walls of the sanctuary, in the community. They may also work in arts programs that take place within the physical location of the sanctuary and may use the language, artistic style, and theological themes associated with the sanctuary. The agape arts are primarily relational in nature, and the motivation of agape artists springs from a compassion for "the least of these."

Agape artists draw on *agape,* the word meaning "to love one's neighbor," and have a primarily outward and horizontal theological orientation and practice. Unlike celebrative and sanctuary artists, the goal of the agape artist is not necessarily to maintain the congregational culture, though their work may be in harmony with that culture. Their purpose is to love one's neighbor through and with the arts. Agape artists are holistic and communal, in that while they understand the spiritual nature of the arts and strive for excellence in artistic presentation, they place equal or greater emphasis on caring for the needs of people, including improving their quality of life and their sense of worth as God's creation.

Agape artists seek to bring about holistic personal transformation that includes behavioral change, spiritual development, physical well-being, and personal, family, and social responsibility through healthy relationships in the community at large. They may also work for holistic social transformation through art produced in community for economic, political, social, and spiritual change—work that may result in social and economic benefits, such as in community development. While similar work may be done within the church, the focus of agape artists is on the broader concept of realizing *shalom* and the kingdom of God in the present through a compassionate and incarnational ministry.

Larell, a young musician in junior high school, was about to quit his drum lessons and give up playing. Though gifted, he couldn't find an outlet for his talents and often doubted his gift. Vivian—who happened to be Larell's Sunday school teacher—sensed this, and, wanting to encourage her Sunday school students, especially young musicians, she asked Larell if he would play for a combined choir that would be singing for their church's Family and Friends Day (the church's name for the traditional Back Home Day of many black churches). No one, including Larell, had ever thought to have him bring his talent into the church. Vivian consulted his mom, the pastor, and the guest organist who would be playing for the choir. No problem with them, although the fairly conservative congregation would have to get used to more "noise" in the church service, and that would be an issue, but it was Larell who needed the help right now. Larell played and did "good"—like when God created the birds of the air and said, "That's good!" Larell was that kind of good. He was then asked to play for another service, then another and another. Larell then volunteered to travel every Thursday night and most weekends to play for Eastern University's gospel choir; then he went to Egypt to witness in music with the group. Recently Larell traveled to Campinas, Brazil, to teach young boys and girls—former street children—how to play drums. He teaches in a community music school near his church and on his own has recruited some boys and girls whom he is raising up as young protégés who are walking in his footsteps. He sits beside them during services and occasionally lets them accompany a song. The choir tolerates the slight offbeat and dragging of the younger ones, whose feet can hardly reach the bass drum peddle. At a young age, Larell found his *eschaton*—his place and his artist ministry, working both in the church and in the street, never once having asked for any reward or remuneration but accepting the gifts that came.

LIMITATIONS OF THE AGAPE ARTS

From an apostolic or ecclesial theology, the agape arts may appear to dilute or avoid the theological concerns of the church congregation. Further, because the art forms used are often those most acceptable and accessible for the constituent community, they may be considered too secular or outside the boundaries of acceptable art. They are not the arts typically considered "sacred" arts.

Depending on one's theological and congregational orientation, the agape arts may be regarded as either "non-Christian" or "unevangelical." This criticism may come because artists of the Christian faith may work in nonchurch institutions where the term "Christian" is either not appropriate (separation of church and state) or unwelcome (negative view of Christians and Christianity). Open Christian witness (especially proselytizing or evangelization, in fundamental terms) is either not allowed or not appropriate. Criticism from the left may also include the fact that the agape arts are not involved enough in the work of social justice. Criticism from the right may come because some agape artists are not winning souls. We want to state clearly that we believe *all* the categories of arts and artists discussed here are worthy and necessary for the holistic work of the arts throughout the sectors of the kingdom of God.

Agape artists live in the spirit of Hosea and live out the commandment to love our neighbors. For the agape artist and for the true Christian, love is not an option; it is a commandment. As with urban prophets, a strong calling compels agape artists. But unlike urban prophets, true agape artists are compelled to make the Savior known not only through word (Rom. 10:14–15) but also through good works (James 2:15–17) and through an example of a new character (Matt. 5:16, 20). Unbelievers are compelled to glorify the Father when they see Christians generously giving their time, resources, and love.

BIBLICAL IMPETUS FOR THE AGAPE ARTS

What characterizes the ministry of the agape artist? Let's look at Hosea as a biblical example. Hosea lived in a period of political instability and moral decline, a time when idolatry was institutionalized and when unfaithfulness to anything or anyone was the norm, a time when Israel looked to her known enemies for help instead of to the One who had loved them always. Such conditions are not unlike those of our world today, nor of any time in human existence for that matter. Hosea was not speaking to the public that did not know Yahweh. He was speaking to believers and to the religious and political leaders of the land, the priests and kings. Hosea did so through both word (metaphoric story, rhythmic poetry) and action. This latter point is very important. The uniqueness of Hosea is that his life story "acted out" the very message he was bringing from God—like a play within a play. And the power of the message came from the fact that Hosea had up close and personal experience with what he was saying to others.

EMPATHY

In other words, the power of an agape artist's ministry through love often comes from their having experienced tragedy, pain, and injustice similar to that of those the artist works with or similar to the issues the artist is struggling to address publicly. The resolution of your own personal situation allows you to empathize with others and understand the emotional pain and heartbreak involved as well as the details of the transformation process others will need to "go through" or endure. Personal experience lends integrity to the message of the agape artist.

INCARNATIONAL LIVING

But *must* one be poor and from the city to serve as an agape artist? No. First, no matter where life circumstances and God have taken us, we have all experienced tragedy and pain, if not injustice, which we can draw on when working to help others. Second, if we have ever truly felt the healing, saving hand of God, and have recognized it as such, we are then under the same command as Hosea and other agape prophets and artists to love our brothers and sisters as God has loved us. There are many artists who live in the suburbs and who, by choice or design, cannot live among the poor. That does not mean they cannot find a ministry to the marginalized that is incarnational in the principle of building lasting relationships.

Joanna, a wealthy but humble woman mentioned in Luke 8, is a good example of incarnational living. Married to Chuza, the manager of Herod's household, Joanna (meaning "Yahweh's gift") was no doubt used to a rather comfortable and luxurious lifestyle, complete with mansion, silks, perfumes, and leisure time. But after being healed of an unnamed infirmity or evil spirit that no doubt controlled her life for some time, she joined Mary Magdalene, Susanna, and the other women who traveled with and ministered to Jesus. As a follower of Christ, Joanna made the decision to sacrifice her privileged and comfortable lifestyle. She gave of her time, energy, and resources to live what must have been a hard but fulfilling adjustment to an incarnational life of ministry "on the road." We can only think that this may have put an emotional strain on her marriage and created some political conflict, given her loyalty to one who was considered an enemy of the state, a state that her husband served.

SACRIFICE

The stories of Zacchaeus and the rich young ruler, both of whom Jesus loved, let us know of the hole in our spirituality if we are not using our wealth and resources to give to the poor. Whether to the rich young ruler or to the lawyer who stood to test Jesus in Luke 10:25, Jesus' answer to the question "What must I do to inherit eternal life?" was consistent: serve/give what you have to the poor/those in need. This message is especially poignant for the agape artist who lives in the suburbs and wants to work in the city.

There is a place for this kind of agape artist, but it requires commitment and sacrifice and requires more than a monthly visit to marginalized communities in the cities. In our work with volunteers, we find that many have a vision and interest in working with the poor in the city, but they don't have the commitment to sacrifice the time and energy it takes to develop the necessary relationships and to live even a modified incarnational lifestyle, which still involves a true sacrifice of time, energy, and money. Even in the short run, these "missionary tourists" may do more damage if they build relationships based on false expectations than if they had never begun.

Hosea's life experience and his prophetic work were inseparable and interwoven. He married a woman who, after the birth of their first son, betrayed and embarrassed him. You can imagine how much ridicule Hosea had to endure from his friends and neighbors, who likely told him to ditch his wife or even to kill her. How the other children must have made fun of little Jezreel, teasing and taunting him for being the child of a street prostitute.

In addition to reputation and embarrassment, Hosea also knew the sacrifice of personal resources. He paid a tangible ransom for Gomer's freedom. So plan to be significantly out-of-pocket for those whom you say you serve and love.

We have witnessed agape artists like Ann Ostholthoft spend their inheritance supporting their projects, and others like Scott Parker (see the case study at the end of this section) living on less than $10,000 a year, and still others like Tom Sullivan and John Russell contributing large portions of their incomes to minister to others.

Rejuvenation

One more significant thing about Hosea as a prophet of action who demonstrated and used true love as his major prophetic vehicle: after paying a heavy price for the one he loved, he saw to love's primary aims (3:3)—provision of time for self-reflection in safety, forgiveness of insult and injury, restoration to former position and responsibilities as wife and mother, and absolute recommitment. Like Hosea's ministry, an agape artist's aims are to bring reconciliation, redemption, and forgiveness through actions, activities, and relationships that provide just and safe environments, renewal, comfort, and hope for those in need; these are provided in the context of a continuous, committed (faithfully showing up), incarnational ministry. (See Hosea 2:14–3:5.)

In contrast to Amos's harsh, gritty, confrontational language and in-your-face style, Hosea, while truthful and forthright in charging his audience with their bad, unacceptable behavior, nevertheless dramatized the message by sharing his own life story and led a prophetic ministry primarily through the simple, repeated act of gentle, merciful (giving a person more than he or she deserves) love.

Loving the Unlovable

Jesus did all of this and is, of course, the greatest of agape lovers. His defense and healing of those held in disgrace and disdain by the self-righteous social order of the day always included a statement of acceptance and forgiveness of sins, the result of which was a new life full of hope and commitment. The woman referred to only as a "sinner" in Luke 7:37 (NKJV), most likely one of Nain's street prostitutes, is a particularly poignant example of the Prophet's intentional relating with, and encouragement of, the poor and rejected. We can picture the boldness of some of today's street people coming up to the car window at the stoplight and asking for a dollar, people whose genuine hearts and searchings are never seen or heard by us because of their outward appearance and off-putting behaviors that violate our rules of civilized engagement. Like these street people, our sinner woman of Nain dared to walk uninvited into the proper house of a Pharisee! What's more, she takes down her hair in public—a definite, disgraceful no-no for a woman of those times—and begins to kiss and wash Jesus' feet with her tears and her hair. Most of us would cringe at the thought of being touched by the probably unwashed dreds of a street woman or man. Through the lens of agape love, Jesus saw and validated the woman's gestures as those of one with need and longing, but he also saw her capacity for great love, service, faith, and humility. The agape artist, through the medium of their art, has a powerful tool to expose the heart, talents, gifts, capacity, and potential of the "invisibles" and the "throwaways" of our cities.

Risky Love

Jesus holds up yet another standard for our modern-day agape artists: that of loving with risk, risk that is more than the usual sacrifice. Why? Because the knowledge and memory of moments when we have been loved with a risky love sustain us and will sustain those with whom the artist works, especially when things are going badly.

Risky love is what caused the street woman to put down the iron pipe that was poised to bash someone's head when Mark Sandiford, a.k.a. Mark Y Rage, appeared in the back alley of the club at which he was playing that night. He had often shown her love in spite of her street filth and drunkenness and had convinced her of her worth, to the point of her being able to testify to wanting a new life. And now he called her to practical proof of her earlier words. "You don't want to do that," he said. "If you want a new life, act like it."

Risky love is why, when Ann wonders why she blew all of her inheritance on the Chicago school, she remembers the impact of her sacrifice on a little girl: "Miss Ann, are we going to have art next week?"

Risky love is what compelled the white high school teacher to stand up in a meeting to defend the work of a colleague of color, knowing that it would end his advancing career since he would be considered a "nigger lover" and a deserter of his own kind.

Will you love by touching disease, dirty bag people, blind beggars, and bleeding women? Jesus' unique method in healing the deaf mute was just short of fringe alternative medicine. Would you love enough to stick your fingers in someone's ear, spit on your fingers, and touch their tongue (Mark 7:32–35)? The love touch of Jesus on the blind beggar in John 9 got the beggar excommunicated, caused much family tension and division (the parents wouldn't stand up for their own child for fear of their own loss of status), and gave the religious leaders another three counts on the arrest docket for Jesus (using saliva, making clay and working on the Sabbath, healing non-life-threatening diseases on the Sabbath).

Agape Artists Cross Barriers of Race and Class

It was risky love that motivated Jesus to cross the boundaries of race, ethnicity, culture, disability, and religion. Like the street prophets of the Old Testament, Jesus loved mostly outside the formal boundaries of the temples, synagogues, structures, and systems. He loved in the streets, through conversation, dialogue, questioning, empowering, and encouraging self-examination and through physically touching the forbidden, the castaways, the untouchables. Risky love is a love that is uncomfortable, inconvenient, anxiety provoking, and sometimes scary.

Jesus forbade sectarianism when he reminded John that "he who is not against us is on our side" (Luke 9:49–50 NKJV). Through his own barrier crossing, Jesus modeled reconciliation across class, gender, ethnicity, religion, and disability. Upper-class noblemen, religious leaders, Samaritan women, Gentiles, Greeks, wealthy women, and rich young rulers all consulted and begged for time, wisdom, and healing from this blue-collar, Middle Eastern carpenter, who also sought them out.

Dana Velps-Marschalk is the director of the Moving in the Spirit dance group in Atlanta. Early in her career she felt a call to the poor of Atlanta, mostly African-Americans—a call affirmed by the poor community when they asked her to stay, but a call that her parents could not understand or support. It was not until many years later that her parents began to understand her call and support her work in dance with the kids of Moving in the Spirit. Moving out on her own and living in the projects alongside people on welfare, Dana struggled to raise support for her ministry. One year was unusually bad, but she refused to give up. She calls it her "four-thousand-dollar year," for that is exactly the income she had for the entire year. One night while praying for enough money to pay her rent and buy groceries, she heard a knock on the door. It was her neighbors. "We know you are starving," they said as they handed her bags of groceries they had purchased with their meager incomes. When Dana once related this story to a group of artists, they became concerned that Dana was taking advantage of her poor neighbors. But this story illustrates that when one becomes a part of a community incarnationally, not only does he or she bring a blessing, but he or she is often blessed in return by that community. It is the nature of true community.

COMPASSION

Compassion, another aspect of agape love, is often taken as evidence of God within us. Such is the case shown by the "certain man" who threw a great supper party. Rejected by his probably well-to-do friends, he held an open-house feast for the lame, the homeless, the poor, the hungry—the lower social classes that most of us would never think of inviting into our churches or our homes. Such were the people that Jesus loved and encourages us to love, through whom he often chose to reveal himself (Luke 14:15–24).

We watched with awe as the young dancers of the Duende Dance Theater troupe performed director Amanda Lower's lyric and inspiring choreography. They were preparing for their first community/church performance and wanted to perfect the somewhat complicated entrances and timing. "OK, Frank. Get ready . . . and . . . take your place (she paused to wait for the music to reach the right spot) *now!*" Frank promptly positioned his electric wheelchair at the spot right of center stage as practiced. Earlier we had spotted Frank sitting off to the side of the dance studio, never once thinking that he was a dancer in the troupe. But here he was, moving skillfully in time to the sacred music with the only parts of his body that would move: arms, head, and feet.

Those with disabilities were always among the objects of Jesus' love. A point not to be missed in the story of the paralytic man is that Jesus noticed and commended the four friends of the paralytic (Mark 2), friends who loved the man enough to persist in finding creative solutions to gain access to healing for him. While not creating quite the havoc of John Q in the movie by the same name, they did destroy a roof in their attempt to move past the often-encountered architectural barriers (still found in many places of work and ministry today), not to mention the attitudinal barriers, faced by our friends with disabilities who desire to be included in our worship and our ministries. And so here is Frank, dancing among able-bodied dancers, fully integrated with others, just as the paralytic's friends had attempted to ensure he was fully integrated with others.

The dance rehearsal was called to a halt, and the dancers scurried off to their next task of the day. One of the dancers stayed behind to attend to Frank—to assist with his clothing and to help him travel out of the complicated maze of buildings that house the studio. We considered the gestures of the dancer, Amanda, to be unusual and special. Not so. Such actions are required of agape artists who claim to do what they do because they "love Jesus." They must comfort, embrace, have compassion for, and love unconditionally those whom others would exclude or forget.

Separation and isolation of the so-called unclean was prescribed by Levitical law and was to be strictly adhered to, lest one become unclean themselves by association and become an outcast. The unclean were stripped of dignity and privacy, having to shout out their uncleanness to ward off any possible contact with humanity. Jesus hung out in the dingiest of town outskirts, encountered the leper, was not repulsed by having to touch his raw sores, was moved by compassion to heal him, and even more, had to remain outside the city in "deserted places" because of the stir created by the leper proclaiming the news of his healing.

How do you know you love your neighbor? The parable of the good Samaritan is as instructive to us as it was to the lawyer who asked Jesus the question that sparked the parable. We of course know that the hero of the story was not the expected Christian—the Levite or the priest. These men, focused solely on preserving their own well-being, crossed to the other side of the street like many of us do in order to avoid contact with the unpleasant people of the streets. No, it was the Samaritan, the so-called pagan and enemy of "God's people." This unknown, patient advocate, with no regard for the ethnicity or faith of the victim, lifted his brother from the gutter, covered his wounds, used his own donkey as an ambulance, took him to the emergency room, stayed the night with him, and paid the bill. That is loving your neighbor, nothing less.

So, if you want to be an agape artist, what needs to characterize your ministry?

- A call and a commandment from God
- A propensity for action
- An ability to draw empathy from one's own personal pain and heart-break
- A goal of redemption through incarnational relationship
- "Out-of-pocket" sacrifice of personal resources of time and money
- Risky love
- Compassion for the unloved, the forgotten, the rejected, the excluded
- A spirit of reconciliation and forgiveness that crosses ethnic and other boundaries
- Faithfully showing up
- Knowing your limits and seeking rejuvenation

Celebrative Artists

Praise the LORD!

Praise God in His sanctuary;
Praise Him in His mighty firmament!

Praise Him for His mighty acts;
Praise Him according to His excellent greatness!

Praise Him with the sound of the trumpet;
Praise Him with the lute and harp!
Praise Him with the timbrel and dance;
Praise Him with stringed instruments and flutes!
Praise Him with loud cymbals;
Praise Him with clashing cymbals!

Let everything that has breath praise the LORD.

Praise the LORD!

Psalm 150 NKJV

Celebrative art and celebrative artists, as we are defining them, provide an opportunity to celebrate renewal for people, community, church, and society. In the A.R.T. model, celebration comes at a significant point of goal completion, where the working out of a significant problem or goal gives pause for rest, reflection, and praise for the accomplishment. Celebrative arts are those forms of artistic expression that are performed, presented, and viewed within this context. Traditionally these include music, icons and other visual arts, dance, and drama. More recently technology could be considered a celebrative art when it enhances the liturgy of worship and public celebrations.

Celebrative artists play an important role in the NU JERUZ as those who lead the community in celebrating renewal. They celebrate accomplishments with and for people. The celebrative artist often strives for an excellence in art that most typifies the standards of the community. Celebrative artists also take artistic tradition into consideration and represent the core values of the community. They design and perform for events that are often orchestrated with precision and dramatic flair. Through their art these artists help us to rejoice, reflect, recognize and honor, lift up, and give thanks.

Sometimes the celebration happens spontaneously in the street, as in the case of Norris Square. Imagine a street so drug infested that children pass scores of drug dealers on their way to elementary school classes every morning. Imagine a community so held hostage by drugs that parents are afraid to send their children out on the streets at night because of the gun violence that erupts as dealers vie for control of territory in a block of twenty-three houses. Imagine a place where cars from out of state drive in to purchase drugs. This is Norris Square, a neighborhood in north Philadelphia. Or at least, this was Norris Square until the women got fed up—so fed up, so brave, so driven that they rat on their husbands and sons, confronted city politicians, and marched in the streets. Before convincing federal and city police of the depth of the evil, the local churches and community organizations banned together to fight for their neighborhood.

Then one morning it happened. Police moved in, arrested nearly fifty-five dealers in a single block, bulldozed all their houses to the ground, cleared the debris, and towed away twenty-six cars. The neighborhood was so elated, people danced in the streets. Old women brought their chairs to the vacant lots to sit out under the evening stars, while mothers lined their children against a wall and painted an impromptu mural of their forms to declare victory and to celebrate life. (You will read more about Norris Square in chapter 8.)

At other times the celebration is more formal. Celebrative art is an important and vital part of the Christian life and is also shared by society at large. Celebrative art within congregations provides aesthetic experiences where the faithful rejoice at the personal victories of life and join in the grand celebration of the meaning of the cross. This celebration propels the cycle of spiritual renewal onward. We agree with de Gruchy that prophets like Isaiah received their vision and call to a prophetic life from an aesthetic worship experience (Isaiah 6). It is our desire that from the worship of the church artists will be propelled into the public square in prophetic and agape ministries.

LIMITATIONS OF THE CELEBRATIVE ARTS

The primary limitations of the celebrative arts have much to do with a tendency toward artistic "idolatry," in which the focus on the art form itself limits creative congregational participation and the art becomes the magnet for spiritual direction. True to our Western culture, we are prone to celebrate the actor rather than the story, the performance rather than the meaning. We find this same concept in the concert hall, museum, and theater of the broader society, where the focus is on the performer and the art form. Because, as Freire, Boal, Small, and others have indicated, our art forms are laden with the values of our culture, and because they represent the symbols and icons of our identity, they can quickly become symbols of the powerful and the sacred icons of the elite.

Art within the walls of cultural enclaves that focuses on the predominant cultural value and quality we refer to as *sanctuary arts*. This concept is discussed in detail in *Music of the Common Tongue,* by Christopher Small.[7] In the extreme, such enclaves must be confronted and re-created in order to allow for transformation and for celebration of renewal versus celebration of tradition. Consider the picture of a European Jesus on many church walls. Jesus was a Jew, and possibly a dark one at that. White Christians have had to adjust their "image" of Jesus as a person of color in order to accept Christians of color, just as Christians of color have had to "learn" that "whiteness" is not the superior view. It is interesting that some black churches still exhibit a white Jesus in their Bible study classes, just as many white churches have yet to make a paradigm shift in favor of a more accurate Jesus. When we discuss the celebration of renewal in chapter 12, we will look at the sanctuary as a place in need of renewal and in need of working out a substantial barrier to the NU JERUZ—in-group solidarity.

Celebrative arts can also celebrate unjust values. Consider the amount of money spent on redecorating sanctuaries and building museums and concert halls. While we would expect cultures to erect buildings of praise and monuments to heroes, when the money spent is disproportionate to the millions who live in poverty, one must ask the question, Why? Who is really being served?

Biblical Impetus for the Celebrative Arts

From Genesis to Revelation, life in biblical times was full of festivals, holy convocations, feast days, commemorations, banquets, and celebrations. The idea of celebration was first ushered in by God himself, when he rested on the seventh day after his creative work of the first six days.

> Then God saw everything that He had made, and indeed it was very good. . . . Thus the heavens and the earth, and all the host of them, were finished. And on the seventh day God ended His work which He had done, and He rested on the seventh day from all His work which He had done.
>
> Genesis 1:31–2:2 NKJV

God's concept of rest includes not just the cessation of work but a time to pause and reflect and evaluate the work done (it was very good). The pomp and circumstance of commencement ceremonies for grade school, high school, college, and university students afford celebrative opportunities for looking back over a time of work and saying, "It was good."

God's example has led humankind to set aside times of resting from work, with that rest including reflection on God, his goodness to us, and our work to serve others in honor of that goodness.

> Six days shall work be done, but the seventh day is a Sabbath of solemn rest, a holy convocation. You shall do no work on it; it is the Sabbath of the LORD in all your dwellings.
>
> Leviticus 23:3 NKJV

The Sabbath rest is in honor of God, in remembrance of his creation, and in praise and thanks for his love and blessings. It continues to be a time of reflection and re-creation, spiritual and physical renewal, and in the more charismatic churches, a time of emotional catharsis. That it was originally considered the first day of the week suggests that the Sabbath prepares us to begin the next period of productivity refreshed and with anticipation. The idea of rest and reflective celebration, then, points us toward more activity. Many of Israel's Old Testament feasts had prophetic New Testament corollaries. For example, the Year of Jubilee, when many rejoiced for their freedom and release from servitude and for the return of their land, is considered the prophetic anteced-ent of the Christian's deliverance through Christ from the bondage of sin. An emotion closely related to celebration is also one of the gifts or fruits of God's Spirit: joy. One of the purposes of joy is to provide blessing and reward for the faithful believer, but it also produces hope, another aspect of celebration that points us toward future work.

> Now may the God of hope fill you with all joy and peace in believing, that you may abound in hope by the power of the Holy Spirit.
>
> Romans 15:13 NKJV

Similarly, then, our celebrations today help point us toward future hope, continued renewal, the next phase of assessment, and critical awareness, work-ing it out, and accomplishment. For example, the Sandtown Children of Praise gospel choir (see chapter 8) is the prophetic result of one man engaging kids in an after-school music activity one hour a week. The after-school music led to a little musical production to celebrate the end of a summer camp. Each small, celebrated triumph encouraged the next and eventually led to the creation of what is now one of the region's most energetic and effective community children's choirs.

The Year of Jubilee celebrated the release of the Hebrews from debt. Passover celebrates and serves as a remembrance of God's deliverance. The Feast of First

Fruits, the Feast of Weeks, and the Feast of Tabernacles celebrated and consecrated the first barley and wheat crops of the year and the completion of the harvest. All of these days were celebrated cyclically and established traditions that gave the Israelite people an identity in and a tie to their Creator, affirmed their core values, and documented a continuous history of a people. Like every other culture, Israel created and practiced traditions to commemorate significant events in their history. One of the most significant is God's covenant with them—relationship. Communities and cultures create their own traditions as significant conveyors of their identity and history but also to celebrate new and strengthened relationships.

Leisure days and feasts in the Bible were associated with food, gift giving, singing, and great joy. In biblical times, the arts were at the center of the celebration, as they are today. After the miracle of the parting of the Red Sea that allowed the Israelites to cross to freedom, Miriam led the women in singing and dancing in praise and thanks to God (Exod. 15:20–21).

Music and dance were a part of the celebration feast held after the return of the lost son (Luke 15:25). Who doesn't celebrate the homecoming of a child who has long been away from home? King David danced at the return of the ark of the covenant to Jerusalem (2 Sam. 6:14), and the Levites appointed their brethren to be singers raising their voices with resounding joy and players of stringed instruments, harps, cymbals, horns, and trumpets (1 Chron. 15:16–29).

At the news of David's victorious battle over the Philistines, the women came out of all the cities of Israel, singing and dancing, with tambourines, with joy, and with musical instruments (1 Sam. 18:6–7). The psalmist expresses spiritual joy and praise at being heard and healed, and he uses the metaphors of dancing and singing to do so:

> You have turned for me my mourning into dancing;
> You have put off my sackcloth and clothed me with gladness,
> To the end that my glory may sing praise to You and not be silent.
> O LORD my God, I will give thanks to You forever.
>
> Psalm 30:11–12 NKJV

Nehemiah dedicated the rebuilt wall of Jerusalem "with gladness, both with thanksgivings and singing, with cymbals and stringed instruments and harps" (Neh. 12:27 NKJV). The artists participating in the celebration came from near and far and built villages all around Jerusalem in preparation for this important landmark celebration (vv. 28–29).

Adornment of the tabernacle and the ritual clothing of the priests with ornamental needlework was important to the Old Testament temple culture, worship, ceremony, and celebration and depended on those gifted in fabric arts. The creative weavers of the time transformed plain materials into works of art for the tabernacle door, the court gates, and the priests' garments, for the beauty and glorification of the Creator.

> You shall skillfully weave the tunic of fine linen thread, you shall make the turban of fine linen, and you shall make the sash of woven work. . . . And you shall make hats for them, for glory and beauty.
>
> Exodus 28:39–40 NKJV

These products were also a valuable part of the economic trade community and were of value as an inheritance for the next generation. They could easily be the forerunners of banners, decorative choir and pastoral robes, and other artistic icons and artifacts of today's sanctuaries and worship traditions.

The wedding at Cana, recorded in the Book of John, adds an additional dimension to the purpose and role of celebration. Such celebrative events lasted a week, and the festivities, gifts, wine, music, dance, and food were all part of celebrating the commitment of two people grounded in the love of God. Weddings and other celebrations are therefore times to reflect on the gift of a permanent relationship.

The greatest rejoicing, both of angels in heaven and people on earth, comes when people choose to follow Jesus. "It was right that we should make merry and be glad, for your brother was dead and is alive again, and was lost and is found" (Luke 15:32 NKJV).

"Do this in remembrance of me" are words that most Christians recite at least once a month. They are a part of one of the most solemn sacramental traditions of the Christian faith: Holy Communion, which remembers and celebrates the death and resurrection of Jesus. The focus of the remembrance is not sorrow but the love of Christ. One of the traditions of the African-American church is a dinner repast that follows funeral and burial services. (Having grown up with a mortician for a father, Vivian is always reminding us that such rituals are always for the living, not the dead.) The funeral service celebrates the removal of the last barrier between us and God—death—while the more celebrative repast in the company of family and friends starts the healing process and turns us toward the future.

In and of themselves, music and dance (whether folk, bee bop, or waltz), theater and textiles (whether banners or fine linen, beadwork or fireworks, culinary spreads or floral arrangements) can be aesthetically joyous. However, they are also the festive centerpieces of most of our celebrations. In celebrations today—whether we are celebrating anniversaries, the Fourth of July, a hero's birthday, or a remembrance of the end of a war—the arts, more naturally than any other discipline or area, are the focal points.

The purposes of celebration in biblical times were the same as they are today: worship, praise, thanks, victory, accomplishment, life, birth, death, relationships, and affirmation. Of all the aspects of the celebrative arts that we have mentioned, perhaps the most important aspect in the context of the A.R.T. model of redemptive transformation is their ability to continually point people toward the future. Churches have been faithful in celebrating the accomplishments of their congregations and their ministries. Remaining too long within those traditions, however, means that celebrations become stale and draw the church's attention toward the past. A "new song in [the] mouth" (Ps. 40:3 NKJV) comes from new acts and new accomplishments.

We will not discuss the nature of the celebrative artist in this section, other than to comment that celebrative artists play an important role in the NU JERUZ. Much has been written about those who lead worship and "perform" worship arts. We prefer to give our attention to those about whom little has been written. Below is a summary chart of our typology.

Typology	Characteristic	Value
Prophetic Art	Confronts hypocrisy Exposes evil Brings judgment Propels to action Instills courage	Justice, confrontation, criticism, salvation
Agape Art	Trains and educates Builds community Empowers	Compassion, love, hope, faith, redemption
Celebrative Art	Reflects and evaluates Remembers Recognizes and honors Affirms and renews Lifts up Gives thanks Points toward the future	Praise, thanksgiving, honor

Artistic Gifts

Through our research it became clear that while some artists were involved in community mission through the agape arts or were prophetic voices for justice, they had certain other spiritual gifts and talents that allowed them to be effective in their particular ministry. Though not exhaustive, following is a list of gifts found in 1 Corinthians 12:28–31.

Administration—Art Architects. Art architects demonstrate excellent administrative skills. They know how to organize a structure for delivery of arts programs. An art architect: is a Nehemiah in administrative gifts and a Jesus in vision for the NU JERUZ; is a visionary "big picture" person; understands structures and how to build them and work within them; is gifted in administration; and networks within the broader community of artists, businesses, and churches.

Performance (Proclamation)—Performing/Preaching Artists. Performing or preaching artists use their art form excellently as a communicative tool.

Service—Servant Artists. Servant artists are most concerned with serving others through their art.

Ministry—Arts Ministers/Liturgists. Art ministers or liturgists are excellent choreographers, composers, dramatists, and others who know how to plan and design an artistic or worship experience in which a message is communicated clearly and out of which community is created.

Teaching—Educator Artists. Educator artists understand the teaching power of the arts and are adept at integrating the arts in relevant ways to teach a subject to a particular audience.

Healing—Empathic Artists. Empathic artists, not confined to a professional therapy model, understand the healing power of the arts and are able to utilize and heal spiritual and emotional hurt through creative expression.

Part 2

Proclaiming the NU JERUZ

Creating Critical Awareness

6

Arts as a Voice of Justice

In this chapter we will explore how art is used as a prophetic voice calling the church (internal) and society (external) to social justice. While the message of the prophetic arts is based on biblical principles, it is adapted to society at large, and the artist may not use "Christian" language or images to comment on problems of poverty, injustice, the environment, and so on. But in addition to commenting on a problem, effective prophetic art also presents a solution, calling both the institutional church and society to task.

Urban prophets give evidence of a faith engaged outside the sanctuary. As did Amos, the biblical antecedent of the urban prophet, these prophets have a *vision* of a just society and a *call* to action based on a life of *compassion*. The prophetic arts create critical awareness—an awakening to the truth as taught by Jesus and an awareness of our need to live lives of worship and devotion in the world God has created.

Why artists as prophets? "The arts remain an important forum for debate in our culture. Although it is not the primary concern of all artists to make statements about the human condition or to create commentary on the times, it is inevitable that many will do so simply because the instinct of the artist is to ask questions about origins, identity, behavior and destiny."[1] In communities where the arts are part of the communication process or community, the arts are inherently relevant. When artists are isolated from the mainstream community, they cannot speak to society with integrity. Christian artists who isolate themselves from society cannot speak to society with relevance either.

As Nathan demonstrated in his book *The Sound of the Harvest,* "artistic prophets stand on the edge between the sanctuary and the street and provide a vision of God's future (and present) reign. [Art] is prophetic when it leads people to truth and justice. It is not a fortune-telling device but a tool that foretells the future consequences based on present realities." Such art is at the heart of Christian faith according to Michael Eric Dyson, who calls Christianity a prophetic faith, and Nicholas Wolterstorff, who points to its emphasis on social change when he writes, "This formative religion seeks the reformation of the social world and finds life outside of the sanctuary and in the streets of the city."[2]

In this stage 1 of our transformation model, artistic expression and the artists who create it aim to create critical awareness of a problem and to call people to transformation. This occurs on three levels: personal, community, and societal. We will deal with the personal awareness and call to transformation more fully in the next chapter. Here we will examine how the arts call the church and society at large to the NU JERUZ.

> Then Jesus said to his host, "When you give a luncheon or dinner, do not invite your friends, your brothers or relatives, or your rich neighbors; if you do, they might invite you back and so you will be repaid. But when you give a banquet, invite the poor, the crippled, the lame, the blind, and you will be blessed. Although they cannot repay you, you will be repaid at the resurrection of the righteous."
>
> Luke 14:12–14

"Today, this very day, 5,500 Africans will die of AIDS. If this isn't an emergency, what is? We're supposed to love our neighbor. The Bible tells us to love our neighbor. We're not. We really are not. God is not looking for alms. God is looking for action."[3] These are not the words of a preacher, though they sound like it. They are not even the words of an AIDS activist, though they sound like it. They are the prophetic call to justice of a musician—Bono, the lead singer of U2—as he called on Christians to participate in his new nonprofit organization, DATA—Debt, Aids, Trade for Africa.

Bono, a popular singer turned activist, has always integrated his faith into his music and his life—a life lived under the microscope of the media, which often point out the seeming dualism of his life and faith and his fame. Bono has no illusions about the criticism or his role and has taken advantage of his fame and wealth to speak out against the injustices committed in the developing world, many committed by the developed world. He is an artist who has used his music and his fame to be a voice of justice. And although Bono may be the most famous example of an urban prophet, he is not alone. In cities all across the United States, urban prophets are working out justice where they live and living a life of compassion where they work.

The Great Banquet

Jesus once told the story of a man who was giving a great banquet. The man sent his servant to tell those who had been invited that the feast was ready. The servant returned, saying that all had made excuses based on their busy lives and that they could not attend. The man became angry and again sent his servant out, saying, "Go out quickly into the streets and alleys of the town and bring in the poor, the crippled, the blind and the lame." Having done this, the servant reported there was still room. So the man told his servant, "Go out to the roads and country lanes and make them come in, so that my house will be full. I tell you, not one of those men who were invited will get a taste of my banquet" (Luke 14:15–24).

Throughout the Gospels, we find Jesus describing the kingdom of God, the NU JERUZ. In *Jesus Before Christianity*, Albert Nolan explores the nature of Jesus' ministry and message to a highly structured society. Nolan points out that the concept of "heaven in the time of Jesus was a synonym for God. The kingdom of *heaven* meant the 'kingdom of God.'" The good news of the kingdom spoke of a "future state of affairs on *earth* when the poor would no longer be poor, the hungry would be satisfied and the oppressed would no longer be miserable. To say 'Thy kingdom come' is the same as saying 'Thy will be done on *earth* as it is in heaven.'"[4]

For the kingdom of God, as opposed to the kingdom of Satan, to be the present reality of people on the earth, those who follow Christ must be concerned for the poor and oppressed, without concern for wealth, status, in-group solidarity, and power.[5] In other words, they must live out social justice. The kingdom of God referred not to a quantitative time in the future but to a qualitative time in the present, an *eschaton*. "The time has come. The kingdom of God is near" (Mark 1:15). The call to those who would follow Jesus was to participate in the great banquet, to experience the *metanoia* (repentance), to follow the call of their *eschaton*. This repentance is one of a change of heart, mind, and allegiance. "True faith is not possible without compassion. . . . People's compassion for one another releases God's power in the world, the only power that can bring about the miracle of the 'kingdom.'"[6]

It is the role of the prophet to announce the kingdom of God, the NU JERUZ, and to confront the kingdom of Satan. The prophet's message is never timeless but is spoken to a particular people living in a particular context with particular needs, to awaken them to their time, their reality, and their call.

In August 2002 the faculty of the Campolo School for Social Change (CSSC) of Eastern University instituted its first residency course, Urban Issues in a Global Context. Thirty-two incoming graduate students in counseling, nonprofit management, and urban economic development spent an intense weekend with an interdisciplinary faculty team, studying theological and theoretical foundations for working with the poor of the city and the nature of social transformation. Brother Viv Grigg, New Zealand author of *Cry of the Urban Poor,* was a featured faculty speaker as we prepared to spend a full Saturday at Norris Square Community Center, a comprehensive community initiative (CCI) located in what once was called the Badlands of north Philadelphia.

The CSSC is located on the sixth floor of an office building on Buttonwood Street, just northeast of the city center and a few blocks away from Chinatown. We share the building with a number of city offices. At the edge of the building is a discontinued railway line that passes over Tenth Street and runs into the city. The cobbled street under the railway bridge and a nearby vacant lot are home to a group of transient and homeless men. Just north of our building is a homeless men's shelter and hostel for people suffering from HIV/AIDS. Our location is perfect for learning and working in the urban context.

On Friday evening, students and faculty gathered for orientation to the CSSC and for opening lectures, all of which centered around a banquet. It was a perfect beginning for what would be a surprising and informative experience for all of us.

As we entered the building, a homeless man was quietly sitting on the bench near the main door. He held a sign reading "Will work for food," with his head bowed in what looked like either exhaustion or drunkenness. His long, curly hair fell about his face and shoulders like a dirty mop. We thought nothing of it until our banquet had started.

After opening remarks and prayer, we heard a very loud commotion in the hallway. Apparently the homeless man had found his way into the building and up the elevator and was now standing in the hallway outside the banquet room door, demanding to eat with us. A number of us remembered a similar incident that had occurred early one morning and had ended in the intruder's virtually destroying the small kitchen near the entrance to the building, crashing coffeemakers and cups about the floor.

It didn't take long before one of our guests went to the hallway to try to usher the homeless man back to the street. He called security on his cell phone and then began to verbally scuffle with the homeless man. As tension began to mount, someone suggested we go ahead and give him a plate of food to keep him settled until security arrived. He calmed down, a faculty member handed him his plate, and the homeless man sat at the front table with six of our female students. He sat quietly and ate his food, while those around him sat quietly and wondered what would happen next.

Our agitated guest that had called security was still uncomfortable, however, and he encouraged the homeless man to finish his food and return to the street. He felt that this disturbance was rude and disruptive and was very concerned for the growing discomfort of the young women next to the homeless man. But the homeless man was not about to be "manhandled" and began to raise his voice as he answered back. A shouting match erupted, and the homeless man arose from his seat, saying, "I just want some food!" He finally walked back to the buffet table to fill his plate a second time. With his plate full, he then walked to the center of the room and began to speak to the entire group. Our residency group silently listened.

> I feel your pain
> When the person that was close to you left this earth
> Before they were supposed to
> Hoping that they made it into heaven's gate
> Say my Lord did he wait too late
> For goodness sake
> And expressions on peoples' faces
> Are saying those are the breaks, kid
> When your pocket's empty
> And you're living by faith kid
> I feel your pain.[7]

"I want to thank you for giving me food, and I am leaving now."

The man's departure seemed to give our students and faculty freedom to vent their frustrations, fears, and concerns.

A young woman who had been sitting next to him confessed, "Today was one of those unexpected experiences that shattered any notion I may have had about my ability to identify with Christ, as he comes to us in his distressing disguises. I am sorely in need of another shot at redemption."[8]

Then we revealed the truth. We had arranged for what Augusto Boal calls "invisible theater,"[9] enlisting the help of Phillip Brown and his street theater company, SaltWorld, Inc. We wanted to use drama to set the stage for the urban issues course by creating critical awareness among our students and faculty of the need for personal and social transformation and of our important role in working with the poor and oppressed around the world. Phillip had enlisted HansSoul, a local rapper, to play the homeless man, and Phillip had acted as the agitated guest. The rest of the script was created by the response of the students and faculty, and the improvisational response of the actors: a homeless man, an agitator, and a student actor planted at the table. It worked well enough, as evidenced in a student's essay about the experience.

Urban issues of injustice and oppression were not abstract lessons reserved for textbooks, but were realities we should expect to encounter in this line of work. For a moment I felt duped, as if I were on candid camera. My silence and passiveness was not the way I wanted to be observed. I longed for Isaac (the homeless man) to return so I could replay the scenario and this time I could talk to him and show him I cared. But he had long gone. My heart sank. "But Lord, when did we see you hungry?" and I thought of the words of the Great Teacher himself. What if I did all the right things to demonstrate my ability to recognize Christ in his distressing disguise just like St. Francis, St. Martin or Mother Teresa? Would I have grown smug? Was it possible they ever failed on occasion? At that moment I did not know which was worse, my inability to recognize the tattered Christ or my desperate need for repentance. On a prophetic, but more comforting note, I am reminded in the Scriptures of the importance of hospitality because some have entertained angels unaware.[10]

We are unashamed of our educational goal at the CSSC: to create Christian change agents, or social transformers, who are not only called, capable, committed, and competent in understanding the urban world but who have the skills to bring about godly transformation in often ungodly places. "People get ready for revolution by changing the way they look at themselves," George Lakey writes. "Private problems become political issues as people develop a collective will and understanding of struggle."[11] This critical awareness—or *conscientización,* as Boal calls it—is the first stage of cultural preparation for change. It is an awareness not only of ourselves but also of our place in the world.

Part of this godly revolution is the awareness that people should be treated with dignity and respect, no matter who they are or what their status in life is. We were not surprised to find that several women from the third floor of our building, not related to the CSSC, had passed our homeless man Hans on their way out the door at the end of the day. They were on their way home from an office party but had returned to the party to prepare a plate of food, which they delivered to Hans on the steps of the building before he came to our floor.

Critical Awareness: Do the Arts Transform?

This story illustrates the use of the arts to create a personal awareness of social injustice. We had used the invisible theater to expose the social injustice right outside the doors of the office building in which we work. While some students felt they had been "duped," others were quite moved by the experience. Not only do we ask our students to be aware of the problems involved in social injustice, but the university is called as an institution that sits in the midst of the problems to be aware of them and to become involved in them.

Using the arts to create critical awareness is not new. In the Old Testament Jeremiah, Isaiah, Amos, and other prophets used drama, allegory, and poetry to jolt people and nations into thinking about their lives in the world. Jesus, by his presence and his storytelling, often confused and angered those around him who did not want to recognize their own role in oppressing the poor. He created critical awareness among the poor by causing them to see and act on the new life of freedom that was possible outside the accepted cultural boundaries based on status, wealth, power, religion, gender, and ethnicity.

Arts of protest and confrontation are not new to American society. The years of the civil rights movement and the antiwar protest are familiar to most readers. Some of those who protest do so out of an acute political conscience and others with a biting sense of humor. While not always motivated by a Christian belief system, often urban prophets have been influenced by experiences in the church and possess a commitment to social justice. But what does Christian justice that creates critical awareness look like? We will begin to see the picture as we look at the lives and ministries of urban prophets we met in the past year.

Critical Awareness of Faith

Barbara Nicolosi trains Christian writers who wish to work in the entertainment industry. She believes that movies can intentionally create critical awareness through what she terms "Christian script." Christian scripts are redemptive in nature and move the viewer in a godly direction. Barbara discussed her thoughts on this when we interviewed her:

Does this movie, by the end, convict someone of their possibility of light/darkness, their need to be loved, their longing for transcendence? Does it connect them to God, does it convince them that there is order, there is mind in the universe, that no matter how chaotic things look that there is something that comprehends it all and is separate from it all? Does it make them hearken for heaven, for beauty, for permanence, and for all the things that can only be found in God? If it does, it's a Christian script. And finally, does it connect them to other people? Does it make them want to be a hero? Does it make them want to be someone who'll die for other people? Does it make them want to be kind? Does it make them be compassionate, merciful, and gentle—all of the goals, you know, of the gospel. If the script, at the end of that movie makes someone want to be kind, . . . we say it's a Christian script.

We tell our students that you need to create projects that have what we've called "haunting moments." And haunting moments that will get stuck in people's consciousness and bother them and make them brood and simmer and question. And that somehow if their projects don't have that, then why do it? But in the idea of creating entertainment that would make people pause, and that would in some way lead them to church or lead them to their knees, or lead them on a search, or validate their search, or validate what happens at church. That's what we're looking to do. But more than that, you lose the power. It's a humble task, creating entertainment like this, in the span of someone's whole journey to God.[12]

Hoodlum Church

You'll find Rev. Anthony Motley creating awareness every time he fearlessly confronts the boyz in his 'hood. He is known for walking the streets of southwest D.C. at all hours and, more than anything, for building relationships with the down and out, the high and out, and the lost. He is a lover of the arts and has an acute understanding of their power to attract, preach, and heal in the church where he pastors—a church that traditional Christians sometimes mock as the "hoodlum church." Redemption Ministries is more than a church; it is a holistic ministry center located in a converted grocery store and supports after-school programs, youth activities, job training, a business incubator, a photocopy store, and the arts.

In a community of approximately seventy thousand people, many of them youth and young adults, the ministry was formed in 1993 "to provide alternative ways of living to the young people in the community and to provide them with hope—hope and the deliverance from many of the social ills that many of them have become the victims of."[13] Rev. Motley has what has been featured in many public reports as a model outreach to the drug community. The conventional church would consider his ministry nontraditional. Once involved in drugs himself, Rev. Motley's *eschaton* came when one of his friends died. His commitment to the young people of his community has continued to grow. One of Rev. Motley's strategies is his use of large music concerts to draw the crowd he has a heart for.

> [See] all of these posters? Hundreds of people come to see the concerts. This last one we had over a thousand folks out there. On the posters it says nothing about faith, it says nothing about altar call, it says nothing about Jesus. It says gospel on it, you know, real small. Matter of fact, even the Junk Yard Band—that's a secular group. And many of the folks that follow them have no faith, no faith in nothing. But we put them there because we want to draw them to the place.

Rev. Motley does not feel that these concerts are in conflict with the gospel.

> Oh, of course not. You know, where was Jesus? Jesus went to where the people were. He went to where the sinners, the disenfranchised, the downtrodden folks that had no idea about nothing about God, that don't wanna hear nothing—that's where he went. So there's no conflict, even though folks get on us about doing it, and I tell them, "I read my Gospels every day, and my Gospels tell me that we're on the right track." And Saturday one of the [well-known secular music groups] said to me, "I wanna be like the [Christian

group]." And I said, "You know how you gotta be. You gotta clean your act up. And they were here Sunday in church. Matter of fact, they asked me to pray with them before they played. And when they were in church Sunday . . . they sang a song after the Word called "Requesting Ears." And they sang that song, and then we did the altar call.

Rev. Motley and Deborah Nicholson—the founder of Redemption's Timothy Ministries, a theater arts ministry that encompasses drama, dance, and music—both believe that the arts in the midst of the service not only prepare us to hear the Word but can also *bring* the Word. Says Motley,

Oh yes, the drama has to bring the Word. I mean, you know, the drama—I mean because even when Deborah does [the drama] Ruby, you know, it's a preaching experience. It's a moment of exaltation. It's a prophetic utterance. It's revelation. It's all of that. And then it's an altar call.

Voiceless Art

Todd Farley is the president of Mimeistry International, an arts organization he founded in 1978. Todd considers mime a prophetic form of art. "In Scripture you capture the concept that the arts in the Old and New Testament alike were a prophetic voice. 'I've spoken to you by the prophets, and have multiplied visions for you, and have appealed to you through parables acted out by the prophets' (Hosea 12:10)." Todd is quick to point out that biblical prophets challenged nations, societies, and peoples. Isaiah, Jeremiah, Amos, Elijah, Hosea, and other prophets "acted out in physicalization and drama their message, their prophecy, their transformational words."[14]

You find Christ using forty-nine parables. You find two hundred and fifty parables in the Old and New Testaments. I think the arts can't avoid being prophetic. Artists of popular society and culture are forming our culture and our society because of the prophetic function that art contains.

One of the things that's wonderful about mime is we are able to approach the issues of rape, brutality of women, concepts of divorce and alienation, and social prejudice from a parabolic form. A lot of times society doesn't want to look at these issues because they consider these issues ugly. They consider these issues repulsive. Every artist should know about their social voice, and through their art form, help people look at an ugly thing and face it with such poetry that it hits the soul with its beauty. And inside of that beauty you see the ugliness of what has actually taken place. And yet it's presented in such a way that we don't shut our eyes. I mean how many people want to go to downtown, to the inner city? They don't. They avoid that. They get on the highway and skirt around it. Where the artists who express in beauty and movement can take that tragedy and capture it in such a way that moves the soul to compassion and causes us to see that which we would not normally look at. And the poetry of it allows us to embrace it more fully. And then after being embraced by it, lets its theme reveal itself.

Look at the social justice of Nathan dealing with David's treatment of Uriah's wife and Uriah being killed. He does it through story, and why? Because David was blind to his own stupidity. He was blind to his own sin; he was blind to his own violence of the family structure. His social structure allowed the king to kill who he would, and so you couldn't rebuke him with lectures and spoken words. And so what happens? The prophet Nathan comes and he pronounces a story that emotionally riles the King David to make him mad. That's what all of us artists are out there to do. To take these things that everybody has walls around and allow them to get mad about it. And then we can turn. Like Nathan says, "You are the builder of the wall. You are the one who has slain Uriah. You are the one ignoring that downtown, you are the one driving around. You are part of the problem. And you need to be part of the solution."

If we as Christians cannot offer hope to the prostitute and the drug addict and to the down and out, to the person on the street as well as in the palace, who can? Art, mime, dance, drama, has the potential to speak to everyone. I mean, our art is known as poor man's theater. And we're able to represent the poor man. And at the same time, because of the tradition of Marcel Marceau, we're able to do it in front of the rich man. And we have. We've mimed on top of outhouses and in the Sydney Opera House. And at the same time, our message stays the same. We deal with the human tragedy as well as the godly hope in the midst of that tragedy.

We discovered through our research that nearly every artist we interviewed was involved in both the prophetic and agape forms of art. They had a strong realization of these qualities and potentialities in their art. Driven by a desire to impact the world, these artists began to encounter God through people in unusual places and began to love them through their art. We turn now to listen to the voices of some of the urban prophets we met, as they tell us how they encounter the world.

All Things Bright and Beautiful

At the edge of Central Park in New York City is a historic black church with a mission and ministry for the streets, All Angels Church. John Bjerklie, a muralist and sculptor, attends the church and is involved in a unique arts ministry with the homeless. His equally unique artistic endeavors provide a perspective on the arts and social justice.

For the past year John has been working in Bridgeport, Connecticut, as a result of a call for sculptors to do public works. He found a gorgeous beach with a huge landfill right next to it, which was perfect for his theology of art. He has been working on an installation on the top of this mound for about a year, and it may be several years before the work is ready for public viewing. He works on this landfill because "To me, art is not necessarily something that you put in a museum or a gallery."

> In fact, I find those places to be void of art most of the time. My work, my art, is taking things which the world or society considers useless and discards. Since I started making art as a teenager I would find something that somebody had thrown out—a scrap of something—and I'd start painting on it or drawing on it. The subject matter of my work is always about that. My work actually led me to this place where I was open to the Christian idea that the things that society throws out, that people discard, God actually sees the value in that which is lost or considered to be unimportant.[15]

Several years ago, John began attending All Angels Church as a result of the help he received from their Artists' Assistance Network, a grant program that funded in part his work in Marseilles, France, a project similar to the landfill installation described above. He began attending the evening Bible study, which is primarily targeted for the homeless of New York. "I just found that this was a place [where] I could worship, and I had a very hard time finding a place to worship in New York."

At the invitation of a church member, John began to lead the Bible study through art, which he has led for five years now.

> One of the things that I always did that helped me in my growth as an artist was I would read the Bible and I'd try to draw. So with the homeless people, we read the Bible and try to draw, I mean it's about as basic as it gets. We would say, "What's the picture that comes to your mind?" And then we'd sit down and we'd try to draw it, and it was just mind-blowing what would come out.
>
> The most important part of my work as an artist has become doing service. It's about sharing my gift. Not to make some big, great piece of art, but about opening up my spirit in a community with other people, because everybody has gifts. Everybody has gifts, and if you sit down in a community of faith and say, "How can I express my faith visually, or in word or in song or in dance?" To me, this is the soul of my work as an artist, and without that, I can't do my big grandiose projects. It keeps me in check. To me they're incredibly beautiful, and my heart is in this so much, because I think this is the most important thing I do as an artist. And I don't walk away with cash in hand, a line on my resume, or something that's gonna last for a thousand years like a pyramid. What I come out of this with is spiritual growth for me, a communion with other people who are at the same place I am. They are coming in need . . . coming in and saying, "God, thanks for getting me through last week. Man, I hope you can get me through next. Amen."

(John Bjerklie produces a Christmas calendar each year featuring the work of the members of his Bible study group. All profits are used for the needs of the homeless members of the group.)

A Compassionate and Prophetic Presence

An Open Door

On the drive to the end of Forty-sixth Street on the southwest side of Philadelphia, one is jolted by the underside of America. Trash on the streets, abandoned houses, and fear of the shootings in this area that are reported in the news on a regular basis make one approach this neighborhood cautiously. But for a fleeting moment one is aware that God must be there. At the end of the street, among the many houses that are collapsing, one sees stylistically painted houses with colorful flower boxes on the steps.

On the east side of the street an open (unlocked) and colorful door is an odd surprise in a community that otherwise appears locked down. A short, unassuming, and gentle Catholic sister is engaged in her ministry at the arts center of the Southwest Community Enrichment Center.

> Definitely it was a very strong call, almost a second calling, in my vocation as a sister of the Immaculate Heart. I studied liberation theology at the Maryknoll School of Theology and was lucky enough to hear Gustavo Gutierrez talk about liberation theology and becoming immersed in the lives of the poor. And I was sitting, listening to him, and I thought to myself, "Here I am in the city, and I'm not acting out my faith. I need to do this." I needed to be pushed to go beyond the words, to actually enter into the city and do something with people. So that's how the idea, the seed, was planted for this place.[16]

When Sister Helen first began to work as a volunteer at the arts center, nearly ten years ago, she refused to lock the door. When a neighbor came to warn her of the violence in the area, she still refused, insisting that she wanted to welcome the community in, not to keep them out. This simple act, an unlocked door, was an incarnational act of love and trust and a prophetic witness of God's presence in a community marked by violence and poverty. Sister Helen's life points people to the peace of God. For nearly ten years, the arts center of the Southwest Community Enrichment Center has been a safe place for children, youth, and older women to create art, develop social relationships, and bring hope to people through the arts.

Apostles in Hollywood

If prophets live in the margins of our society and speak to both the kingdom of God and the kingdom of Satan, where would they most likely be found in the United States? Where would you expect a prophet to work, and who would they work with?

The answers to these questions are clear to Barbara Nicolosi, whom we introduced to you earlier. Barbara is a professional writer and the director of Act One: Writing for Hollywood, which is housed in an office of the Hollywood Presbyterian Church. Act One, a program that trains writers of the Christian faith for careers in the entertainment industry, now has 130 alumni working in Hollywood and in other cities of the United States and Canada. A no-nonsense organizational executive, Barbara articulates with passion and clarity a need and a vision within the most influential power in American society: the entertainment industry. She is an apostle to the industry and a prophetic voice to the church. She is working to bring transformation and renewal, a renaissance, to our society.

> The culture will be renewed because entertainment is at the center of our culture: what we laugh at, what we consider heroism to look like, what we consider a healthy human life, and what we consider to be meaningful in life. We're allowing them to be defined right now by the entertainment industry. It's the most powerful way to visualize a life choice. The first difference would be that we'd have a culture in which a lot of the choices that people make would be spoken of in a more truthful way.
>
> Take, for example, a show like *Friends,* where you have six promiscuous beautiful young people who jump in and out of bed with anyone and everyone and each other. They mirror for the world life without a moral compass outside of yourself. And yet it's a false mirror because there are no ramifications to their choices in the long term. They're still beautiful, and nobody gets a disease. Nobody gets AIDS on *Friends.* But that's just one thing. Beyond that it's a lie, that you could have all the things they have on that show and not pay any kind of price for it. And to live a life where you're just not concerned about anybody but your own self and your own needs and gratification. To me, the kind of person who really lived that out would be a despicable human being; they wouldn't be funny, charming, somebody you'd like to call your friend. So those are kind of lies as far as we're concerned. I don't mean to be harping on *Friends*—it's a tremendously well written show, well acted, well produced, and obviously it has an audience. But I *don't* consider it to be a truthful show, and I consider it to be detrimental to the culture. We would like to see some more truth telling out there. And not to say that that would be bad, because there's a flip side, which is the peace that comes from having God in your framework, which is never mirrored in our culture in terms of entertainment. People who have God in their framework [are portrayed] to be people who are fanatical, crazy, fearful, intolerant, uptight—people who throw bombs at things. There are a few exceptions. But for the most part, that's the perception in the entertainment industry. And that's a lie, so we'd like to correct that.

Founded in 1999, Act One began as an intense training session, or "boot camp," for Christians who wanted to have writing careers in film and television. The program has since been expanded to include two-month-long boot camp sessions, a script critique service, a consultation service for production companies with projects that have been given the green light, a series of weekend seminars on topical issues pertaining to screenwriting or adaptation, and an ongoing formation series for program alumni.

The faculty consists of over seventy-five writers and producers who work in Hollywood in all different genres: comedy, television comedy, television drama, soaps, and so on. Some of the faculty have been nominated for Academy Awards. The students come from all over the United States and Canada. Barbara says, "They have to have a college degree, they have to be a talented writer, they have to convince us that they're a committed Christian, they have to understand the goals and the principles of the program and want to kind of throw their hat in the ring and be part of that."

Through their programs Act One believes that "a renaissance in Hollywood will come about through a commitment to artistry, professionalism, a conviction, a concern for the audience, a concern for substance in the product, and prayer, to have a personal relationship with God, and especially in Christ."

Nicolosi's strategy is clear: "Our goal is to bring into Hollywood alternative programming sources. The script is the blueprint for everything in this industry and . . . it all starts with the writer. And the problem is there just aren't enough products, there's not enough healthy alternatives being written right now. Healthy entertainment comes from a healthy heart. We encourage people who have their spiritual act together to then learn what the industry knows and requires on a professional and artistic level so that they can be taken seriously."

Act One takes a proactive approach to changing the culture, one in which they expect the highest in preparation, craft, and work ethic. They are in a highly competitive market where whining or criticizing will not cut it. They are looking for a few good writers who are willing to throw their artistic and spiritual muscle into the writing pit.

Act One began with a confrontational strategy that has, after four years of teaching Christian writers, now become an agape strategy. We have observed that this transition is common in the ministries of urban prophets who become involved in the lives and communities of those outside the four walls of the church.

When we started Act One, we were concerned about the need to replace the ungodly with us godly people. But as we've gone ahead, we've grown in love and compassion and prayer. We pray so much for this ministry and [for the] entertainment industry. And [one day] in that prayer we had a paradigm shift. . . . We do not perceive people in Hollywood to be the enemy anymore, but we perceive them to be the mission field, and that's our job.

God could have good movies tomorrow if he wanted—he could make movies. But then we think what he's more interested in is the hearts and the souls of the people in this town. Tremendously creative, tremendously intelligent, tremendously driven, tremendously beautiful, articulate, funny people. That's who the people are who keep this business going. And the idea that we could take them to our hearts and kind of one-by-one witness to them a life with God at the center, as artists, and thereby win them over. And when we win one of them over, you know, we win over their audience, which can be in the millions and millions. That's the second part of the strategy, to put our students in the heart of the industry: on the sets, in the writers' rooms, in the studios, in the offices, just being who they are as believers, loving people and witnessing to them by the work that they do and by the lives that they lead. If we can just up the numbers, that will begin a renaissance.

Act One is seeing results and a change in local Christian communities.

Fifteen years ago there were no ministries for Christians in Hollywood, and there was no God in prime time. Christians in this town were very much in the closet, you know, completely in the closet. Our faculty would say, "I couldn't out myself because I'd lose my job if people knew I went to church." And they're very serious, and a lot of them were very persecuted. They experienced a lot of persecution for the fact that they just believed in God. In the last fifteen years there have been this whole new spate of ministries started in Hollywood now. So we have Media Fellowship International, Master Media, Intermission Actors Co-op, Associates in Media Premise, Open Call, Slate, and Act One. All of these are ministries formed by Christians in Hollywood for Christians in Hollywood. And what they've done is they've given us a visibility. Christians can come together and realize you're not alone. They've given us the ability to figure out what it is we're doing here: how to present ourselves, how to function in the industry, how to be an apostle in Hollywood. The fact is that everybody is like, "We love these people. We feel compassion for them, for the most part."

I'm working with a woman now; she's an executive producer on a prime-time show. She was profiled a couple years ago in one of the trades as one of the top ten women in television. She's become a Christian. You just listen to her story and you have nothing but compassion, you know: two failed marriages, a couple other failed relationships, children here and there—you know, I mean, terrible life messes. The woman has everything money can buy, all the power you could ever want, and she's beautiful. It's that paradox that you find in Hollywood like nowhere else, where you have people that literally have everything the world has to give, but they're not happy, and in fact their lives tend to be a mess. So I love this woman and I feel a lot of compassion for her. I'm not going to look at her as the enemy. To me, she's the reason I'm here.

Nicolosi is not satisfied with just impacting the secular culture of Hollywood. She is equally vehement and strong in her crusade to call the church into the task, though she is often weary of trying to convince the church of the mission nature of her work.

I find that most of the Christians in Hollywood have lost patience with the church. They feel abandoned by the church. Act One is completely supported by the entertainment community of Hollywood, the Christian community. My faculty work for nothing; they'll teach three hours for a hundred dollars. And they'll mentor a student for an entire month for nothing. They're doing it because they believe it's important. But we're sick to death of trying to convince the church that this is not the throne center of the devil. This is just another mission field, and it's a tremendously powerful mission field. And it's not the Holy Spirit that has made the church think that Hollywood is the enemy. It is not. I think it's Satan that sold that line to the church. Because it makes the church not take it seriously. You don't have to evangelize Satan, do you? You don't have to send missionaries to Satan, to hell.

I gave a talk last year at a conference in Delaware to 250 Christian writers. I started by saying, "Greetings from the church which is in Hollywood." And everybody laughed. And I stopped and I said, "Why are you laughing?" And they said—well, this lady up front looked at me and she said, "Well, that's because it's like saying 'Greetings from the church which is in hell.'" I was like, "Hollywood is not hell. It's people that I love and know and that God loves." And they're just lost. They're tremendously powerful, wealthy, creative, beautiful people. They don't look lost, but in fact their lives are a mess. They have no hope; they have no lasting peace or promise of it. And the problem is they have a forum in which they can blast to the entire planet their no promise of peace and no conviction of joy. If we win them over, then we win over their audience.

Is Act One transforming society? It is too early to tell.

We've made a difference in that we've made them aspire to be great writers—not just good writers, but great writers. We've made them aspire to be apostles, to be part of the church community, to be plugged in, to have a vibrant life of faith so that as their career unfolds they won't lose it all, lose their spirit. I see among them tremendous bonds of friendship and charity. They go help each other move, they work with each other on projects, they collaborate, they love one another—and that network of our alumni is astounding. I've seen tremendous things in our faculty. Act One has forced the Christian writers and producers in Hollywood who are kind of undercover, in the closet, to come out and articulate what it is they're doing, and to want to do projects that they can come and show the students every year and say, "See, this is what I made."

We've learned that we will achieve nothing as a church within the culture and the arts without a posture of respect. . . . You need to be able to see the presence of the Holy Spirit where he is already active and go and baptize that.

We've learned that the hardest challenge we have is finding Christians who have something to say as parable makers. And to get people who are willing to be readers, brooders, reflectors, and then roll up their sleeves and put in the time in the darkness in front of that empty screen and try to come up with something that will work as entertainment and also work as a parable—this is the hardest thing. I can't find people to do for God what Hollywood has found people willing to do for money. We've got to find those people. I think the whole thing is kind of wrapped up in the missionary understanding: "Will you come here as a missionary? You won't do it for money because it's not worth it to you. But will you come for God?" And that's the challenge.

Christians are like refugees because they're artists from other places, because they haven't found a home in the church, and so you have that situation. The good thing in Hollywood is there's so many people out here working in the entertainment industry that many of the churches have fellowships for entertainment people. There's a great openness to them, but once you get out of Hollywood, there's almost no support for the arts in the church, for Christians that happen to be artists. In fact, they're considered to be the problem in a lot of places.

The church needs to completely repent, reexamine and repent of the way it treats these artists that God sends to us. They're not to be used for an agenda; they don't belong to the church that way. You know, they're a gift to the church, they're to make our faith experience more beautiful, they're to decorate our faith experience. The problem is artists are quirky, they're demanding, they pay a price for their insight and their art. And they can be hard to live with, and they can be outside the box and a little crazy and have rough edges. But that's where beautiful art comes from, that kind of person who's kind of a victim and trauma and integrated and distracted and thinking of other things. And there has to be room for that in the church.

Potential for Renewal

Practicing for the Revolution

George Lakey is a sixty-four-year-old grandfather who has spent the last forty-five years working for peace and social change in the world. Founder and director of Training for Change, a nonprofit organization, Lakey has had plenty of practical experience in facing violence and working for peace around the world.[17] In 1989, when Sri Lanka was in the midst of two civil wars, many leaders, including lawyers, were being assassinated. Lakey, along with other volunteers, was called in by an association of lawyers working for human rights and was asked to serve as an unarmed bodyguard to those threatened with assassination. The belief was that the assassins would not shoot an unarmed international bodyguard for fear of creating an international incident. When this proved to be a success, the work was extended to other vulnerable human-rights activists. George's ministry was a true ministry of God's presence. During the nine years George worked in Sri Lanka, not one human rights leader accompanied by the Peace Brigades team was assassinated.

George advocates and uses role playing in preparing people to respond in situations of conflict and uncertainty. Role playing (related to playback theater) allows people to gain an awareness of an issue and develop options for action, and it significantly raises consciousness of the extent of injustice in the world.

In a simple example, Lakey explains how he would help a group know how to handle an owner who is abusing his or her dog. Dividing the group into two lines, he asks each person to select a partner from the opposite line. One line is to play a tired and frustrated owner of an obnoxious dog. The other line represents a person walking in the park. Once they visualize their roles, they are asked to interact. Following this interaction, the group debriefs by listing options for stopping the violence. Then they reverse roles. This role-playing experience prompts profound discussions on issues of responding to evil.

Learning about Life

Brian Joyce is not what he appears to be. His earring, booming voice, and omnipresent personality might cause one to guess his creative power. One might not, however, suspect his deep spirituality, his commitment to his local church, or his status as a part-time student at Eastern Baptist Theological Seminary. Joyce is the director of Children's Programming at the Annenburg Center on the campus of the University of Pennsylvania and the director of the Philadelphia International Children's Festival. Each year this festival is host to over twenty thousand children and nine theater productions from around the world.

Brian lives out his role as an artist of faith through the choices he makes for justice in his life and in his theater. He almost left the theater for the pastorate several years ago, but two of his seminary professors recognized his gift, talent, and potential for impacting change through the arts and confronted him.

> The calling took place in my job while I was in the secular arts, and so then when I got to seminary, a series of individuals convicted me about whether or not I was taking an enormous amount of training and throwing it away, as if God hadn't given me the training to begin with. Ian Scott and Ron Sider [seminary professors] really forced me to think about what it meant to have this training, to have this gift and this ability and want to use it.[18]

Brian's calling and his "outing" as a Christian had occurred in a very public and secular environment several years before. While attending a national theater conference where he was a guest speaker, many of the attendees began to make disparaging remarks about born-again Christians, which is not an uncommon practice in secular artist gatherings.

> The conversation became about the enemy, and the enemy was the born again. That's what they kept saying. "Ya know, the people that are the enemy are the born again. They're these fundamentalists. They're the religious right." The compacting of these terms together became uncomfortable for me, so it came

around to my turn to talk, and I said, "Before I begin this conversation, I need to let you know that I'm the Enemy. It would be wrong of me to sit here and deny my God." And I said, "So I want you to know that I'm born again, that there are places in which my theology is fundamental, and there is no way in which I am right wing. So, you have not described your enemy very well, because you have described your Enemy to include the entire church. And you need to look at this as a political question, not a religious question."

What shocked Brian was that the most critical of the group was a friend of his who had not admitted until that day that he was a regular churchgoer in Manhattan. Following this incident, many people stood waiting to talk with him. Brian thought,

> "I'm about to have my head taken off here, and this is going to be unpleasant."
> Because I saw people in this group that I knew well. People I've known for years.
> But I had come out publicly, and I was ready to take the heat for it, so I went over
> to talk to these people, and to a person, every one of them said, "Thank you. I'm
> a Christian, and I'm afraid to talk about my Christianity to my colleagues."

Since that simple, painful, and courageous act to be who he really was in public, Brian has provided a friendly space "so that Christian artists know that this is a safe haven, a place where they can admit their faith and talk about how their faith drove them into the arts. And so that launched me into a desire to actually heal the break between the church and the arts." Part of that healing has to do with how Brian makes choices in his work.

The arts have been and continue to be an activity for the elite. So Brian sets the ticket prices for the children's festival artificially low. The ticket price is about 30 percent of its actual value. He raises money to pay for the other 70 percent for every ticket. He works to involve kids from underprivileged schools and neighborhood groups "so that you bring people into performance, and you make it seem like an organic part of their life."

In 2002 Brian purposefully selected dramas on death and dying—not a subject one would think appropriate for a children's drama festival. But Brian understands his audience, which comes primarily from Philadelphia.

> At any given time, my audience is going to contain people who are dying,
> children who are dying, children who have known someone who died, have a
> parent who just died. . . . My audience comes to me in hundreds of types of
> pain. So, I program art, specifically when I can find it, that addresses those sorts
> of situations.

Brian does not believe in prescriptive drama, in which easy and pat answers are given to difficult problems. He prefers to challenge people to come out of their comfort zone and strives to transform their ability to see the context of their own lives. He takes the symbols of their lives and reshuffles them so that the audience can look at these symbols in new and different ways.

Brian believes real learning occurs once people are pushed out of their comfort zones. "I prefer they leave with a question and pointed towards the right direction. Performance leads you to questions but points you in directions. And I'm looking for shows that point people towards Scripture, *point* people towards God. I would prefer, however, that performance—especially for children—not *take* people there, because it's an intrusion on both the family and the church."

Brian attempts to respect people's—especially parents'—boundaries. He presents family art and believes "that family art should be put into context by parents, because they're the other voice that I need in there." He believes "every child has at least one parent who can help them interpret the world." He has a rule that children cannot attend his shows without an adult, even threatening to cancel the performance if adults are not present.

> Part of what you do as an adult with a child at a performance is to witness the validity and the importance of that art. A child sits next to an adult and takes cues. And without that, you've got incomplete communication, and then I can't finish the prophetic theology because I don't have the person to guide that person, because the parent or the teacher has to be part of the prophecy. They have to talk to that child. And as I said, the art's only there for an hour; it goes away. Who is going to witness for that art and the questions raised once the art leaves? That's very important to me.

To place sensitive issues in perspective for children and adults, Brian produces study guides for the performances and assists local teachers and parents through workshops to answer the questions that arise from the drama. While he does not believe in prescriptive drama, he does prepare teachers and parents for the major themes of the drama. It is in the dialogue with children, parents, and teachers that transformation takes place.

Summary: The Prophetic Power of Art

Does art have real power to change lives, communities, and societies? We can see, from the examples given, the latent functions of art creating critical awareness through an action potential in personal lives, communities, and the broader society. Unfortunately, or maybe fortunately, life is too complex for a simple solution. Without an eye to see or an ear to hear, prophets are indeed crying in a vast, dry, and lonely desert. The barren soil has not been watered with enough love and care to even receive a seed of hope that can grow in faithful joy through the presence and power of God.

But it is in the lives and ministries of the silent ones like Barbara Nicolosi, Brian Joyce, and the many others who labor in "secular" society, confronting and loving those outside the NU JERUZ and calling them into what God is doing and can do in the world that we hear the voice of Jesus saying, "Come to me, all you who are weary and burdened, and I will give you rest" (Matt. 11:28). Jesus calls us to heal the sick and give power of capacity to the poor. These artists are also called to love with great compassion, to incarnate, to have the empathy necessary to understand those in need, and to develop the courage of compassion to speak out against the winds of contemporary culture.

Their courage to "come out" as followers of Jesus in a hostile environment serves as a prophetic act to the many who work in government offices, social and educational institutions, and community organizations outside the four walls of a church.

Their call to the church to become involved and to use the gift of the arts to serve others is a mixed blessing for the church. While living in the margins has provided these urban prophets with a unique perspective of justice, it has also at times forced them to be at odds with the church.

If there is a lesson here for the church and for Christian artists, it is the call for intentionality. Justice and social transformation require vision, excellence, planning, and courage, but they also require action. These urban prophets, without exception, not only speak out but continually act to bring about transformation and to provide solutions. And they also carry out their work through an ongoing agape work of compassion within the community they serve.

We become worldly not by engaging with the world but by allowing it to shape our thinking.[19]

Steve Turner

7

Arts as a Call to Redemption

In this chapter we will explore the characteristics of artists who use the arts as a prophetic voice to call people to critical awareness and to provide a message of redemption and God's saving grace to individuals and to societies, more commonly referred to as "evangelism." We will look at the direct and indirect methods employed by a reggae musician, a street-theater artist, a hip-hop artist, and a mime artist, who often brave the danger of the streets to share a message of hope and redemption. Prescriptive art brings a person to the point of a particular decision. It bristles the aesthetic artist, challenges the communicative one, but is standard fare for the urban prophet who calls others to personal accountability and responsibility.

As you read this chapter, the case examples we present should help you compare the characteristics of urban prophets and agape artists mentioned in chapter 5. To review:

Urban Prophets

- Have a strong calling from God
- Have a vision for justice
- Identify with the victims of society
- Preach a specific message of redemption
- Unmask hypocrisy

- Evoke hope
- Act and cause others to act
- Use the language of the streets
- Live a life of compassion
- Suffer for their ministry

Agape Artists

- Are called by God
- Have a propensity for action
- Empathize through personal pain and heartbreak
- Have a goal of redemption
- Live incarnationally and cross-culturally
- Make personal sacrifice for their ministry
- Know how to love with a risky love
- Have compassion for the "forgotten"
- Have a spirit of reconciliation and forgiveness
- Show up faithfully
- Know their limits
- Seek rejuvenation

In relation to our Arts in Redemptive Transformation model, we are at stage 1 in the process of transformation, in which art and the artist confront personal sin and the injustices of a society, create critical awareness of the need for change, and ultimately call both the individual and society to action and responsibility. We recall the four barriers to the NU JERUZ—personal and social desire for money, status, in-group solidarity, and power—that are at the root of collective oppression of the poor. In the last chapter we looked at how the arts play a prophetic role in society to confront and create critical awareness of the NU JERUZ. It is the urban prophets' *eschaton,* the call to a time and place, the understanding of their role and their purpose in bringing about the kingdom of God on earth, that leads artists to critically reflect on society, identify with the needs and plight of society's victims, unmask hypocrisy, and evoke a hope that results in action.[1] As we have seen, while a particular work of art is sometimes effective in confronting society with the need to change, the form of confrontation that most often leads to action is both incarnational and long term. This is especially true of urban prophets who prophetically call for redemption and salvation. Some might know them as arts evangelists, but their methods may not fit traditional categories.

Leaving the comfort of one's cultural walls, as the urban prophet and agape artist must do, means that one must not only use the artistic language of the street but must also, through a strong personal and spiritual autonomy, be in the world but not of it. While these artists may hold many values of the majority culture, values that are present even within the sanctuary, other values they believe to be important differ from those of the majority culture or may not be practiced in the same way. God came in the recognizable form of a human so that we could understand and relate to his message. The sacred artist uses a similar approach to reach those in the secular world—through art with a familiar beat and form that will enage their audience but that also contains seeds of the sacred message of redemption.

The Role of the Arts

A word of caution is in order here. Too often the church has expected art and artists to act as the church. There is often a misunderstanding of the role of artists, their creative impulses and lives, and the role of their creative aesthetic experience. Barbara Nicolosi, whom we met in the last chapter, expresses the concern well:

> It's not supposed to replace the church. The arts do not replace the church. The arts complement what happens at church. In the evangelical Christian community when [we] get the power of media, we tend to use it like we are at church. Talking heads, blaring out overt theological formulations. This isn't where the power in media is, especially entertainment. Entertainment has another job to do.
>
> Evangelicals often ask, "When does somebody kneel down and give his life over to the Lord Jesus Christ?" And somehow if that isn't there, then it isn't a valid Christian entertainment project. The arts are to mirror [society] . . . or they are a living out of a particular theological view. They're to show people what a theology looks like in human life and in application. And they're also just to fill the world with delight, to connect to one another, with the experience of community, sharing in joy and laughter and beauty.

While we agree with Nicolosi that the arts mirror society, we also agree with de Gruchy that the arts construct a reality for people. This is one reason that the arts, especially participatory art, as in the work of Boal, provide an opportunity and rehearsal for change. People get to try on the experience of a new life and, through critical awareness, make a change of allegiance. An important role of the art and the artist is to provide a redemptive alternative to nonredemptive thoughts and actions. The prophetic role of redemptive art provides "a way out" by offering a call to redemption through an allegiance to the NU JERUZ.

The Role of the Artist

Brian Joyce, whom we met in the last chapter, responds to another common concern and misconception about the role of the artist:

> One of the problems with arts is that art is an hour or two hours long and then it leaves. Artists [may] have a tendency to make claims that I find abhorrent. So, for instance, "I'm going to come into a community and I'm going to transform that community." Well, no. No you're not, unless you're going to stay. You're going to come to that community and perform for them and then leave and [the community] is going to transform the community. You've done nothing except perform.
>
> I expect evangelizing artists who are going to the street to not be dropping in to hit people and then leave. If nothing else, they're going to leave the Book. So I expect them to make the commitment. I can't ask a performing company coming from France to stay for six months with these people and nurture them. If I do, if I bring a longer residency in, then you can get closer to prescription as far as I'm concerned—as long as you're staying to take the heat when it's difficult. And I expect preaching art, I expect street art, to be part of a ministry. And a ministry involves commitment. It involves good shepherding. It involves discipling.

Brian's concern for incarnation is a critical component of the prophetic arts. As we have noted, artists who are not related to a community often have little communicative power of identity and relevance, two key components of effective communication. As you read the case examples below, consider how these artists mirror life, construct reality, and exemplify the relational principles of effective social and personal transformation.

A Call to Transformation

To most evangelicals, bringing the Good News means preaching the Word and calling people to a personal commitment to Jesus Christ. This includes a confession of one's sins and may take place anywhere, but it eventually brings people to the church, where they join the church community through the covenant of baptism.

We were curious, in our search for urban prophets, what "preaching the Good News" might look like in the street. It is still not uncommon to find street preachers. We have seen them with microphones, preaching in Chicago, Miami, and Philadelphia. This role within the public square of American life has been critical in raising awareness of the gospel of Jesus since the time of Jesus himself, and long before, in the voices of the prophets.

We found artists with this same passion, call, and vision to change the world through a personal message of redemption and salvation. These urban prophets are passionate and courageous and at the same time quite vulnerable, having come to a real point of humility through Jonah experiences, in which they were headed in a direction far away from God; but God was there, waiting to meet them.

Often these prophets have a disdain and mistrust for the institutional church, and at other times, a deep appreciation for the support that some church congregations have given them. Their lives are no longer focused on the pursuit of money or fame but on bringing about the NU JERUZ in the lives of the down and out, the oppressed and marginalized, and "the least of these." We discovered that while these artists often presented very strong messages in their art, they were very gentle in spirit and worked with the poor within their own neighborhoods. As in the last chapter, all of these artists displayed characteristics of both urban prophets and agape artists.

The Heist: SaltWorld, Inc.

Pennsylvania Avenue, Baltimore, Maryland. Four thugs walk out of a local bank and begin to argue. A gun is brandished as they argue about the getaway. Either these thugs are stupid or their conflict is more important than the robbery. People begin to gather.

In the ghetto when you start to stir up confusion and conflict, people stop. People watch. You get people's attention. We started performing the piece, and folks realized, "Okay, this is a play." Two things began to happen. People started coming around, and they were ticked off at first, because they thought that there was really gonna be some real ruckus or some real action. But they got over that really quick. Then they start watching the piece.

[In the play] one guy shows up late and wants to get out of the game because his son was miraculously healed by the Lord, and so he accepts Christ as a result and becomes a martyr for the Lord. He walks out of the game, even if it means he catches a bullet, which he does at the end.

Following the show, there was a brother standing there with a neck brace on. The brother had tears in his eyes. We had started to pray with various audience members, people on the street after the show. He comes over to one of the actors in the play—Shy Lyn. Shy starts to pray for this brother. Immediately following the prayer, he takes off his neck brace, and in tears, he reaches into his pocket and he pulls out crack cocaine, and he says, "That's it. That's it. I'm finished. I'm finished." And he throws his crack down on the street and starts weeping. And of course, we're shouting, "Hallelujah!"

We're kinda amazed. We're kinda in shock at the same time. We don't run a "miracle, healing crusade." So we're not expecting to see miracles like that just happen. We're performing; we get caught up in the performance. And sometimes as artists, just as human beings, God is working a miracle right in front of you. And it really makes you say, "Wow. God is all powerful." And when this brother pulled crack out of his pants, that was an immediate testament as to the Holy Spirit working and God working through our ministry in a very practical and real way. Not just people going home with the message that they should receive Christ, but actually receiving Christ right there on the street. And then not just receiving Christ, but even getting healed and delivered from something as entrapping and as devastating as crack cocaine.[2]

Phillip Brown, who played the part of the "agitated guest" in the last chapter and who is the narrator of this story, is a tall, lean, and attractive man with an intense, charismatic personality. You might expect to see him on a Broadway stage or on a movie screen. You may have and you might again. Phillip is a professional actor and playwright with a call to bring the gospel to the streets, literally. His two passions are his art and his calling to preach the Good News.

Phillip founded and leads an itinerate guerrilla theater organization called SaltWorld, Inc. A company of ethnically diverse actors with a call to bring quality drama and preaching in the ghetto streets, SaltWorld's mission is to bring salt and light, hope and peace, into communities void of art and the peace of the gospel. The troupe goes into the "dead parts of the world" and into places that have "lost their flavor, their potency." They want to wake up the ghetto, bring it back to life, and preserve what is good. In places filled with misery, homeless people, prostitutes, drug addicts, corner boys, stray dogs and cats—that is where you will see Salt. Phillip says, "Frankly, poor people, it seems, always have an ear to listen. They always have an eye that will stop and watch, because there's hope that they can get something out of it that would better their situation or better their lives, and a lot of times because that's all they have."

While SaltWorld preaches Jesus, they are also aware of the vision for the community. They want a world that is beautiful, a world where there's no vandalism, no blight, no graffiti, and no garbage on the streets. And through good art and Good News, they want to make a difference.

Phillip tells us that the communities they perform in are often without a church presence or Christian witness. People in these communities feel marginalized by "good" Christians who are often bound to the exclusivity of the sanctuary. And then Phillip code switches his talk:

We don't have a formal altar call at the end of our productions because, one, we want the Holy Spirit to do what the Holy Spirit's going to do, and two, we don't want to emulate, if you will, orthodox Christian evangelism ministries. In other words, we don't want people to see the piece that we perform, have this great experience, and then all of a sudden feel like there's a hook at the end—feel like, "Oh, okay, here it comes. Here's the altar call. Here's the old tent revival. Here's the old . . . This is where they're getting us. Now they're going to put us in church, indoctrinate us, and we're gonna sing hymns and we're gonna take communion every other Sunday and we gotta pay our tithes." All this traditionalism and religiosity. That phobia comes over people. Gets 'em timid. Gets 'em fearful. Gets 'em . . . their trust is lost a lot of times. Now, do I have a basis for my theory in this? Yes. Experience, that's all. I've experienced both sides of it, and as soon as you start putting rigid boundaries and borders around the performances of what we do and it starts to look and sound and smell like traditional church, traditional Christian outreach, people are innately, instinctually perceptive. They know like animals, "Oh, wait a second. This isn't honest now. This isn't sincere. This isn't genuine."

They don't like the traditional church because the traditional church in their opinion has failed them, because the traditional church has put church culture, church religion, religiosity, first and not Christ alone first. They don't like church culture because they feel like they've been hoodwinked. I think what started to happen is as the culture began to change . . . and we kinda got more sophisticated, if you will, we kinda moved away from this sincere coming to know Christ as [a] person and building a spiritual relationship with Christ. All of a sudden church became an act, a production, and the real substance was no longer there, because the only substance is Christ alone. [Our generation] would see our parents going to church, and some of us our grandparents going to church, praising the Lord, shoutin' on cue, dancin' on cue, singin' on cue, get right home, cuss you out, open a pint, start all kind of gossipin'. And so all of a sudden we're sayin', "Wait a second. Church isn't . . . is this what they expect me to go to and believe in when it's not even helping them?" Well, so now who trusts the church? People say, "I'm getting as far away from the church as possible, because I know if God is all truth, and what I'm supposed to be seeing is truth in my parents and all I'm seeing is hypocrisy and lies, God can't be there, can't be in that church." And so what we've done is we've stigmatized . . . we have a whole generation of young people who have stigmatized the orthodox church, quite frankly.

SaltWorld follows a modified incarnational principle: to be with. So rather than staging a hit-and-run evangelistic drama, they stay around to talk, pray, encourage, and listen. And then they connect people with local mentors.

It just amazed me, and we've had people come up on the street and just give so much love. A brother will come up and just say, "Look, I have a problem. I have a drinking problem. Could you just pray for me?" Absolutely! That's all it's about. After the show it's all about just fellowship and meeting people where they are. And they feel comfortable. And I haven't seen a random group of people, artists of any kind, just walk out and just start performing based on anything. Not just Christianity, but just anything. So when you come out and just perform in an area where there's nothing going on but sin, prostitution, drug dealing, drug smoking—when you come out into an area like that on somebody's block and just start performing anything, they immediately say, "Why do they care so much about us? Who cares that much to come out? Look, . . . the mayor doesn't care enough to come to sweep the streets most of the time. Trash doesn't get picked up on time. People aren't coming to set up businesses in these places. Who cares so much to come out and to perform, of all things?" Well, that gets people's attention. So if we perform, usually they wait until the show is finished and then we fellowship after the show. And that's where the praying takes place. That's where people are healed; people accept Christ. And that's how we know that we're making a difference, that we're being effective.

SaltWorld does, however, recognize the importance of the church, the community of faith, and comes at their invitation. A single performance often raises more questions than it answers for members of their audience. Critical are partnerships with local churches that are already working in the community and can provide a safety net and ongoing support for those who respond. The crack addict Phillip mentioned was immediately introduced to a minister from a local church who stepped in to get the man into a twelve-step program.

This type of ministry of confrontation is not without its perils and dangers, especially since SaltWorld strives to be as authentic as they can in the language and the style and sound of the culture. Phillip describes a performance in Baltimore:

> You heard a lot of commotion, characters speaking in loud Ebonics that only if you're from there you could probably really understand, and then he pulls out his gat, which is a 9 mm gun. And he's waving it at his friend like he's about to shoot. Interestingly enough, my character hadn't made his entrance yet around the RV. When I do come around the RV for my scene, I see one of our lead actors—literally now, this wasn't part of the show—up against the RV with his hands up. He's getting frisked down. Two police officers were there. One police officer was sayin', "Don't move. Be real slow." Well, I was shocked. Everybody in the audience they were sayin', "Nah, nah. It's a play. It's a play." But the police weren't playin' in Baltimore. They were literally proceeding to arrest one of the actors in the middle of the show, and we had to actually call the minister over. Timothy Warner, the director of Holy Boldness in Washington, had to say, "Look, this is just a play. They have their permit. They were cleared to perform." So that was a compliment to us as actors that we were able to [create such a realistic scene] . . . but then I guess it's not that difficult if you just pull a gun out on the street and go at anything I think police would stop. That's how . . . we like to push the envelope a little bit.

SaltWorld partners with churches because they recognize that everybody in the church isn't a hypocrite, insincere, disingenuous; that "everybody in the church isn't wearing a mask." SaltWorld is not antichurch, but they do struggle. They stand between the traditional church and a secular society that does not support or understand them or the power of their art.

> The orthodox church loves what we do and what we profess to do on paper. They love the vision, the edginess to what we do, and who we're trying to reach. They like the evangelism part. They like going out to the dark places and saving lost folk—on

paper. But when it comes down to it, I think the orthodox church is scared to death to partner with Salt, because they feel like somehow we're a little bit too street. We're a little bit too on the edge. We reflect a little bit too much of what real low-class, low-life culture is all about. Frankly, I don't know if they wanna get dirty—ya know, really get dirty—and I think it scares them to a large degree to go to places that they say they know but that they really don't know. And so we don't really get the funding from the traditional churches, with the exception of the United Methodist churches—God bless 'em—in Baltimore, Maryland, through the vision of one person: Timothy Warner.

On the flip side, we can't work in a commercial world because we're preaching the gospel of Jesus Christ. So secular folk don't wanna give us money because they feel like, "Well, we can't support religion. We can't support Christianity. You guys are too spiritual. You're too Christ centered." So here we are stuck in the middle.

In our empathy for Phillip, SaltWorld, Inc., and the urban prophets who are literally on the street, our first impulse is to pull out the checkbook and write a check. Here are these folks with such strong calls and giftedness who suffer in the margins to call people to a life of faith and personal transformation. They need support, and we hope Christians are compelled to support them. A more important level of giving, however, involves the church taking its own message of hope seriously. Phillip and artists like him need both. The message he is sending is that for there to be real social and personal transformation, the church must back their words with action in the tough places of the world by becoming involved in partnership with those who know the streets.

Must Come Correct: Mark Sandiford

> Bible inna mi han' and word o' Jah in mi mout'
> Hail up all I bredren while mi sip up mi stout
> Tho' mi ah bruk pocket still ah me run de rout
> Temple Yard we ah go bus up inna de North and South
> Come fi praise de Father mek de devil skin out[3]
>
> Mark Sandiford

Mark Sandiford is a reggae musician, or in his words, "a warrior in the kingdom of God . . . to fight to reclaim not only music and culture, but to reclaim the streets for Christ."[4] And that is where you'll find him daily, "being salt and light in a dark place where salt and light will not be found." He is either leading worship at Safe House, a homeless shelter in the business district of Atlanta, or playing at underground clubs where people are smoking, selling, or packing. He is a prophet who lives in two worlds and wants those worlds reconciled.

I wanna see them transformed the way they are. In other words, I want to see the body of Christ get to the point where a guy doesn't have to cut his locks off to come to a Bible study, and a guy doesn't have to think that he has to stop smoking weed to come to hear the Word shared at a Bible study. That a guy can come into a Bible study environment that allows him to be himself and have the Word of God change him by its sheer power and not by religion or by legalism, by tellin' him you gotta do all this to become ready to receive Christ. I feel like my responsibility is to transform people's lives by, one, writing what God gives me to write and, two, being there.

Husband, father, preacher's son, minister, warrior for God, member of the group Temple Yard, Jamaican, man of color in a primarily white society—Mark Sandiford, a.k.a. Mark Y Rage, praises the Father that drives the devil out, as his poetry says. His life bears that out in his call.

Mark earned his name Rage at an early age because of his temper. He appears to have been at war with the world and with God for the first part of his life, until God called him out. Born into a conservative Jamaican church culture, where as a preacher's son he was "shut out" from the streets, his music was the one thing that gave him respect.

It was out of anger and rebellion that Mark Y Rage eventually robbed his parents and left Jamaica to find his fortune in the world of reggae. Like Jonah who was called to preach in Nineveh, Mark was running from his Nineveh and God would not let him go. In New York he turned to witchcraft, buying oils and potions to put on his guitar-playing hands. On a London tour, not only could he not get the necessary visa for travel but neither could the members of his band. Riding on a tour bus across Europe, door after door was closed. Like Jonah, Mark confessed, "Guys, it's me. I shouldn't be here."

I remember calling my wife and telling her. And she just said, "Well, we'll just stay here in frustration until you get ready to obey God. I'm waiting. It's cool. Take your time. Do what you got to do, but I just want you to know that your family and your life is going to be miserable until you let go, because God's got an incredible purpose for you, but it calls for you letting go of all the things you've learned about the music industry and all the things you think you need to pursue and just hold on to the heart of Christ and being Christlike. Being selfless and being humble and being broken and giving away your music and going to places and playing for free where you know you're not going to get paid at the end of the night beyond the fact that somebody's gonna say, 'Oh you guys sound great.'"

Mark's wife is a strong influence in his life, and he jokes about the old musician's saying "A musician without a wife is homeless." It is no small matter to him that his wife has supported him throughout his career. Mark eventually moved to Nashville and became a part of the Christian music industry, but that would not end his own transformation journey.

And so I came off the road and I came to Atlanta. I spent the rest of the year home in the Word and on my knees, just building up my devotional life again, because everybody knows as Christians you struggle to spend time with God. I was in Christ when we played at Safe House for the Olympics. One of the events we played in was the Olympic Village in Atlanta in '96, and I connected with pastor Philip Gray. I would come down and speak to the guys occasionally, but when I moved here God immediately directed me here and [Gray] said, "Man, we were praying for somebody like you for months now."

I couldn't receive it, because how do you go from being a Christian artist in Nashville to being part of a ministry playing music to homeless guys. I didn't wanna do that. Homeless guys can't buy no CDs. And God just broke that whole thing and just taught me more and more about what Christ was about. What was Christ after? What was he seeking? What did he mean by the foxes had holes and the birds got nests, but the Son of Man doesn't have a place to lay his head? What was he trying to communicate with that? And the more I learned, the more I didn't want to do music anymore.

I wanted to get out of it and be done with it. And as my heart started to transform towards being a hand extended and being more of the heart of Christ, I saw in my life God saying, "Okay, you can start doing music again." And all of a sudden my music took on a different meaning for me, and I saw myself coming here and playing on Sunday mornings for worship and playing for free and just getting out of the concept of being a musician for hire and getting the concept of being a prophet in music, to hear from God—to spend time hearing from God so when you get onstage to say that one phrase that radically impacts somebody's life, that one piece of Scripture that you quote that radically impacts somebody's life, and it's like those moments I'm always searching for.

It is out of this personal transformation that Mark now has a "missionary zeal."

Let's also have an industry that hones and develops musical prophets. Musical Levites that go out into communities, and you know that you're not going to be paid, and you know that the returns are not going to be that great, but you know that you're exactly where God wants you to be, because if you don't go, who will? . . . We need to go where those people [in the clubs] are at and provide an alternative to what they think happiness is and peace is, and like I said, not to provide it by preaching necessarily but to provide it with good music that they can get down to, and within that music the Word of God, which will not return void.

Mark Y Rage has both a prophetic voice and a prophetic word to others. His open social consciousness and his nationality as a Jamaican have in many ways allowed him to fulfill a reconciling role as a bridge between the white and black worlds of the United States. He is very concerned for the plight of people of color in this country and acts with an attitude of humility, whether considering the "man or Babylon [the system]."

Mark's concern, reflected in his prophetic vision, is clear.

As a Christian, you do need to be a voice of the hurting and the helpless, and I like the fact that Christ said the Spirit of the Lord is upon me. He anointed me to preach good tidings unto the meek and to bind up the brokenhearted and proclaim liberty to the captives who are bound, to preach the acceptable year of the Lord. This is your time for freedom. My fight is not against flesh and blood but against principalities and powers. So I need to in my music to be writing songs that address the demonic warfare that I'm engaged in. And in the context I think that I'm at war with the social injustices. I don't think that God is happy about the homeless situation in our country.

Mark learned his heart from his mother, and this heart is reflected in his music.

The cool thing about being a reggae artist is this: that reggae has always been synonymous with spirituality, so I can quote two chapters of Scripture in between songs and people love it. But the thing is that my mom always would say, "Demons can quote Scripture." So, it's all about the person, the heart of the person. That's a beautiful concept to me—the heart of the person quoting the Scripture, because if I'm going into Christ with intimacy every day, then the Word then becomes quick and powerful and sharper than any two-edged sword coming from my mouth, because my life is a living testimony that backs up the Scripture I'm quoting and there's something that happens, I believe, in the spirit realm with a man who's trying to walk uprightly before God as he shares the Word of God. And that's where the prophetic happens, which I'm not in control of. All I'm doing is telling you what the Bible says.

How does this work out in Mark's life? He does not believe in what he calls "undercover CIA Christianity," where one hides his or her identity. He guards against being a "moral terrorist," as many people in his world think of Christians. He believes and lives as if the Holy Spirit provides the people with whom he should come into contact. So guided by the Spirit, his boldness can be both alarming and admired. He may ask club revelers to be silent and say the Lord's Prayer before his set, or he may give a word of encouragement to a homeless woman behind the club who is about to grab a pipe and attack an enemy, calming the storm before it happens.

One can see in Mark the ideals of a street prophet, not unlike an image of Christ himself—bold of word and gentle of heart, with truth ever on his lips. It is a life not easily led or understood by most in our society but is not unlike that of other urban prophets on a journey to make a difference in the lives of others through the power of the Spirit on the streets of the NU JERUZ.

Holy Hip-Hop and the NU JERUZ: HansSoul

I would like the world to look like the blood of Jesus.
I would like God to look down and see people covered by the blood.
They're saved.

It's educating people on how to gain resources.
Educating people that God wants them to prosper.
Educating people that God wants them to be healthy.
Educating people that God wants to use their gifts,
whether it be rap,
break-dancing,
graffiti.
Whatever it is,
the gift is from God—because they're good gifts.

I would like to see a world that's not splashed with violence and tinged with all
    these other things that bring down society.
I would like to see a world that speaks life,
that blesses the city,
that blesses its mayor,
that blesses its president,
its government.

A country that has prayer in schools and no abortion.
Where family is valued and people are in unity in family and households.
Where the fathers are turned to children and children to their fathers,
and they grieve the heart of God. They grieve God.

I'm first for the Lord,
I'm also for myself and for this ministry and for my family and for people.
That's the good for everybody.
All those things are good for everyone.

I'd like to see a world where there's great music praising God,
speaking positive things,
edifying things to lift up society.
No world hunger, starvation of children.
That we would be able to allocate our resources in a way that would touch the
    world.
That we could utilize our resources and not hoard up our resources.
And that countries would be held accountable for how they manage their
    resources.

And my goal is to minister the gospel, but not just speaking Jesus, because that's
    the critical thing,

'cause Jesus was a politician.
Jesus dealt with issues, real issues.
Jesus dealt with how people felt,
'cause he's touched every infirmity.[5]

The interview became a litany of a vision for the world. When HansSoul, or Hans Nelson, begins to speak, words roll off his tongue with the speed, rhythm, and clarity of a prophet with a word from God. Like Mark Y Rage, that word comes from a calling deep in the hip-hop culture of the streets. Now you can see and hear Hans with his partners King Glover and Clarence Clay Brigade as part of HansSoul and the Tribe of Judah singing in clubs, prisons, churches, college campuses, and on the street. But that was not always so.

Hans was not born in a Christian family as was Mark Y Rage. Born in Philadelphia to fairly well-to-do parents who later divorced, Hans discovered in his teenage years his gift of "freestyling," a hip-hop term for expressing lyrics on the fly. He was not without Christian influence, however, as his mother, who eventually returned to her native Sweden, had taken him to church and taught him Christian songs. It was an influence that would stay with him in his journey to the present.

Discovered by hip-hop artists in 1986, Hans was drawn "deep into secular hip-hop." By 1991 he signed his first recording contract with Epic Records and was eventually seeing his rap singles on the Billboard charts. In 1994 he started his own label,

And my personality began to change. Not that I was a bad person, but you know you deal with pride, you deal with a lot of things. At that time that I signed the album deal [with RCA], I didn't want to record it because I kind of knew God didn't want me to do it. And I would tell the lady I was dating at the time, "I don't want to do this." I had the money and everything, I just didn't want to do it.

I moved to L.A., and then I came back in '94 and started my own label. And the only reason I'm saying that is I saw my life going from a pretty happy young man that didn't have a lot of guidance spiritually [to a time when] I was wretched and miserable. I was a bad person. I was hanging with people that were selling drugs. I was funding my label with drug money. I was promiscuous. I was speaking anything out my mouth that I thought . . . because people don't really understand what the concept of freestyling is. They don't realize that hip-hop can deal with a lot of witchcraft and a lot of demonic things. And if you say the first thing that comes to your mind, you'd better check what spirit is leading you to say that. And what I learned was that . . . I learned from there that I was in the wrong camp. I mean, the Lord allowed me to get physically ill.

And in '95, March, like sixth or seventh, I flew to St. Thomas and I went and took a vacation, and I was trying to get away. And I came home on the eleventh, which is a Saturday, and I prayed to the Lord. I said, "Lord!" . . . on the whole way home I cried out—from San Juan to New York. And I said, "Lord, just take away this illness, take away this depression, even if you don't heal me just take away the depression, because

I don't wanna live no more if you don't." And I ran into a church the next day. God allowed me to get up to church, they laid hands on me, and I believe it was in the name of Jesus. And I knew that I was healed; I was whole. I felt just a burden, a depression, hurt, wounds, illness . . . things lifted off of me. I knew that the Lord was real, and I knew I had been healed. I knew that God was true and that what the Bible said was real. And I could look in people's eyes and see, like, in their eyes I could see the Spirit of God in people.

Following this experience, HansSoul heard God tell him to ante up. He collected his current project and threw it in the trash and set out to be an encourager to others through his music, "speaking words of encouragement through my songs to encourage people to hold to their faith."

While his last album, *New Jerusalem,* is one of "gospel psalms," his current project, *The Unthugged Life,* speaks of personal transformation and is music of freedom—spiritually, physically, socially, economically. One can see this freedom in his life as well, though it is not the kind of freedom he had in his secular hip-hop years. Far from it. He and his partners eke out a meager living, not bound by success, and put most of their money into their ministry, Fisherman Entertainment, in order to finance their projects on CD and video. A video project can cost $130,000.

Hans credits Philadelphia's New Covenant Church and its pastor, Bishop Grannam, with giving him the support he has needed. Hans is a graduate of Temple University and is now enrolled in Eastern Baptist Theological Seminary.

Is he making a difference? Is he bringing about transformation? In the music industry, success is most often measured by CD sales and airtime, but Hans seems more concerned with writing his music and giving his words of encouragement than with success in sales. His words of encouragement are heard outside the studio as well. Hans holds an annual vacation Bible school in his house for neighborhood kids, sings in his church choir, spends time with kids in the park, and witnesses on the street. "Somebody accepted the Lord today!" he told us on the phone. It is difficult to know the exact impact of his work, but to Hans and others like him, that is not important. It is speaking the Word and living a life of example that matters.

Prophets without Words

I spoke to the prophets, gave them many visions and told parables through them.

Hosea 12:10

In the last chapter we introduced you to Todd Farley of Mimestry International. As much as his ministry is one of justice, it is also one of calling people to redemption. To some, mime seems an unusual way to communicate a prophetic message of salvation. Imagine, if you will, a busy city street. A barker begins to announce a performance. A crowd gathers and white-faced, white-gloved actors begin to move to a song. Through what Todd calls the universal language of physicalization, he and his students and colleagues announce the kingdom of God and tell the stories of God's redemption. Through an encounter with this physicalization of the Word of God, many come to have a "heart experience" and come to see visibly the invisible God. And in that heart experience, they are transformed. Not unlike many performing artists, Todd wants to "reintroduce the concept that the arts are primarily an expression of a [human] relationship with God, first and fundamentally." It is through this spiritual connection to the arts that the stories are told.

> The concept behind the ministry of mime is that the issues and the subject matters aren't just crosses and crucifixes but are also the story of the passion of humanity, the struggles of humanity, the fatherless child. One of my mimes is called "My Father's Chair," and it deals with a child who finds his father absent at a young age. And the chair where his father once sat now sits empty. And it's a human issue; it's a human problem. And inside of that human problem, we introduce the concept of God as father. We introduce solutions, or rather dialogue, with the Christian family, the Christian faith. So what we can do on a street, on a street venue, is show multiple levels of expression, where we might express a religious theme such as a crucifixion.

Todd believes that his silent stories communicate in a universal language, to any culture, and his experience seems to authenticate this, as he has also done street mime in many parts of the world.

> The first step that usually takes place is that the mime gathers a crowd, because the mime looks different. The mime has the white face. The mime has the costume. The mime has all that different rhythm of life. And it arrests the passerby by that different rhythm, by that difference, by that stylization, that suspense. And they watch them.
> The first thing the mime does is usually entertain: grabs them, does illusions, moves like a robot, to something that wins the audience. They participate with us. And in the process they start to sympathize, interact with the mime artist. And we take them into a story: a human story, a comedy, a tragedy, something that captures the imagination. And after capturing the imagination, the human aspects, we can start to dialogue with the human questions of "Who is God? Why are we alive? What are we doing here? What's our purpose?"
> We're able to draw from a myriad of stories that capture those different truths and those different questions and present back to them our reflection on that answer, to present our faith, our faith in God, our faith in what he can do in reaction and relation with our struggles and trials. Usually twenty minutes, thirty minutes, you might set up a stage, it might just be on a street corner where

you've got a raw audience that's transient—off to buy butter or meet a friend. But within that five minutes you can plant a seed, or if you've got a stage somewhere with seats outside, you can actually give a fuller message.

In a way, the street mime is an advertisement of a larger program or concert. People are invited to the two-hour "concert" where the gospel message is presented in mime and word. People on the street may feel violated if an appeal is made on the spot, although Todd and his troops will cooperate with a local church and enter into dialogue with those who seem inclined to stay afterwards and talk.

On the street, people don't need to know anything other than that they've been stopped for five minutes and they've enjoyed five minutes of the day. We have three different agendas on the street. One, we might have the agenda of just going and making that place have fun with us, and at the end of it the barker will call out, "Hey, we're Grandview Christian Center, and we're just here to make you laugh for an afternoon and just say if you wanna come and say hey Christians do have fun, here we are, and we're just here to be part of you." That's [the] first agenda.

The second agenda might be to invite them to an evening event. "Hey, we're Puget Sound and we want you to come out to an evening concert that we have tonight. You've seen a little bit of what they're gonna do. Come for our two-hour presentation." At that point you've identified yourself as a Christian organization or a Christian-based thing. The mimes themselves have already probably given a couple of examples of that. Or a third one, you're actually trying to do a full evangelistic package where you're presenting gospel messages: "If you would like to know more about what this God is that we've presented, this invisible God we have now made visible, come and talk to us." And at that point you start dialogue and conversations with the people.

Because of Todd's focus on the art of mime and excellence of performance, he finds a responsive audience wherever he performs. So his goal of making people aware of fine Christian art succeeds and leads people into a discussion of the message. He gains respect for the performance and, because of this, is able to dialogue. Fine art wins an audience and communicates a message. He has been received in the ghettos and barrios of American cities and also in the elite thoroughfares of Europe.

Saving the Net

We would not be faithful to our understanding of the arts if we did not include one example from the Internet. In a previous chapter we briefly discussed the web site of the Adbusters Media Foundation, www.adbusters.com. Their eighty-five thousand subscribers is no small number for their topic, which is both politically and socially volatile.

Web prophets have a unique opportunity to reach an audience that is not reached by other forms of art. A list of links for these Web prophets can be found at our research web site: www.urbanprophets.org.

Summary

Each of the artists we have highlighted in this chapter wants to bring people into a right relationship with God and also understands the holistic nature of faith in a journey toward God. They meet people where they are, and through a spoken word and a kind deed, they are God's messenger for a time and place—often places that are uncomfortable for most Christians: clubs, ghetto streets, and bars. They speak in allegory in their art and through action on the street.

They are struggling, like many artists, to make a living and often live below the poverty level in order to be true to their calling—a calling they have received from God and a lifestyle that brings honor to him in the streets and in the public square. They have given up the notion of fame (though one assumes the heart may still yearn for it) and seek instead to give a message from God to those around them, often to a very specific audience. They are interculturally competent in that they understand the dimensions of race and class and can work in and across cultures. They are both streetwise and churchwise. Because of their experience in the secular world, they have no illusion about the glitter of fame or the perfection of the church. They are real. And yet one senses a vulnerability and genuineness about them, for they know how to play, how to have a good time, how to be comfortable in almost any situation, and how to speak a word of kindness or confrontation when led by the Spirit.

They have a vision for the good life. While they want people to know Jesus, they recognize that part of the holistic NU JERUZ is clean streets, safe communities, opportunities for employment and education, whole families, and healthy bodies. They have no illusions about what keeps the NU JERUZ from being realized. They observe that for many in our self-medicated society, a party in a club often brings more relief than a worship service in a church. But they also know that a party in a club will not bring relief any more than will a constrictive and often judgmental faith community that has little value for the arts and their power. At the same time, they fully understand the power of a risen Lord, to whom they have given their allegiance and who has literally called them, often in specific acts, to be salt and light in some of the darkest and toughest places.

They are under no illusion about the power and nature of art. They express what they are given by the Spirit, and then they let the Spirit move. By and large, they do not take a prescriptive view of their art, as do many evangelicals who sing and leave. They guard their witness, even refusing to use the name "Christian," in an effort to build relationships where their lives can be a witness outside the stereotypes of a constrictive faith that continues to hurt and oppress those who may not fit within mainstream society—a society that is more often white than of color, middle class than poor, materialistic and safe than giving and risking a faith that meets the needs of the poor of our society.

After talking with each of these artists at length, we wondered how they might fare in the years ahead. Can they maintain their prophetic role and meager living for a lifetime? Will they, as they grow older, keep the vision, stay the course, and speak the truth? There is a difference in the work of professionals like Todd Farley and those of the hip-hop world. Whereas Todd has developed an international organization that now resides at Fuller Theological Seminary, where he teaches the art of mime, those involved in the arts of popular culture do not have institutional support for their ministries, except as provided by their local church community. The organizational demands of managing new parachurch nonprofits, such as Phillip Brown's SaltWorld and HansSoul's Fishermen Entertainment, can be overwhelming and may sidetrack the artists' true giftedness and calling. Their ministry, because it is in the margins of society and church culture, does not carry the respect, support, or understanding of the traditional "fine" arts. Yet one has to appreciate the call, vision, and courage these artists have to minister on a regular basis to the marginalized of the urban world.

While we have focused on the Christian concept of personal redemption in this chapter, the reader should be aware that street drama, hip-hop, and other forms of our contemporary culture are used in community development, health education, and public awareness campaigns to call people, in a prescriptive manner, to become aware of health and lifestyle issues and to make an allegiance to change. The following principles can apply to both secular and faith-integrated strategies for transformation.

Principles

Using the brief case studies presented in this chapter and drawing from interviews with other artists, we can see the following principles for those who would use their artistic gifts in transformation. Urban prophets

1. Understand the communicative power of their art form.
2. Possess a deep respect for people of all backgrounds, which is reflected in their relationships, both onstage and offstage.
3. Understand that the context of their performance changes the meaning or function of their role. For example, though they may use decidedly

Christian words, the context of the performance changes depending on whether the message is a prophetic call to those outside the sanctuary or a celebration within the sanctuary.

4. Have reached a level of competence that gives them credibility with their audience.
5. Are committed to relationships that extend beyond the performance.
6. Speak of a strong calling and commitment to God and the message of salvation.
7. Speak of a reliance on the Holy Spirit as how they receive their words and define their actions.
8. Have a deep understanding of the Bible. This has partly to do with the power of the language but also the power expressed in the meaning of the cross.
9. Understand that their calling is to draw people into a closer relationship with God.
10. Are involved in some kind of ministry besides performance, be it ministry to the homeless, working with children, or training others.
11. Tend to be rooted in a faith community for support and collaboration, even though they may have complained about the institutional church.
12. Have a strong understanding of social justice. Prophets of color and others who have experienced injustice often understand the broader and more political nature of justice issues and seek to express it in their work.
13. Are concerned about bringing people into a community of faith.
14. Partner with local faith communities in their ministry.

Conclusion

We found that many of these artists—SaltWorld, for example—are underutilized by the church. Eager, brave, and committed and having a message of hope and the creativity and talent to enter the streets, many of these urban prophets are living a life of poverty in order to proclaim their message. If they are successful—and success is always based on their own terms and not by society or the institutional church—it is because they have heard the Spirit speak and have followed the Spirit's voice without regard for affirmation or results.

Part 3

Building the NU JERUZ

Working It Out

8

Arts as a Community Builder

In this chapter we will learn how art helps to build community by bringing a community together and by providing community identity and a means of conflict resolution. Using two case studies, from Philadelphia and Baltimore, we will learn how people of faith have collaborated in and across ethnic, faith, and organizational lines to effect a holistic transformation of their communities.

As you read, this chapter should answer the following questions:

1. What is community?
2. What are some of the indicators of healthy communities?
3. What characterizes the role of the arts in bringing about community transformation? What characterizes the role of faith?
4. What are the critical features in the two case studies that increased chances of success?

The Nature of Community

What is a community? While a neighborhood is a geographically defined entity, primarily residential, a community may be referred to as a physical entity or a salient value.[1] When we use the term *community* in community development, we are referring to community as an essential value.

The key elements to any definition of community are:

- Clear boundaries—geographic boundaries and also boundaries presented by a set of beliefs, a special-interest or affinity group, and so on. Some anthropologists would say that a community consists of no more than one hundred people who know each other by name.
- Purpose or sense of belonging, shared values, and common interest (for example, maintenance of a safe place to live and/or work).
- A sense of connectedness, interdependence, and acting together around common interests and goals.

Many would agree that these elements are not enough and that true community exists only when there is a demonstrated commitment to, or caring for, the "other." St. Augustine's often-quoted definition of community provides an understanding of this: "A community is a group of people united by the common objects of their love."[2] In other words, community is made by a set of shared values. If those values are good and godly, a godly community will emerge. If not, an immoral community emerges. While these "objects" vary among communities and over time, love amongst and for the people of a community is not optional. *Community development,* then, is the working out of a sense of purpose and connectedness within a neighborhood based on the common principle of love, caring for one's neighbors.

Working out community requires love, commitment, and self-determination. Without the element of love, we might just as well be talking about a mob, a gathering, a team, or an organization. The unique contribution of agape artists to the building of community is their ability to contribute to an essential community "spirit" through incarnational, unselfish giving in service to others. Carol Anne Ogdin terms this essential spirit "Commitment."[3]

Ogdin adds a fifth element to those required for community: self-determination. This implies that communities not mobilized and empowered to determine, or to attempt to determine, their own direction and destiny are not yet fully "communities." In many neighborhoods where there seems to be no visible effort on the part of the inhabitants to rid its blocks of the dirt, trash, and drug houses, this may be because in fact there *is* no sense of community spirit or shared values for cleanliness. They are just a neighborhood, people residing together without community.

A Biblical Image of Community

In the New Testament, particularly the writings of Paul, we find the value connotation of community among the faithful within the world. Christians are to be salt and light, in the world but not of it, bringing about the reign of God as the people of God and the body of Christ. The church has a responsibility to develop community within itself and to bring a sense of community (peace and reconciliation) in the world.

In Acts 4:32–37 we see a beautiful sense of community, in which the believers were of one heart and mind. No person was needy; all members of the community shared their belongings, even selling property so that everyone was cared for. In the letters to the Corinthians, as believers began to form communities of the faithful, Paul's letters were both a reporting and an encouragement to build communities of faith and love. Paul told them about the grace of the Macedonian churches: "Out of the most severe trial, their overflowing joy and their extreme poverty welled up in rich generosity" (2 Cor. 8:2–5). He encouraged the Corinthians to give generously in service to those in need so that God would be praised by all those who experienced and witnessed it (2 Cor. 9:6–15).

The community is to function as a body—an organic image of community—in which each person serves a particular function in the body's development and life (1 Cor. 12:12–27). There is a need for cooperation and collaboration within the members of a community. It is love, however, that is at the center of this organic community where patience, kindness, humility, politeness, other seeking, and forgiveness are to form a life of hope, trust, and perseverance (1 Corinthians 13).

How do we know, then, that community has been developed—that there is a sense of community? In the minds of our artists describing the NU JERUZ, and in most disciplinary definitions, the physical indicators of a healthy community include:

- Safe and clean streets
- The presence of incarnational leaders
- Job opportunities
- Affordable, decent housing
- Effective education for its children
- Cultural establishments
- Accessible transportation
- Functioning municipal and social services
- A pleasing environment in which to live

The World Health Organization adds to this list

- An environment with a sustainable ecosystem
- Access to health care services that focus on prevention and staying healthy

There are also outcomes of the value, or sense of community, that are much more difficult to quantify:

- The absence of violence and abuse (peace)
- The presence of cooperation (harmony)
- The presence of forgiveness, patience, sharing, and politeness (love)
- Integration of race and class (reconciliation)
- A sense of awe and the presence of God (redemption)

As we will see in this and the remaining chapters of part 3, artists play a role in impacting the community and make significant contributions to many of the above outcomes and indicators.

Developing Community

Asset-based or capacity-oriented approaches to community development, which follow directly from the biblical examples of community, are replacing deficit- or needs-based models in the enlightened programs providing education and training for community development. In their classic text on community development, John Kretzmann and John McKnight point out the negative consequences and problems inherent in portraying a community over long periods of time only through the lens of its needs. They rightly argue that the revitalization of most devastated, low-income neighborhoods will come about through the efforts and investments of its own residents rather than from outside help, funding, or corporate and industrial relocation to these areas.

Kretzmann and McKnight site needs-based strategies as a major cause of the sense of hopelessness in discussions and planning for many low-income neighborhoods and conclude that moving beyond mere survival and maintenance of status quo can only be attained through identifying, mobilizing, and connecting the local assets of a community "in ways that multiply their power and effectiveness."[4] They recommend an asset-based approach that builds on the gifts and abilities found within the community.

Listed among the local institutions, citizens' associations, and gifts of individuals on the "Community Assets Map" template of Kretzmann's and McKnight's text, are artists. Indeed, these local "creators" are among the unique combination of gifts of just about all communities. Not only are their talents linked to community-building efforts, but their vision can create "new possibilities for community growth."[5] As we will see in our chapter on economic development, art can also become the basis for microenterprise and cottage industry.

Asset-based strategy suggests the importance of first "mapping" or discovering the artistic and cultural assets of a community and then connecting the vital artistic resources to the other segments of community assets: churches, businesses, schools, hospitals, youth, elderly, libraries, parks, block clubs, and so on.

Mobilizing a whole community depends on thorough completion of these two steps: asset mapping and building relationships among and between asset groups and individuals. The process used in achieving these steps can convince a community of its ability to be self-determining and to solve its problems with resources from within rather than always looking to the outside for help, which results in hopelessness and dependency. In addition, finding leaders who will work from an assets framework and who will work together with other community leaders to develop a shared vision and plan for the community's future is vital to the success of the revitalization process. In the following two examples of "whole" community development, the arts and artists were at the center of the vision. Inherent in asset-based models of community development are the principles of the community development theory of John Perkins—relocation, reconciliation, redistribution—which we will describe more fully later in the book.

Community Cultural Development Theory

In the introduction we introduced the field of community cultural development (CCD), which links cultural development (broadly defined and including more than just the arts) to action that is empowering and that leads to the self-directed development of a community, as opposed to development that is imposed, and which is marked by participative and collaborative approaches. Whether the community is one of proximity (neighborhoods), interest (for example, homeless populations, AIDS victims), or affinity group (senior citizens, ethnic youth), CCD work focuses more on the group than on the individual.

Much like the family therapy movement in clinical psychology, the issues of the individual are not ignored but are always considered in the context of the community or group. One of the cornerstones of CCD is the belief that "there is a higher and more socially useful role for the artist than to decorate the surroundings of wealth."[6] Again, consistent with family therapeutic goals as well as with stage 1 of our A.R.T. model, the task of CCD is always to bring about a consciousness of community. A.R.T. goes further than CCD theory, however, and recognizes the role the arts play in working out this awareness of a new and better reality, which must then be celebrated, assessed, and reexamined.

Like the A.R.T. model, community cultural development theory and practice sees culture and art as political, transformational events—not as merely aesthetic activities. Only in this way does CCD see art and culture playing an effective community-building role. The role of the artist as an agent of change is, in CCD theory, more socially valuable than mainstream art-making roles and is just as legitimate as those in the mainstream, though not always treated so by the traditional church or governmental and funding powers. The CCD practice posits principles with particular value "biases," which are necessary for playing out this transformational role. CCD theory and principles value:

- Action over passivity, on the part of both the individual and the community[7]
- The "right" to culture, or "cultural democracy"[8]
- Process over product, emphasizing participative and collaborative approaches— open-ended projects, with content determined by participants—marked by improvisatory nature[9]
- Diversity over homogeneity[10]

The CCD movement suggests several questions by which to judge arts efforts that are truly community building.

- Is there self-determination and dignity?
- Is the project's goal one of expanded liberty of the particular community?
- Are pressing social problems being addressed through *cultural* responses?
- Does the leader possess the combined skill sets of an effective organizer *and* those of an artist, or an understanding of the artistic process and its potential power?
- When art takes on what we call a more prophetic role, does the work offer solutions and present a vision for transformation along with the criticism of institutions?
- Is the presence of "success" indicators related to community building?[11]

The indicators of these value questions suggest that there will be true collaboration, participants' cultural knowledge will be broadened, participants will feel satisfaction regarding their expression through the project, and participants will register heightened confidence and be disposed toward further social action involvement.

Specific Plan

Building Community through Collaboration

In 1993 the New England Foundation for the Arts (NEFA) began a regional movement to heighten the visibility of existing collaborations and encourage the development of new ones between artists and civic and community leaders. The foundation's April 2001 report on the Building Communities through Culture project recognized the power of existing art efforts in combination with civic activity. The report noted that this central or partnership role for the arts is not new.[12]

As our country and the world became increasingly industrialized, specialized, and professionalized, the integrated nature of community living diminished and its various components—faith, art, government, and work—became separated. There was a strong reemergence of art and artists as catalysts for social activism and social justice, particularly in the music and art of the 1960s and 1970s.

NEFA established the Building Communities through Culture project, over a period of seven years, to restore and support the central role of the arts in building communities through facilitating the integration of artists, arts organizations, and community developers. Examples of their regional collaborations include the following:

- A program for fifty court-involved, at-risk youth that engaged the youth in job readiness programs, in designing new uses for vacant lots, cleaning the lots, working with an architect to learn the basics of urban design, researching the neighborhood's history, learning basic quantitative and demographic analysis, and photographing their community while learning photography
- A program that introduced children to live performances and film to create an appreciation for the arts and also secured capital improvement monies for the renovation of the Academy of Music building
- Cultural programming aimed to encourage residents to visit the downtown area and patronize local businesses
- A program that created affordable housing for artists and low-income families, as well as program and gallery space in historic firehouses

NEFA's work supported the knowledge that the most effective art project collaborations are those that involve strong leadership; include local individuals, agencies, and officials; seek long-term benefits for a specific geographic or demographic community; and draw on the people and places of the neighborhood for inspiration.

Building Community across Cultures

The Social Impact of the Arts Project (SIAP) of the University of Pennsylvania provides useful definitions of economic and ethnic diversity for community-building investigation. According to this study, we have diversity if (1) the poverty rate and the percentage of professionals and managers in the labor force are both above average for the metropolitan area as a whole, and (2) the largest ethnic group in the neighborhood makes up less than 80 percent of the population. A neighborhood can be considered *revitalized* if, in addition to the above two conditions, there is a higher than average decline in poverty without loss of population.[13]

The SIAP study concluded that diversity and the presence of arts organizations in a community are correlated. The study found that (1) diversity is a strong predictor of the concentration of arts organizations, and the presence of such organizations means that the community is more likely to remain diverse; (2) for-profit arts firms (for example, community music schools) are critical to the economic support of artists and to the emergence of natural "cultural districts"; (3) networks are critical to the success of community cultural providers; (4) community participation by youth and families is more related to the concentration of arts organizations than to education or income; and (5) well-off or affluent neighborhoods have greater participation in "mainstream" arts, while diverse neighborhoods have greater participation in alternative arts.

SIAP helps us conclude that social diversity, artistic vitality, and community strength are strongly related. That is, there is a strong and significant relationship between the presence of arts organizations in a community, the community's participation rate, and the degree of diversity of the community; all of these factors are related to the chances that a block group will undergo revitalization. Revitalization also occurs through the breakdown of the barriers that separate rich and poor neighborhoods. In the SIAP study, 80 percent of the participants in community arts are people "outside" the community where the program is located! The arts foster participation across class and ethnicity; thus, arts make a unique contribution to overcoming exclusion and fostering community revitalization.

In the following two case studies, see if you can spot the principles, values, methods, and indicators in their development discussed in this chapter.

If God Be for Us

It is 1990. Sister Carol Keck shouts to the other sister in the car to get the kids down in their seats. The nightly shooting is erupting the streets. The drug addicts that shoot up in nearby Needle Park—the center of drug use in this part of Philadelphia, known as the Badlands—are also beginning to appear.

But soon the incredible coming together of events on a single day, what Sister Carol calls "the providential blessing of God," will reward the two years of singing, praying, marching, and acting of God's people.[14] Their battle cry will show itself to be true: "If God be for us, who can be against us?"

In 1990 Norris Square in north Philadelphia was populated with 50–60 percent Puerto Rican unemployed and working poor and was bordered by an African-American population just as poor. Norris Square boasted the worst schools in the city and the highest quality heroine. Neglected by the city, the "official" plan was to deliberately keep the drugs contained in this and other poor neighborhoods of north Philly. This community was a "throwaway"—a dumping ground. Seventy drug dealers were residing and operating in one block. Buyers were driving in from nearby New Jersey, New York, and Delaware.

Sister Carol, like the other church, nonprofit, and community leaders, lived in the neighborhood. She moved to the Norris Square community in the early 1970s and served there as a teacher/principal for thirteen years. Moving to Tampa to assist a school that had just failed to get accreditation, she returned to Norris Square when she was invited to be the executive director of the Norris Square Neighborhood Project. All totaled, Sister Carol has been living and working in Norris Square for thirty years.

In a community plan the United Neighbors Against Drugs (UNAD) began meeting with the police. The group decided to march on a block weekly, late at night after the drug action started. The nonprofit organizations in the area and the churches (the Episcopal church, First Spanish Baptist, St. Boniface Catholic Church, the Presbyterians, and the Mennonites) cooperated and collaborated to stage a big late-night rally in the park. Each organization brought designated numbers of people to insure impact. Initially, the police were not encouraging, but a sympathetic police captain drew in favors from everywhere he could and provided protection: police on foot, police with dogs, police in vans.

For two years UNAD met with police every Monday and rallied every Friday. Each Wednesday night they met with business leaders in the community, who depended on the neighbors for their livelihoods and on the town watch for the safety of their shops. UNAD began to speak out to a city that was not delivering services to the neighborhood: trash was not being collected, sewers were backed up, the park was not mowed, and the Department of Recreations had created no programs in this area. The mayor at the time (W. Wilson Goode) came out to the neighborhood once a month with his commissioners in an attempt to effect some change. The community residents were direct: "They aren't doing anything!"

Around this same time, the Federal Drug Enforcement Agency was being besieged to do something besides arrest people. The Weed and Seed Program (weed out drugs, seed in social services) came to Philadelphia in 1992 and from one of the "cleared" lots of Norris Square announced their sixteen-city program kickoff, this section of Philly being one of them. A three-by-three-block area was targeted for improvement. Houses would be demolished or rehabilitated, and lots would be cleaned of garbage and debris.

Norris Square would reap one of its greatest victories—the day the notorious 2200 block of Palethorp would become the target of local and federal police. The federal and local police were communicating. A raid was scheduled for 4:00 A.M. There were twenty-eight houses on the block.

In nearby Needle Park, Father Butch, Father Kelly, Rev. Luis, and his brother Dr. Danny Cortes led the songs and prayers and sermons that challenged the people, "Do you want to live like this in your community?" In a show of the unity of the many groups and different faiths that were now committed to the common cause with common grace, the congregants adopted as their rally cry a passage from Romans: "If God be for us, who can be against us?"

The group left the park and made their way over to the school, another location of heavy drug action, where children would pass scores of dealers each day on their walk home. In the meantime Lt. John Gallo, one of the officers people had begun to trust and give information to, was throwing a net around the perimeters of the targeted blocks.

Twenty-three houses were raided. Fifty-five people from five different drug gangs were apprehended. At 8:00 A.M., twenty-six cars seized in the raid (out of which the dealers did business) were towed away. The bulldozers rolled in behind the tow trucks, and by 4:00 P.M. houses were flattened and lots were totally cleaned up. The night's work was productive and led to many arrests, thwarting $250,000 in drug sales.

The next evening, for the first time in years, neighbors were not afraid to come out of their doors. There was so much energy that evening, reports Sister Carol. The old women, who were used to farm life in Puerto Rico, ran out with their chairs to sit and see the stars in the sky and to experience the peace and quiet they had not experienced in twenty years. They lined the children up against the wall of the house bordering one of the vacant lots and painted a mural of their silhouettes in celebration of the liberation of their neighborhood and their future, symbolized in the children.

But, then, the next challenge: How could they maintain the peace, save the children, and change the image of their community from that of drug-infested Badlands and regain the image of their residents as "good" people that count? They reached back to the community's organizational mission of thirty years ago: education and literacy through interactive, experience-based learning focused on the environment. Thirty years ago two teachers had endeavored to improve the literacy of the most difficult students at Miller, the oldest school in Philadelphia (founded in 1896).[15] They feared that many of the students in this school, for whom English was a second language, would never achieve grade-level competency under the current circumstances. The usual "See Spot Run" readers would not be appropriate, but perhaps studying nature and using it as a vehicle for learning would prove to be more interesting for the children.

The two teachers began in a basement space, next to the boiler of the neglected neighborhood school building. They developed a nature museum and wrote science and other lessons to be used by the children with the help of Eastern College education majors. When the school building was condemned a few years later, the two teachers each added $2,000 of their own money to the $2,000 remaining in a fund that supported the project, and they purchased a local house.[16] The small after-school program moved to the first floor of that house under the name Norris Square Neighborhood Project. The program took over all the space in the house and began to serve as the base of operations for the neighborhood transformation efforts of UNAD. Today it provides day care during the seventeen official school holidays so that parents can continue their work schedule; they also run a seven-week summer day camp.

As the teachers began working out community development, they decided to use the environment as the vehicle through which to rehabilitate the neighborhood and educate the youth, in the hope of keeping them on productive paths. They reasoned, "If we teach them about trees, and trees become their 'friends,' perhaps they will discontinue their mischievous pastime of setting trees on fire and waiting for the fire trucks to come and put the fire out."

After the raids, the Norris Square community remembered these two teachers and drew on the work they had done. Forfeiture legislation said that confiscated drug property, while usually divided up between the enforcement agencies responsible for the captures, could also be given to community organizations for "good works." And so, with persistent advocacy and as land was reclaimed from drugs and cleared, extensive flower and vegetable gardens were started. Now, twelve years later, Las Parcelas (the Parcels) is the main garden on Palethorp Street, and the families of the community tend to their plots in season. They receive oversight, lessons, and training from Iris Brown, one of the younger Latino women, who is now a trained horticulture specialist.[17]

The Norris Square people were not raised in violence and drugs in their homeland. They were a clean, moral, and hardworking people, proud of their Taino, African, and European heritage. This is the image and heritage they wanted to give back to the children. So they integrated the greening of their community through the gardens with the teaching of their tricultural heritage through the murals, artifacts, and re-created villages that form the themes for the gardens. La Casita village and its fixtures reflect Puerto Rican heritage and is reminiscent of earlier days, with its outdoor kitchen, or El Fogón.[18]

In good weather La Casita is where the ladies cook the fresh tomatoes, herbs, and eggplant just picked from the adjacent Las Parcelas. The harvest from the gardens is never sold. What is not used by the families for their homes and for the youth programs is given to others in the neighborhood and to the shelters and homes serving those in need. The traditional "mud huts" being constructed in the plot across the street from Las Parcelas will be the centerpiece of the African heritage garden.[19] Raices, or Roots, is the children's garden and has the community's main mural, reflecting their African, Taino, and European heritages. Finally, El Batey garden honors their Taino heritage. It displays a ceremonial space (Parque Ceremonial Taino) and includes a long, freestanding, wood-carved and painted "wall" relief of Taino people at various daily tasks. There are cutouts where people's heads would be so that the children can go behind the wall and fit their own faces into the relief, imagining, becoming, and reclaiming a part of their past identity.

Grupo Motivas (the Motivated Ones), the women of Norris Square, gather strength from their group. Many of them lost husbands, sons, and daughters to the drug activity in the park and in the subsequent raids. But they too have renewed vision. The still largely Spanish-speaking older women—Las Motivas—harvest the gardens and cook food for the children in the after-school program, for children in the summer camp, and for visitors like us after a several-hours walk and oral history of the transformation. They have formed a vision for yet another former drug stronghold—the closed-down pizza store on the corner. The raids gave that building over to the Norris Square Project, and Las Motivas are planning to start a catering business and café in the space. They will extend the café out into the adjacent gardens and ask local guitarists to play at the café.

"What about the men in the community?" asked one of the Eastern University graduate students visiting the site with us.[20] Sister Carol offers a familiar response. "The structure of the welfare system mitigates against males in the community. And now they're in jail." She goes on to share that there are some success stories of men returning to the community and learning skills to rebuild and repair houses and cars and to do plumbing. Some work on the barter system. Others sell their cooking and sewing services.

Señora Tomasita, at seventy years of age, has become a neighborhood councilperson. She boasts a quiet, spiritual demeanor. A stately woman with white hair and a dark complexion, Tomasita came to the United States from Puerto Rico in 1948 at the age of seventeen. Like other people of color, she came to work in the Campbell Soup factory and at farms. She relates that this kind of work, along with washing dishes, was all that "minorities" were allowed to do. She later worked in hospitals and worked in the clothing industry as a hand seamstress when she was twenty-two. When St. Boniface opened its bilingual kindergarten, she joined Sister Carol there for twenty years. She has borne the loss of a family member to the drug enforcement effort. But she recounts that she "had to live in the mess and just got tired of it." Her power in the community, won through her personal sacrifices during the transformation and through her strong resolve of faith, is used to keep the community in constant dialogue with city government and to increase the voting power of the community as a strategy for maintaining services for their neighborhood.

September 8, 2002. We strolled through Norris Square Park (formerly Needle Park) on a perfect, eighty-degree, low-humidity day full of sunshine and hope—little children soaring in the air on a homemade tree swing, children roller-skating and falling, running and laughing, going up and down the slide; old men in wheelchairs taking in the warmth; younger men standing under a tree, admiring the evenly cut grass that makes a soft bed for others sitting on blankets; a family picnicking under a small pavilion; preteens tossing a football; a child playing gleefully with her pet dog.

A huge, three-story butterfly adorns the wall of the garden at the other end of the block. It was painted with the help of the children who worked on the tiles for the mural. A Cuban artist, Salvador Gonzales, came to Norris Square with funding from the city's mural arts program to assist the community in discovering an appropriate symbol for the community's transformation and emerging identity. After consulting with neighbors regarding the spirit of the community, he proposed the symbol of the butterfly. The choice was perhaps also providential: the butterfly is the symbol of resurrection in the Christian community, and it is also a religious symbol in the Yoruba faith of the Afro-Cuban artist.

The park and its surrounding structures are now "a community gathering place," according to Sister Carol. "It's a whole spiritual experience, although some don't name it that." Catholic Social Services has joined with the Norris Square Civic Association to develop the senior citizens' home. The association has rehabbed or built twenty units of housing and is working on building another twenty units. Hospitality House now provides drug-rehab services for youth. And a former drug house is now a community center. The Quakers at Fourth and Arch Streets are partners with the women of Norris Square in transforming yet another former drug corner store into a café. Other social and youth service nonprofits have come together with the faith community in a holistic transformation effort; all of the nonprofit leaders live in the area.

For the people of Norris Square, the Badlands have become the green lands. For the people of Norris Square, the NU JERUZ is come, and it looks every bit like heaven. The leaders at the center of this renewal are Sister Carol Keck and Señora Tomasita.

While people still tell Sister Carol how "lucky" she was to have everything come together in just the right way and with perfect timing, she and the women who suffered and sacrificed know it was not luck; it was God, blessing and rewarding their faithful shoulders to the plow. The decision to move against the drug gangs was a sorrowful and difficult one for many of the women in Norris Square. Giving critical information to the police meant that many of their sons, husbands, and daughters would go to jail. But the scourge would never end unless they did so. And only the power and strength of an unwavering and united faith would move them through the fear, long hours, loss, and darkness. Sister Carol said, "There is something about people of faith coming together—the Muslim

Palestinian group is now here too—that whatever the power, whatever this God above us is, planning and living together and calling on God."

And where do you find Sister Carol each evening? Walking the streets of Norris Square, in constant vigilance and joy.

Summary

In this case study we can find the arts as a collaborator in transformation. The prophetic songs and sermons of the marchers and faith leaders called the fearful neighbors to critical awareness—to recognize, admit, and take a stand against the evil in their community. There was the intermittent celebration, with the immediate painting of the outlines of the children on the wall as a victory symbol—as a first, joyous, almost impulsive, act of celebration.

The arts took on, and continue to take on, the larger agape role in the working out of the community's transformation through the beautifully planted gardens of herbs and vegetables. Flowers have replaced garbage-strewn vacant lots, abandoned houses, and a drug-infested park. The gardens grow minds and community identity as well as flowers and food. The children's silhouette mural has now been replaced with a mural titled *Neighborhood Heroes,* depicting the women of the neighborhood whose resolve, courage, persistence, and faith culminated in a providential act of God—God's blessing of their actions and will to dispel evil. *The Butterfly* and other garden murals, the artifacts, and the reconstructed authentic villages all teach the multiethnic history of a people and keep alive the memory of the fight and the positive values of the past.

Norris Square is not alone in the community effort of transformation, nor in understanding the important role of the arts. In our next case study, which comes from the Sandtown community of Baltimore, two hours south of Philadelphia, we discover a group of Christians, including an artist, who intentionally relocated to offer their gifts and their lives as agents of transformation.

A New Song

> I waited patiently for the LORD;
> And He inclined to me,
> And heard my cry.
> He also brought me up out of a horrible pit,
> Out of the miry clay,
> And set my feet upon a rock,
> And established my steps.
> He has put a new song in my mouth—
> Praise to our God;
> Many will see it and fear,
> And will trust in the LORD.
>
> Psalm 40:1–3 NKJV

We found the small church easily enough. The directions took us through much of the small Sandtown community—which of all the places we have visited comes closest to north Philadelphia but still not nearly as dilapidated, trashy, or dirty. We wondered what role the churches had played in the ongoing development of this community.

In looking for the community, we stopped to talk with a bellman at a city hotel. "I live in a community and do volunteer work," he told us. "There are a lot of churches, but they're all a song and dance and a big Bible—glitz and glamour. There's HIV/AIDS, homelessness—they're not interested. And artists working in a community? I didn't know anything like that existed. Artists and the church working in community!" He dismissed the idea.

His comments made us think about the validity of his expectations of the church. What *should* we expect churches to do? Turn their sanctuaries into cots and soup kitchens? Is the church a house of worship (yes) or a place of real refuge—true "sanctuaries" for the hungry and the homeless? But churches and nonprofits don't make policy. They can't solve social problems alone, can they? Doesn't it take a coordinated effort of government and state organizations and local citizenry and businesses?

We pulled up in front of the small but new-looking two-story building bearing the name New Song Community Church. The sanctuary was a small, simple, and tastefully appointed room off of the one-door vestibule that also housed the two rest rooms. That was it for space but not for spirit. We were immediately hugged and kissed on both cheeks by the three or four men and women already in the waiting area. They treated us as if we were long lost friends, shoved programs in our hands, brought us a worship hymnal, and ushered us into the sanctuary to await the start of the service.

This greeting was not the first sign that we were in a friendly space. It had been evident even before we got out of the car. To anyone watching us, we looked like interracial outsiders in this almost all-black community, and people expected that we were there only to attend the church. From across the street, a white woman (who we would soon learn was Mrs. Smallman) raised her voice to greet Miss Gertrude, a black, elderly woman who was coming down the street. Having spoken their greetings, both of their gazes now landed on us. They said genuinely, "Good morning" and "God bless you."

The third sign of welcome came from the half-jazz, half-gospel music sounds already beginning inside the still empty sanctuary room appointed with rows of unattached padded chairs, wood floors, and a low stage area in the front of the room, illuminated with track spotlights. Our souls were rushing quickly toward the soulful, multiethnic chords of the electric piano being played, we were sure, by Steve Smallman. Pastor Steve's journey toward Sandtown began with an encounter in a multiracial urban church in Chattanooga, Tennessee. It was his moment of critical awareness that, in the A.R.T. model, is the necessary beginning for any transformation process. It was there that the church fostered his love of African-American music.

Pastor Steve told us, "My friends were listening to Aerosmith and Lynrd Skynrd and stuff like that, and I was listening to Stevie Wonder. He was my musical mentor, no question about it."[21] At the same time a social awakening was taking place. He and his wife heard Tony Campolo speak as a Staley lecturer at Covenant College, where he went to college and where he also later heard Dr. John Perkins speak.

> There was also a social conscience waking up in us, where we were becoming appropriately outraged by our own country's history and what was going on in the fact that I had benefited from a system which was still a system which was oppressive and which was marginalizing certain parts of our culture. And so that was happening. It was a social-spiritual awakening. And for me as a musician and artist, the music provided me with the context and the glue to respond to what was happening intellectually, socially, spiritually, at the same time.

Steve was to meet up in Baltimore with a committed group of Christians who had a social conscience and commitment to action.

Three of these Christians were Susan and Alan Tibbels and Pastor Mark Gornick. Alan Tibbels had read a few of John Perkins's books, and Gornick had studied with Perkins before the two families set out in 1988 to settle in Sandtown. This west Baltimore neighborhood had been ravaged by the loss of Bethlehem Steel, the riots after the assassination of Martin Luther King, and white flight and black flight. Once known as Baltimore's center of African-American culture, the seventy-two-block community was once a must-do stop on the East Coast concert circuit for Stevie Wonder, the Temptations, Diana Ross, the young boy Herbie Hancock, and all the greats of music and entertainment. The Royal Theater on Pennsylvania Avenue and a couple of other historic theaters now stand in ruin, shrines to a glorious past when forty-five thousand residents and home owners used to vie for the honor of being designated Best Block of the Year. Sandtown is now an isolated desert, the once-busy bridges that connected it to the city proper now eroded and gone.

And now, forty years later, there are only ten thousand residents left. However, according to Susan Tibbels, the community has always had a strong fabric which is allowing its regeneration; it's just that during the seventies and eighties the threads had come unraveled and disconnected so that the mosaic and identity of the community were invisible.

The town still appears to be shunned by almost everyone, including the large churches, whose African-American members commute in on Sundays and then lock and gate their buildings for the rest of the week. A local community woman asked to have the funeral of her child at one of these disengaged churches and met with dispassionate and cold hearts because she was not "one of them."

This story seemed to support the bellman's earlier unsolicited opinion about the church's seeming abandonment of their role in building community.

The youth of the community describe their Sandtown streets as places that harbor drug dealers, child abusers, murderers, and prostitutes. But while the streets still remain dangerous for growing kids, there is much hope and many tangible signs of rebirth, transformation, and revitalization. The mosaic is becoming clear, and the identity is solid. As we entered the neighborhood, it bore all the signs of renewal: rehabilitated homes, people walking the streets, a new school, and an engaged church.

Started as a house church in the Tibbelses' home, the New Song Community Church's multiethnic Sunday congregation has grown slowly, but their followers outside the four walls are significant. Once a grassroots group of neighbors getting together for worship, the little church began to do what the bellman would have expected—they began to meet the articulated needs of the community: housing, education, health care, economic development.

New Song's work has galvanized the interest, attention, and resources of Baltimore's politicians, school boards, and foundations. Following the methods of John Perkins and his "relocation, reconciliation, redistribution" model, they purchased property in Sandtown, rehabbed their houses, and made a long-term commitment to the community. They listened to the needs of residents and began to lead the rebuilding of the community through a series of efforts that eventually became a family of separate nonprofit organizations making up New Song Urban Ministries—a holistic, comprehensive approach to serving the whole person. First, they started a Habitat for Humanity affiliate that led to the construction of 127 new homes, and the rehab of many others, now owned by residents making less than $15,000 a year—home ownership that is stabilizing the community by making it possible for people to own homes who could not otherwise do so. Then they addressed the educational dilemma of the community's children and youth, whose schools left them with some of the lowest standardized test scores in the city. An outreach program of the New Song Community Church, the New Song Learning Center began in 1991 as a half-day preschool and after-school program that together served forty students.

Today the center operates a full-day preschool; a public K–8 school (New Song Academy) that came into being when the Baltimore courts mandated the start of new, innovative schools after tiring of trying to reform the existing, failing schools; and a high school scholarship program—together impacting over 150 young people. The school provides some of the best facilities and classrooms available anywhere. But what is unique about this school is its arts-integrated, expeditionary learning curriculum. Kindergarten students draw in the styles of Picasso and Michelangelo. Elementary students create their own illustrated books about a community figure for an English and Writing class. Students participate in significant field learning and community service that culminates in a to-scale construction of their city, including houses and bridges and electrical wiring (science class) for the train tracks and lights. New Song's graduates are going to private high schools and are being told that they are better prepared and more mature than many other students entering their institutions.

The Academy building is not considered just a school—but a center belonging to the community. School employees are members of the community who have kids in the school. Six weddings were held last year in its multipurpose room. Habitat for Humanity uses the room for corporate lunches, with school going on around them. The building was constructed around the community's greatest felt need: a large community gathering space. The multipurpose room was built first, then the school around it, with administrative and teacher offices taking up the least space in the building. There is no other facility like this in the community. It is open and accessible, and the kids corroborate this. The building now also boasts a greenhouse on the roof, with ripe tomatoes that summon the kids to pick them. The neighborhood celebrates every event in their progress, generating the spirit and pride that has turned the neighborhood into a community.

After the community school came EDEN Jobs, then New Song Family Health Services, and last, New Song Arts.

"Just one person with one good idea that came from God, willing to do one thing about that one idea," Steve says of Susan Tibbels, who started the New Song Learning Center as a very small after-school program. "If there's anything that's transferable or that you can replicate, it's that one person with a good idea from God is in a position to do something about it."

Everything that started at Sandtown was started "tiny" and follows the "start small" principle of social change articulated by Ray Bakke in *A Theology as Big as the City*.[22] Steve relates that it "was one doctor in the church willing to meet one night a week with uninsured residents who needed to see a doctor. And the first night we did it, we called it the health center, even though that was kind of a presumptuous nomenclature." It was like a prophetic attitude, speaking it into being. One house being rehabbed leads to twenty.

Steve came to Sandtown to join the pastoral team at New Song at the invitation of his college friend, Mark Gornick, who was the founding pastor. There "wasn't much of a worship life happening in the community," and through his music, Steve would contribute to more than the revival of the church. Tibbels asked him to provide some music enrichment activity for the kids in the after-school program. So he did: one man, one hour a week, coming in with his keyboard and guitar, creating new, culturally relevant songs for kids who had no context for music anywhere else. Songs about math club or working with computers or walking to camp. "When everybody's singing the same song in the same way, doing the same thing, there's something happening there that's magical . . . and they dug it." Authenticity is what first impresses every crowd that hears the Sandtown Children of Praise. Music after school led to a little musical at the end of summer camp. When Habitat for Humanity dedicated a house, they sang on the sidewalk. People responded.

The repertoire increased, and the group began to receive invitations to sing at churches, senior citizen homes, ball games, mayoral inaugurations, conferences, and even the Baltimore Symphony Orchestra. Their first two CDs were done as grassroots local efforts. As Steve says, "There's something special about what these kids do."

The Sandtown Children of Praise are currently completing work on their third CD, which will be released nationally through Gotee Records, a national Christian-owned recording label. They've also got a "thing" goin' on with Bobby McFerrin this fall and maybe something with Aaron Neville. But Steve is not sure of the group's commercial viability. He does know that they are a community choir, and that's what they'll stay. "What's here at the grassroots level is intact enough and authentic enough that commercial viability will [not] dilute who the kids are. That's something we guard against."

NewSong Arts is Steve Smallman's effort to "dream the dream of kids bringing their talent back to Sandtown," to reverse what he calls the "brain and gift drain" of the last forty years. In his role as founder and executive director of NewSong Arts, and as the first artistic director and conductor of the Sandtown Children of Praise gospel choir, Steve had an initial covenant with the children and with God to have a great performance choir. He wanted their music and presence to say every time they performed that "excellence comes from Sandtown." But as his relationship with the children deepened, the covenant grew to emphasize his wanting to see every kid succeed. "I'm called to this. I'm planting seeds, putting a song in their hearts. Only God knows the end."

The seeds are taking root. On any given day the kids can be heard singing and humming the Sandtown songs in the streets or wherever they are. And on the day we visited the church and the rehearsal studio, we heard them too—amidst their playing and joking and talking—singing a phrase here and a verse there. The Sandtown songs are God's truths expressed musically, and the children who participate are learning "whose" they are.

The whole NewSong Urban Ministries effort has created a church outside the building and includes those who would not identify with or attend regular church. Testimony to this is when unchurched kids are asked, "Where do you go to church?" They immediately respond, "New Song." They have learned, perhaps more deeply than most lifelong evangelicals, that God's "church" is not the building but is in God's people who live and love every day, in every circumstance of their lives. Pastor Steve corroborates this as he too tells us that his faith is expressed in the relationships with the kids and that it is these relationships that lead to discussions of what it means to be a Christian. He explains,

Art defines culture. It tells us who we are, and it helps us process the world we live in. And so it's a vital part of who we are. So that to me as a community developer and an artist and a Christian, it just made sense to begin doing that.

I look for a worldview shift, a paradigm shift where folks value traditional family structure. I'd love to see kids who've grown up with strong adult interaction, adult supervision leading to harmonious relationships and mutually beneficial societal ties, where there's a vibrant economic community happening within our borders as well as trade going on outside, and where there's a vibrant intellectual ground bubbling up, also interaction with the outside.

A vibrant worshiping community is where people really take their faith in God beyond a survival mentality where it's all about daily bread and all about just surviving. I think maybe seeing folks move from a survival mind-set into a forward-thinking, forward-looking mind-set which allows you to . . . I think we're looking for renewal: economic, spiritual, creative renewal. I'd love to see sort of a renaissance take place where [the vibrancy of the old theaters on Pennsylvania Avenue would return to the community]. . . . And I think having community leaders reemerge—lifetime Sandtown residents, born and raised—I think those folks are gonna be the ones to define what a whole community looks like.

Lessons Learned

In both of these case studies we see people of action in unity. Christian people of faith acting out of mission, calling, and love that starts the catalytic working out of the transformation process—people acting and God blessing the action. Though space does not permit further analysis here, a number of lessons can be learned from these examples.

1. The residents of the community are the major stakeholders and must own and lead and carry out the transformation strategies.
2. Faith is at the center of the movement. It is the major force that sustains a long-term effort requiring high motivation, patience, and a vision. Faith values action. They prayed that God would bless what they were going to do. God will bless the just actions of a praying people.
3. Community transformation begins with gathering and listening to the community members. Their needs must be the focus of initial efforts.
4. Multiple collaborations among *all* segments of a community's life are necessary for transformation.
5. Community transformation is a long-term endeavor and involves personal sacrifice and suffering on the part of residents. If they are not willing to put the good of the community above personal interests, the effort will be flawed.
6. Start small. Work with the money and resources you have and do what you can.

7. Work with what you have. Just take your idea and start. Don't wait for the big whatever.

8. Love it enough in a day to do it for a year. As Steve said, "One hour, one afternoon was my start, and I liked it enough to keep on."

9. Artists often approach their work from an artist's point of view. Working with an educator is key to wrapping relationships, homework, and tutoring around the art to impact grades.

Summary: Norris Square and Sandtown

If we analyze the case studies based on the values of community, the principles for community development, and the indicators for success mentioned at the beginning of the chapter, we would affirm that both of these cases exhibit successful community development. These communities are not without their problems, though we have not focused on that here. They can be considered successful and provide models in which the arts have been a part, a significant part, of the transformation process.

Both of these communities had and still do have leaders, community members, and institutions of faith at their center. This faith element is what those involved say allowed them to continue the hard work over the long term, enduring the harsh sacrifices often present in comprehensive community-building work in seriously distressed and marginalized communities. Faith allowed the depth and breadth of change, matching the depth and breadth of commitment that only the motivation of faith and an eternal perspective provide.

9

Arts as Economic Development

Part of community development is economic development. Communities without jobs and without stores to shop for basic needs are difficult places to live. Yet in many inner-city neighborhoods the poor struggle for a very basic life. Many must commute long distances, often to the suburbs, for low-paying jobs. They must walk as many as ten city blocks to find a grocery store, only to find the prices inflated well above the prices of the grocery superstores found in most suburbs. In many urban communities employment for the youth is a primary concern. Educational systems in the inner city—often underfunded because of a shrinking tax base, because those who can move do—cannot and do not provide adequate education and training for college or employment.

What has art got to do with this? The arts continue to provide a creative, though not lucrative, option for employment and for ministry. The arts as an industry are a significant part of city revitalization, not only by creating jobs but also by creating an environment that attracts new residents to the city. Though the arts are not separate from overall community development, in this chapter we will look more specifically at the role of the arts in developing the power of capacity in both the people and the places of the urban poor.

As you read, this chapter should help you understand the following:

1. The key theoretical and biblical concepts related to economic development and wealth.

2. How the fates of urban and suburban areas are interwoven and inter-connected.
3. The roles the arts and artists play in place-based and people-based economic development.
4. The characteristics of effective models of economic development using the arts.

Overview of Economic Development

According to the U.S. Department of Commerce, economic development "is fundamentally about enhancing the factors of productive capacity—land, labor, capital and technology."[1] The goal of economic development is to increase income, jobs, and resources. This involves having a trained labor force; an infrastructure of accessible transportation and telecommunications; business and community facilities for education, industry, and recreation; an environment that enhances a community holistically; an economic structure that facilitates business; and institutional capacity that supports development through leadership, knowledge, and skills.

Economic developers use two basic approaches to development: *place-based* development, in which an environment and structure is created for developing economic opportunity; and *people-based* development, in which skills, training, jobs, and accessibility to employment are key for economic growth. Both place-based and people-based goals are included in our consideration of the arts in economic development.

According to the Department of Commerce, developers concerned for economically disadvantaged and depressed communities seek to stimulate self-sustaining economic growth by creating jobs and career ladders for community residents, producing goods and services that benefit local residents, establishing community control of the development, and broadening ownership within the community. Among many economic developers there is an antipoverty and environmental concern. They seek to improve the quality of life of the poor as well as to find a balance between business growth and environmental health.

In 1960 Dr. John Perkins returned to his hometown of Mendenhall, Mississippi. Confronted by racism and poverty, he watched as the youth of the area left for the "big city" to find jobs. His goal was to begin to nurture these young people in long-term development that included a holistic vision of introducing them to God, nurturing them in their faith, and encouraging them to go to college and later return to their hometown to develop their community. It worked. Perkins saw many young people return from college and build professional careers and businesses. Soon both black and white disciples joined him as he planted Voice of Calvary Ministries and the International Study Center in Jackson, Mississippi. He finally migrated to California and established Harambee Ministries, highlighted below in the work of Rudolpho Carrasco, Harambee's assistant director.

Out of the ministries founded by John Perkins, and the ministries started by his disciples, grew the Christian Community Development Association, which celebrated its eleventh year in 2002 with five hundred member organizations (BuildaBridge International and the Campolo School for Social Change at Eastern University being two of them) in one hundred U.S. cities and thirty-two states.[2] A parallel secular organization, the National Congress for Community Economic Development, has over eight hundred members and includes a faith-based office.

Perkins believes that "more Christians are discovering the simple truth that people empowered by God are the most effective solution for the spiritual and economic development of the poor, and that the very physical presence of God's people is the surest way to begin tackling the problems of our poorest communities."[3] His theory is simply stated in three words: relocation, reconciliation, and redistribution. Advocating holistic evangelism and social action, Perkins calls on committed Christians and their families to *relocate* to communities of need and become part of these communities, working alongside the community, modeling healthy lifestyles, and raising up Christian leaders.

Perkins further believes and advocates that *reconciliation* includes not only reconciliation to God through Jesus Christ and nurture in the church but also the true love for Jesus Christ that breaks down every racial, ethnic, or economic barrier as all Christians come together to solve the problems of the community—"the entire body of Christ, black, white, brown, and yellow, rich and poor, urban and suburban."[4]

When Christians relocate and reconcile, the result is *redistribution*. As God's people with resources live in the community, they apply their knowledge and skills as part of the community. The result is that they find "creative avenues to create jobs, schools, health centers, home ownership, and other enterprises of long-term development."[5] Later in this chapter we will examine how Perkins's model is lived out by agape artists.

Dr. Tony Campolo—native Philadelphian, noted urban sociologist, and professor emeritus at Eastern University—has been a tireless advocate for the poor. In addition to teaching and preaching, he founded the Evangelical Association for the Promotion of Education (EAPE) in 1970. Based at the university, EAPE is a missionary organization committed to creating programs to help the poor in developing countries and in disenfranchised neighborhoods across the United States. These programs exist to educate, train, and model the development of small businesses in poor and low-income areas. Urban Promise, located in Camden, New Jersey, is one of the many programs incubated and spawned by Campolo and EAPE and reaches more than fifteen hundred children and teens a year. Urban Promise gave rise to what is now a thriving grassroots neighborhood graphic arts printing business, one of the case studies we will present later in the chapter.

Campolo was one of the first people to conceptualize and concretize the idea of the church as a major catalyst in neighborhood revitalization, and in particular, in job creation and the nurturing and training of the poor. The graduate programs in economic development at Eastern University, originally developed by Dr. Campolo, bear the mark of this church-based microenterprise theme, which has been successfully accomplished in many places around the world and highlighted in his books on the subject.[6] Campolo has for years pointed to the church as a possessor of resources that can and should provide creative people of the community with a low-overhead alternative for incubating economically viable ideas for income generation and business.

Dr. Campolo is quick to point out the classrooms and open spaces of churches that most often go unused during most days of the week; the phone, office equipment, and secretarial support available for use; the "consulting" services and potential consumers available through the church's membership; the credit unions, a growing phenomenon of larger urban churches, which can often provide start-up funds, co-ops, and low-cost loans; and the marketing, advertising, and dissemination opportunities that abound through the communication vehicles of the church and through members' external roles and contacts.

We also have observed this same phenomenon and have approached numerous churches to open their doors to after-school arts programs. While many churches are interested, quite often these churches have been all but abandoned by the "up and outers" in the neighborhood—people who commute to these neighborhoods only to attend church.

Campolo mentions one other unique role that the church can play in supporting the unemployed in developing their "capacity" for work: calling together selected men and women to form small groups that he terms "koinonia Bible study groups." He uses the term *koinonia* because it refers to the unique kind of fellowship and caring for one another among Christians that is based on shared spiritual experiences and values.[7] This same idea can be used in developing Christian artist co-ops and network groups in a community. Informally, this is being done by Coz Crosscombe and the staff of Asaph Studios, which we will discuss in a bit.

Through the use and study of specific Scriptures, the small group meetings explore and reinforce spiritual values, especially those related to in-group solidarity; Jesus' identification with and good news for the poor (Luke); community-building behaviors (Acts); the role of money (James) and the challenge of materialism; and relationships with coworkers and partners. In addition, the small groups develop a sense of camaraderie that allows members to hold each other accountable for work habits and commitment to work and also to support each other in times of hardship and failure. In addition to the obvious goal of holding up new hope in "community" with others, such groups have the ability to provide a "renewing of the mind," a necessary accompaniment to specific job skills training. As Campolo puts it, koinonia groups have the ability to transform the long-term jobless into "risk-taking entrepreneurs with the stick-to-itiveness that makes for success."[8]

A Biblical Perspective

In chapter 5 we mentioned the story of the rich young man and Jesus (Mark 10:17–31). In this story—well known to most Christians and often quoted in matters related to wealth, giving, and the poor—a rich young man comes to Jesus, asking how to inherit eternal life. The young man has followed all the commandments, though perhaps with smugness and the religious arrogance of legalism. His religion is an external one in which he is more concerned about the rules of the faith than with the values of the faith. "Jesus looked at him and loved him and had compassion for him. 'One thing you lack,' he said. 'Go sell everything you have and give to the poor, and you will have treasure in heaven. Then come, follow me'" (v. 21).

The first part of this passage indicates that we are to give up our wealth to assist those in need. Other teachings reiterate that we are always to consider the needs of those less fortunate than us (see Lev. 19:9–10, for example) and not rely on wealth through hoarding and greed. The problem Jesus points to is not just one of *having* wealth but even more, the issues that surround wealth and the consequences of having wealth—the choices and decisions involved and the time and energy spent seeking and keeping one's wealth. Jesus reminds us in other teachings that we cannot serve two masters and must choose either God or mammon, which in the young ruler's case is devotion to wealth. Devotion to wealth leads us away from serving God through our service to the poor.

The second part of the passage reiterates his lesson to Peter and the disciples that those who forsake wealth will be blessed not only in the age to come (eternal life) but also in this present age a hundred times over (Mark 10:29–30). We are reminded that the first will be last and the last will be first, indicating that the poor are God's kingdom priority.

It is important to note that Jesus' approach to the young man was one of understanding and compassion, not disdain or anger. Jesus is not concerned that we have wealth but with how we use the blessing of riches. He understands how very difficult it is to even consider giving up that which makes our lives easy and pleasurable in order to redirect our life energy: "It is easier for a camel to go through the eye of a needle than for a rich man to enter the kingdom of God" (v. 24). He does not begrudge us wealth; in fact, wealth can be part of God's gift to our lives. It is a gift to be used in the calling he gives us, to be used in what God is doing in the world to bring about the NU JERUZ. The wealthy have the responsibility to "earn much and give plenty."[9]

This passage is problematic for many. Our reliance on insurance, money market funds, and retirement plans might indicate our similarity to the rich young ruler and our lack of commitment to the poor and to the teachings of Jesus regarding reward. (See especially Luke 12:16–21 regarding laying up treasures for ourselves.) However, even if all the money of the rich were given to the poor, it wouldn't take long for all the money of the poor to be once again in the hands of the rich, as we will later hear from one who lives among the poor. Giving of our wealth requires more than writing a check. The poor lack the skills and the understanding to maintain wealth. This presents two goals for economic development among the urban poor and among the rich, both individuals and churches, who often live in the suburbs. First, part of economic development is people based and focuses on developing appropriate job skills, technology training, critical thinking skills, and access to employment. Giving of our wealth is more than just donating money; it is sharing our time, talents, and any other resources at our disposal.

Second, economic development is also place based. Recent studies suggest that "central-city poverty has dynamic effects on the economic development of the suburbs."[10] In his detailed analysis of poor urban communities, *Poverty and Place,* Paul A. Jargowsky shows that the characteristics of local communities and their cultures play a secondary role in reducing community property and that the primary factor is the "overall economic conditions prevailing in the metropolitan area and the levels of segregation by race and income."[11] He suggests that part of the solution to the plight of the urban poor is not only found in improving local neighborhood assets and educating and training the poor for employment; it is also found in a recognition of the responsibility of the broader metropolitan areas and the suburbs surrounding the ghettos, barrios, and slums.

The development of macroeconomic policies by both urban and suburban districts is necessary to ensure a more equitable sharing of the resources held by wealthier districts and to accomplish an integration of the poor outside the ghetto. In other words, social isolation is a major contributor to urban poverty. These kinds of strategies and policies come closer to the type of wealth sharing that Jesus talked about. This is more than giving; it requires a different paradigm for living together, one in which there is a "new and viable structure for metropolitan areas in the twenty-first century; a larger urban community rather than an agglomeration of separate and antagonistic places."[12] Most of us do not care to make personal sacrifices to achieve this vision of the NU JERUZ, thus the camel gets stuck in the eye of the needle.

Jargowsky further suggests that if our policies "raise incomes, reduce inequality, and unite rather than divide our society, neighborhood poverty can be significantly reduced and its effects ameliorated." The consequences of not doing so, Jargowsky states, are that the poor continue to be "warehoused in vast urban wastelands," with a greater risk that our country could descend into internal racial and ethnic conflicts[13]—a type of revolution being called for by gangsta rappers since the late 1980s.

Former Albuquerque mayor David Rusk, author of *Cities without Suburbs,* does not believe America has a poverty problem as such, especially when compared to the rest of the world. Americans have, as a whole, a much better standard of living, as anyone who has traveled abroad can attest. But we do have a real problem with "racial and economic segregation that has created an underclass in America's major urban areas."[14]

Building on the work of Jargowsky, Rusk agrees that segregating poor urban blacks and Hispanics has spawned decaying, revenue-strapped, poverty-impacted, crime-ridden "inner cities." These inner cities are isolated from their "outer cities," which are usually the wealthier, growing, and largely white suburbs. Rusk believes that the real city is the total metropolitan area—city and suburb—and that for the city to grow, it must be "elastic."[15] Cities that are elastic and that encompass the suburbs as part of their growth are able to increase revenue dollars that benefit all residents. Those that are "inelastic," where the suburbs have controlled the growth of the city, tend to create segregation and poverty. As more people flee the decaying cities, the suburbs, once seen as havens of low-density peace, begin to experience some of the same issues of land use, deforestation, traffic, overcrowding, municipal services overloads, and school shortages that the city faces.

The relevant point here is that many people living in the suburbs are not aware or do not understand that a protective lifestyle from the city, a failure to recognize the interconnectedness of city and suburb, and a control of funding all actually help to create and maintain poverty in the inner city. Neither large-scale federal aid for social welfare and economic development programs nor enterprise zones, public housing, and empowerment programs in which the poor are "quarantined" in ghettos and barrios will solve the problem.

Rusk examined the census tracts of areas where community development corporations have worked to rehabilitate housing, provide job training, and create microloan institutions and did not find a single area that had improved income levels over the past twenty years. He does not, however, believe that these efforts are bad, and he recognizes that they improve the quality of life of the inhabitants. The problem is that those who gain the skills and benefits of such development programs move up and out of the neighborhoods, which thus leaves these areas in the same state of poverty.

Rusk believes "sustained success requires moving poor people from bad city neighborhoods to good suburban neighborhoods and moving dollars from relatively wealthy suburban governments to poorer city governments. The long-term payoffs will be an overall reduction in poverty, dependency, and crime area-wide."[16]

Speaking of community development in relationship to the arts, Jargowsky says, "The endemic social problems of poor neighborhoods have left many residents unprepared to take advantage of new economic opportunities. Thus, programs that emphasize culture, values, and self-esteem are important but only in the context of increasing economic opportunities for the poor. But they must not be stand-alone efforts, because the behavior of the poor is not the cause of neighborhood poverty."[17] Thus, a wonderful art program that teaches the arts may not, and probably will not, improve the economic situation of the recipients because of the broader economic reality of the city. They will, however, play a significant role in improving the quality of life for residents and, in cooperation with other organizations, especially for-profit arts organizations, may begin community and economic revitalization.

The Role of the Arts in Economic Development

In chapter 1 we introduced you to Sarah Thompson, a young economic and community developer working in Philadelphia. Sarah is using a place-based strategy of economic development, one that is being replicated in many communities of America. By purchasing and renovating old warehouses for artists' housing and studio space and by improving the streets of her community through a bench-painting campaign in which artists creatively decorate bus benches, Sarah is seeking to create an attractive environment for continued economic growth within her community.

A recent study of the National Governors Association (NGA) confirmed the value of the nonprofit arts industry to the national economy, with $36.8 billion in annual revenue supporting 1.3 million jobs.[18] While much research is still to be done, it seems there is a symbiotic relationship between nonprofit art programs and the commercial art sector of the economy. The nonprofit arts sector includes many small groups that utilize artistic and cultural resources important for tourism, for example. And as in the example of Sarah's work, communities are being revitalized through direct arts strategies.

In our research of U.S. cities in the past year, we have witnessed the power of arts-based economic development in downtown revitalization in programs such as Philadelphia's Avenue of the Arts, Baltimore's Harborplace, and Charleston's Spoleto Arts Festival. Such areas and events around the country attract tourists, spawn businesses, provide beautiful public spaces, and create jobs. According to Richard Florida of Carnegie Mellon University, the arts and the creative class provide a "quality of place" necessary in city revitalization: lifestyle, environmental quality, a vibrant music and arts scene, and natural and outdoor amenities. Research is showing that these creative spaces are attractive and fertile for the "development of new industries that require a high degree of creativity, intellectual expansiveness, and collaborative work among multiple firms in related industries."[19]

We have also observed that these arts-based economic strategies in city revitalization often do not improve the plight of the poor in the neighborhoods surrounding the city. Tickets to a symphony concert can be as much as $40. While construction in art development zones has attracted the wealthy, the poor generally have little access to or interest in the type of art found in museums and concert halls, and often they continue to live in squalid conditions while investment has been made in the center of the city and not in the fringes of the city. When revitalization does occur in these communities, it is sometimes in the form of gentrification.

Arts-based strategies for economic development are not the "drivers" of economic development but are to be seen as the "missing link" in development. Churches often do not think of themselves as part of this equation and the broader American economy. Churches are nonprofit businesses, however, in that they employ people and contribute to the general well-being of the community. For years churches have used the arts to raise funds through presenting concerts and theater productions as fund-raising events for local ministries. They also have provided attractive architecture for the community and a safe place for its residences. Churches have the potential to become much more intentional both in their understanding of the role of the arts and in the use of arts strategies for developing the community. By nurturing the gifts of its members, collaborating with the community and community organizations, sharing its space, and developing the latent resources within the congregation and community, the church can play a more vital role in overall community and economic development.

The NGA study also looked at *people-based* arts strategies through examining the impact of arts education on workforce preparation. As we will discuss further in our chapter on education, the arts help to develop "human capital," an essential component in economic growth and stability. In the new economy that is supplanting a labor-intensive economy, the workplace is demanding people with not only academic skills but also flexibility, problem-solving abilities, interpersonal skills, and creativity.

Arts-based educational programs have been proven to enhance students' learning and preparation for a productive life in society. Unfortunately, most art programs have been cut from poorer inner-city schools, seriously decreasing the early discovery and encouragement of artistic gifts in children and youth, which thus prevents consideration of these gifts for career and life options. The result is that the competitive edge remains with the youth of the suburbs, who have continued access to arts programs. In recent years, however, there has been growth in the number of arts programs for at-risk children and incarcerated youth. The continued development and implementation of these programs will be significant in people-based development strategies.

Camden Printworks

It's been twelve years now, and the printing business that started out as an offshoot of one of the youth programs at Urban Promise is now supporting families and providing a decent living for those working at Camden Printworks (CPW). Begun in 1990 by literally pulling kids in off the streets, the program still targets at-risk youth and young adults and is now also providing work for one or two single moms. Participants receive on-the-job training in office and workplace skills as well as training related to particular aspects of the custom screen-printing business.

Recently, as we left a meeting with people from a large research university who had given us gifts—T-shirts made by CPW—Dr. Campolo gave us an update: "It is now a $500,000 business, with the goal of physical expansion. Some of the young people who were here in the early days have now moved on to better jobs because of the experience they gained there."[20]

Printworks now handles big corporate accounts as well as small accounts but continues to remain grounded in its faith-integrated beginnings and its focus on increasing "human capacity" and economic and employment options for those in the community. There is informal profit sharing in the way of bonuses at the end of a profitable year, with some of the profit going back into the business. The balance goes to support the various youth-focused programs of its parent ministry, Urban Promise.

The idea of starting a printing business came up when a Vancouver graphic artist working at Urban Promise decided he wasn't good with kids. He, along with Tony Campolo and Bruce Main, who directs the larger Urban Promise ministries, suggested that he put to use his excellent screen-printing talents. CPW's current leader is Mary Anne Degenhart, a paralegal for nineteen years who, at the age of forty-two, was convicted to change careers to work with the poor in her community. Mary Anne had read one of Campolo's books, *Everything You Heard Is Wrong,* then took his Urban Sociology course in the Urban Economic Development program at Eastern. A field project was required for the course, and being from Camden (born in the city and raised in a nearby town), Mary Anne wanted to do something there. In the process of completing a marketing plan for the business, she got excited about what was happening. Following her field project, Mary Anne remained involved, and sensing God's call to inner-city economic development, she moved to full-time leadership of CPW in July 1996.

Mary Anne corroborates the impact of the program by telling us of one of the guys who started at CPW, stayed five or six years, and who now owns and operates his own tractor trailer. And Juanita, who's been with the business for ten years, is the office manager. As the business has expanded, Juanita's role has expanded too. She now supervises three part-time staff members and trains them in all aspects of their work, including Quickbooks and various bookkeeping functions, inventory control, and shipping/receiving. Juanita is currently attending evening college courses in pursuit of a degree in accounting. Not all the stories from CPW are as successful. Like all profitable businesses that reflect Christ, CPW has high standards that some find hard to meet. Grace and mercy are in full measure, however, as the CPW staff extend themselves to give a second chance to those struggling against the odds of personal sin and social evil. Mary Anne talks about some of the employees:

> Like Billie, who was a star employee for about three months before he backslid into his cocaine addiction. We met with him and his wife and pastor to help him work through it, but eventually he just disappeared.
>
> And Kenny, who had served time for drug dealing. After his release, he worked successfully for CPW for about six months. He is a very young man, and he enrolled in an evening class at the community college in Camden. But he could not shake the pull of his old friends. He was out all night on the street and was coming in late to work every day; eventually we had to terminate him. Shortly thereafter he was arrested for murder and awaits trial. [A tentative deal has been struck with prosecutors because the shooting was an act of self-defense.]
>
> Jim has been with UP since he was a young boy in summer camp; he later became a StreetLeader [Urban Promise's youth leadership program], sang in the choir, and in 1999 came to work at CPW. He has been through some tough times and his attendance and on-time records left something to be desired. He is currently in a six-month residential drug-rehabilitation program. His job awaits him, but he will be on probation with us until he proves that he is ready and eager to work hard again.
>
> There are dozens who work well for a few months, or a few weeks, or just a few days. If their personal life is in chaos, only so much is possible. Even if they are committed to do well in their job, outside influences continue to pull at them.[21]

Planting Trees

Like so many agape artists and urban prophets, Rudy Carrasco, the energetic associate director of Harambee Christian Family Center in Pasadena, California, has a clear vision of what the NU JERUZ should be like in his neighborhood: "Home ownership, an ethnically diverse community, people with long-standing roots in the community, a strong Christian presence, and changes in academic achievement and college degrees."[22] Specifically, he wants to see "folks who choose to live here and are neighbors." His vision draws on the image from Psalm 1, where there is a "tree firmly planted by the stream, leaves do not wither, bears fruit in season, whatever it does it prospers." To Rudy, the tree is one of the strongest metaphors for describing urban transformation. The tree represents individuals, leaders, who are strongly rooted in the community.

> Throughout Scripture and just looking around at life we see that a tree can provide shade. The birds of the air will nest [in it], in the parable of the mustard seed. A tree is a very good strong thing. I feel like a tree a lot of times. I feel like there are people who take shade under me, people who are weighing on my branches, people who need this strong, firmly rooted thing, presence that is long lasting.

Rudy lives in an area that, like many other urban communities, has lost its strong leaders, which leaves a vacuum. "In a vacuum gangs can get pretty strong. Gangs themselves are not so well-organized. They have this tendency to destroy their own human capital. But in a vacuum a gang can terrorize a community and take over and create the ethos, create the environment. So we think that part of what needs to happen in urban development is replanting leaders, replanting trees." Rudy recognizes that it takes a long time to grow leaders, fifteen years or more. And so he is about the business of planting and replanting trees.

Rudy's attention deficit disorder was a bit distracting in our interview on the run, as he manages multiple tasks at a fast walking pace—talking to this person, calling out orders to another. His love for technology cannot be missed; his Apple laptop is an ever-present extension of his hand. "Here, have you seen this web site?" he will ask as he cracks open the lid and connects to the Internet through a remote satellite connection. He is a disciple of John Perkins, though Rudy would not use the term disciple. His allegiance is firmly in the love of Jesus. He has been at the Harambee Center for twelve of its nineteen years and has watched the four-block community change from one of violence to peace, and one of primarily African-Americans to an equal mix of Latinos and African-Americans. He has committed his life to this community and to planting human trees.

> The problems or needs we're trying to address here are how to reach people in a holistic way and ultimately for them to touch the gospel, touch the love of God for themselves. So we are missionaries in a very traditional sense. We want to share knowledge about Jesus Christ and his saving power, his saving blood. Understanding our context, we know that we need to build trust with folks in the community. One of the best ways to build trust is to offer some basic services, working with their children. We've found that everybody—no matter where you're coming from, what you believe or don't believe, what you trust and don't trust—everybody is concerned about kids and treating kids well. And so our basic outreach is a set of programs that just come around kids, help them with homework, love them, encourage them to dream for the future, and we've

found that that's a tremendous trust builder and a tremendous foundation for the things that we do in the ministry.

Rudy has always had a concern for at-risk communities. Born in east L.A., his call came at ten, when he first heard about the walls of Jericho falling down. Rudy remembers thinking, "If God is strong enough to do something about the walls of Jericho, God is strong enough to do something about east L.A." In Rudy one can see a strong man whose own life walls have been rebuilt. First his father abandoned the family when Rudy was very young, then his mother died when he was seven, and then he was shuffled between relatives, but Rudy never forgot his east L.A. roots. "I spent the first seven years of my life in east L.A., in a community that was thriving, buoyant, struggling, historic, Mexican."

As a student at Stanford University, Rudy heard John Perkins speak to a group of students. Perkins threw out a recruiting pitch; he needed a writer and an assistant to work with him for two years. "And I thought to myself, 'Well, this is great. I know John Perkins; I know the ministries, Christian community development, and holistic ministry philosophies.' I said I'd love to work with this guy for two years; it will be like grad school. Especially since I couldn't, at that time in 1990 . . . see [much] academic or Christian community development holistic focus. Two years with Perkins, then I go back to east L.A. Well, actually it's been twelve years. I haven't gone back to east L.A."

According to Rudy, the Harambee Center is like the movie *The Matrix.* While there are many programs, the teaching and life discipleship happens on a more personal and informal level. Harambee has a highly visible web site and after-school programs that run throughout the academic year, primarily for elementary kids, and include tutoring and Bible studies. In the summer they hold a day camp. Through a junior staff program they take teenagers and teach job skills training, college preparation, and technology. They do anything they believe will prepare the youth for leadership. They also have a program for adults called Harambee Fellows. The fellows are primarily unskilled but learn on the job as they assist with the children and youth programs.

Technology is integrated throughout Harambee's programs. As Rudy says, they understand "the basic idea that technology is going to be a part of everyone's future, including our young people. And to whatever degree you believe that the digital divide exists or doesn't exist, we don't dispute that most urban kids tend to be behind in their access or their practice in gaining technological skills."

Using technology has been a passion and a practicality at Harambee. Both Rudy and Derek Perkins, the director of Harambee, enjoy technology. Rudy manages several web sites and writes prolifically about urban issues. Practically, they realized they could cut organizational costs if they did everything themselves. They shoot the digital photos, lay out brochures and newsletters on a computer using Quark Express, and print drafts on a laser printer. They recently purchased an inexpensive Risograph machine and now produce three thousand copies of the Harambee newsletter every month. Labor costs have disappeared, and young people are gaining firsthand technical experience in a mentoring, apprenticeship relationship.

Informal technology mentoring was not in Rudy's plan. It came about by accident, through something he learned from another youth worker.

One day a group from Long Beach, California, about thirty miles down the way, visited Harambee. It was a multiethnic youth group from, I think, a Baptist church. And our young people were excited to meet them, and they had wanted to get out and do service projects in the community and meet some other young people. And so we got there and as is typical, we challenged them to a basketball game. We have a full-court basketball court in the backyard. And so we said, "Let's play basketball." You know we saw some black kids, some Mexican kids, Asian and white kids, and thought, "These kids [the group from Long Beach] can play basketball." And they said okay, but they were not very excited; they sort of shuffled along, and our kids could tell they weren't excited. So they said let's play soccer, because our kids will beat you down in basketball or soccer, sorry to say that. But it's the truth. We challenged them at soccer; we said they must love soccer. They did the same old, looking at the ground, not very excited about it. And—which really puzzled all of us—and finally we said to them, so what do you guys do? And they perked up and said, "We play golf." Yeah, and they started talking about playing golf. And . . . that was around the time that Tiger Woods was really starting to take off professionally. So we thought, oh it's a Tiger Woods thing. They really got into Tiger Woods. But we asked them that, and they didn't really indicate that Tiger Woods was any big deal. Finally I asked the youth pastor and the youth pastor said, "Well, I never planned this; I never planned to get black and Latino and Asian and white kids good at golf, but I like to play golf, and I just thought that, well, maybe I could spend some time in discipleship and have some fun, and maybe they'd want to play golf with me. So I just made sure that whenever I went to play golf I dragged a bunch of kids along with me. And while we're on the golf course, there's tons of time to hang out and talk and listen and teach and model by example. And the only reason it was golf is 'cause I like golf."

Likewise, Rudy admits that "the only reason that Harambee has really pushed forward in technology is because Derek and I like technology. We have a lot of fun with it. And probably the major reason we have a lot of our technological innovations at an urban level is because that's what we like to do. We drive down costs, but it's fun."

Training his kids in technology is unorthodox and intuitive. It is not program driven like most technology programs but is instead project driven. Eager neighborhood kids seem to wait in the wings for a chance to be assigned a project and learn the technology by experience, always under the watchful eye of Rudy.

The reality is that there's an entire environment of people who are capable of teaching, and when a young person, or any person, has a project with a fixed deadline and a fixed goal, they can not only achieve that, they can hit the mark, but they will learn whatever skills they need to learn to hit the mark. We have witnessed this time and time again.

It's also a lot easier for me to manage, as you might imagine, but it gives a tremendous sense of affirmation as well. So the young person looks up and says, "I actually did that. And I can do it again."

Much of what Rudy does in ministry is driven by his philosophy and his lifestyle. He and his family have chosen to incarnate in the community; they live just across the street from the center. Choices about work, play, and ministry are determined by practical concerns. Until a few years ago, he maintained a computer lab in the center. The management of the lab began to take time away from the primary goal of discipleship and family time, as young people demanded more time on the computers, which meant more open hours for the center. So in another innovative move Rudy decided to put the computers and the printers in the homes of neighborhood kids. So when they knock on his door at 8 P.M. wanting help, he sends them to another kid's house who can help him just as well.

A self-professed sloth and unfocused human being (which he isn't), Rudy is very reflective about his calling.

I want to see the Bible lived out—what I've seen in the Book of Acts, read about in the Gospels. And I want to be close to where God's at, and at some point in my life I figured out that it seems to me I also wanted to be in a place where I would be challenged and pushed to be more diligent and more faithful in my own personal relationship with Christ. I get to see miracles. I get to see the Bible come alive.

Rudy has followed the philosophy of Dr. Perkins—relocation, reconciliation, and redistribution—as a theological framework for ministry. He relocated into the area and began to build trust before he began his work. He seeks daily to bring people into a right relationship with God and with each other in reconciliation. He has redistributed resources by applying and sharing his own skills and abilities with the community through tutoring, mentoring, and apprenticeship. "And you hope by the time you're done that the kid actually knows how to do the math problem for him or herself. We apply that in every piece of our lives."

People at Harambee are open about being a Christian program. They teach the Bible and try to live out their faith, and there are rules of the house. Harambee holds the kids to tough standards. No swearing. And no music, because Rudy believes they listen to enough music on their own and need to learn to listen and think.

They're being ministered to . . . every time you see a young person, don't be fooled. They're not being entertained; they're being ministered to. They're drawing something, they're drawing meaning from that music. And what we're saying is when you're in our environment, draw meaning from someone else. Take a break from that stuff. Mostly holding up certain standards for how you treat people. Having a sense of hope for people.

Is Harambee making a difference? They have not done formal assessments, but Harambee is evaluated every day by the parents, who are quick to voice their concerns and pleasures. They have seen the neighborhood change from a place of violence with thirty independent drug houses to a community relatively free and peaceful today. They have watched as students complete college and take successful jobs, many of whom return to the neighborhood to take up leadership positions. And Harambee has seen their ministry replicated by others.

Rudy states two important lessons for others who wish to be involved in a community ministry:

First, own property. Property is so huge in our ministry. We own nine properties. Eight of them are paid off, zero mortgage. One of them has a mortgage. If we lose all of our funding we can still run programs. We all just run out and get jobs [to pay operations], and here's this property we have. Property is incredible. So it's not just owning . . . it's owning property and paying the stuff off. Pure asset. Second, focus on discipleship.

To Rudy, "this means living your faith, not just calling yourself a Christian, shouting 'Praise Jesus!' and never mentoring a young life by example and involvement. That is what we find in groups where people have some religion and some understanding but don't have the deep whole-life transformation that Jesus is actually talking about. He said, 'Go out and make disciples'; he didn't say, 'Go out and make people who are gonna name me every chance they get and then turn around and do something else.'"

Music of Chance and Opportunity

Coz Crosscombe is an Australian with a practical edge. Trained in business and, by his own admission, possessing little artistic skill, video and audio technology are Coz's tools of discipleship for community and economic development. It is the living, the incarnation, in the community that makes the difference. For ten years Coz has lived as a "missionary" in the community on Allegheny Avenue in north Philadelphia where he has built Asaph Studios, part of the ministry of Bethel Temple Church. Unlike most businesspeople, Coz doesn't measure success in numbers and profits but in changed lives.

Community change can be deciding to run [our] day camp in a park full of drug dealers just because you want the kids to play in the grass. And watching, by the end of the four weeks, the drug dealers actually run security for the park to make sure that no one interferes with our day camps. And then to have somebody who's doing an article on the problems of drugs in this community call me up one day from the newspaper and say that I blew his article because all the dealers were gone from the park when he came to shoot and it was all full of kids. Well, that's a success story.

A young girl comes in that I've known for a long time, and she comes in here because I've convinced the judge to let her get out of prison in order to come here and that we'd work with her. And it's got nothing to do with her productivity here. It's completely to do with keeping her off the street. I went back over the last three months, and said, ya know, I can miss the contracts and the money and all those kinds of things, but nothing comes even close to the change in her. Just the change in how she speaks, and the fact that she goes to a Bible study and gets excited. She talks about working with kids now instead of selling drugs and the other parts of her life that were involved. Ya know . . . that's success.[23]

Coz's goal is ever before him as he seeks to change the "acceptable."

It has to do with the lie that the people are convinced that they don't have to achieve to a certain level. It's becoming acceptable in this community to be a failure. It's acceptable not to go to school. It's acceptable not to get a job. It's acceptable to deal drugs. It's acceptable to have low moral values. We deal with changing people—what people are allowed to accept from themselves. Dealing with people's misconceptions about what they can actually expect from themselves.

Like Rudy, Coz believes community leadership should use a three-pronged approach: discipleship, evangelism, revitalization. He sees the church as part of the problem.

They talk about the "white flight" that happened in these areas in the eighties. Well, after that came the "Latino flight." The strong leadership to the community all moves out. I've heard numbers that say that the church is the first organization to leave the community. People get saved, they get a good job, they get their life together, they get their family together, and they pack up and move to the northeast. And so that's one of our deepest issues that we deal with . . . is convincing the young adults that you can be a success and remain in this community.

To change the community and develop strong leadership, Coz has worked holistically to bring about change. Ten years ago when he moved into the four city blocks of his community, drug dealers were on every corner and no flowers were to be seen on the porches. Coz understands the importance of little things. He takes walks in the neighborhood with his children, in places where young children have been shot. He shops in local stores, often demands better products, and knows that parking on the street is a sign that he lives there and is not afraid of having his car stolen.

Coz wants to see role models in his community, people to look up to. He points to the empowerment of the suburbs, where people call the police and they come. If the trash is not collected, people call and they come. He would like to see this kind of civic empowerment and leadership in his neighborhood. And after ten years of work, it is beginning to happen.

> The first year [my wife and I] lived there, there were twelve people shot on the one block. Obviously, they were not all killed, but shooting on this one half block [he points in the direction of the street outside Asaph Studios]. A time when you know it's changed is when you go there and you see there's been a time when there was no drug dealing and the police were cracking down, responding to calls. But I remember seeing a girl recently, and she was maybe thirteen, and I said, "Are these guys dealing again on the corner?" And she says, "Yes, but we've told them they have to leave." And I was like "Wow!! I haven't heard that before here." And it's empowerment to the people to say, "Hang on, people helped us get rid of them before; we're allowed to do that again." It's going and meeting a crossing guard who won't tell the drug dealer to leave the kids alone but will take fifty people to that same corner and give the power back to the people and say "You know what? You don't have to settle for this. We're going to fight with you on these issues, we're going to battle with you." So people feeling helpless, you start to give them empowerment, but that's lacking, because the people who have the ability to do that have left the communities.

Like many agape artists, Coz's mission is transformation, and art is the vehicle. Asaph Studios is run like a business—a business of transformation. With six employees and a $100,000 budget, they struggle to make ends meet. They have major business accounts for video production and graphic design, but their recording studio also touches the community and provides the context for change.

> Occasionally we have to make some tough decisions on who we let record. You may get a drug dealer come in, pull out a wad of cash—thousands of dollars of cash laying on the table—and ask to record. Those ones get a little trickier as what we're gonna do, but often times we've let people record that we would never put our name to. As a ministry chance, we get these guys coming in and we get a chance to tell them about what we believe. There's this group that the arts field is appealing to, particularly when it's high quality. It gives you opportunity to speak from a different level. It's something that they admire, coming to a recording studio and have a good recording done. They'll start to listen to everything else you have to say. And that gives a chance to share with people about their lives, question about their lives. I've had some guys record . . . content [that] doesn't fit with what I believe at all. However, by the end of four weeks of coming to record, we're having a Bible study at the end of the week, and answering all the

questions they have on God and Christ and what all that means in their lives. And that's the exciting side of it.

The studio staff, who all live in the community, confront in love what they consider as unhealthy and unchristian lyrics.

We could say, "How dare you speak about your women like that? You have a mother." But it's a different story to say, ya know, "I know your mother. How do you think she feels about the kinds of language you use?" "What about the girl that you're with? I know her. She's a sweet girl. Hmm . . . how do you think she responds? Or your daughter that we know you have." Gets a little closer to home. Makes them think a little more.

This ministry is not without its critics, especially some church members who don't like some of the lyrics of the songs or the artists who get high outside on the street and then walk into the studio. Coz says, "At least they weren't getting high in our studio. That was the start, and next week they may not get high on the block, and the week after that maybe they may not get high at all."

One might wonder how Coz goes about people-based economic development. By all appearances, the studio struggles for money, many of his "employees" are volunteers, and he talks more about leadership and discipleship than about employment. As his incarnational life is a transforming agent in his community, so it is in the lives of his staff.

Coz raises his own support so that he can employ people—people who live in the community. He has helped his employees purchase local property, rehabilitate the houses, and become home owners of houses they could not afford to rent.

We don't have any income that helps us get any retirement benefits or any of these kinds of things. We want to be revitalizing properties. The young people in our church have no concept of physical management, so I began with one young guy. We partnered and bought a few houses, fixed them up. He bought my share out, went up to the next guy, and just actually today was on the phone getting things set up for the third young guy to come on board. We just buy out some places, fix 'em up, get some renters in there, have the renters pay off our mortgages in about five years. . . . We work in extremely concentrated areas. The church may say its boundaries [are] a mile or two miles or three miles—it doesn't really matter—but for economic development, my boundaries are two blocks. Absolute maximum. Outside that area, you just get too spread and you can't make an impact. So that's why I bought a house on a small half-block, and then you'd get Christians moving into those places, they begin talking to each other in the street—something that's not often done—ya know, saying hello as they walk around the corner . . . using the local stores, demanding higher quality from the local stores. And that's to make the impact. So for me it achieves a whole bunch of goals. It doesn't take too much of my time. Teaches young people how to manage investment. Give them a really good foothold well ahead of their peers, revitalize the community, and then, hopefully, leaves my family with some future benefits. That kind of comes last on the list, but it's nice to have as well.

Coz speaks proudly about his staff and the accomplishments they have seen nationally. He also says that they would like to see greater support from the church at large.

I'm still trying to understand in this country how politics and religion work. I am conservative in my theology. Very conservative. Yet in the other areas, I'm a socialist. I'm pure socialist at heart. And for a long time it seemed hard to fit in anywhere. If you're into social justice, then you had to be liberal in your theology, and if you were conservative in your theology, then you had to vote Republican.

So I think my place in social justice is we're trying to change it. One of the reasons for having a studio to make money is the model of developing business in the community to keep money there. There's a model of getting other businesses to bring money in. Our model is to go out and take the money from those I think should have given it in the first place. We go to a Christian concert and sell T-shirts to people who wouldn't give us the money to do ministry. But they'll happily buy a T-shirt with someone's face on it. That doesn't reflect Christ to me, but that's what we feel we're called to do. We'll survive without their money. But how?

I could go out and sell product to a large church and they get excited about this product and we could overcharge them for the product. Yet if we said, "Can you give us a couple thousand dollars so we can go tell some kids about Jesus?" they'd say, "I'm sorry, we don't have that money in our budget." But boy I can go out and make a video for them, we could make T-shirts for them to wear around the house, and they'd be happy with that. To me, that's the epitome of social injustice. And it's church-based, ya know, it's really church-based.

Coz refuses to take the credit for any good that comes through his ministry, a lesson he wishes to pass on to others.

All the credits around here point back to God from my aspect, because at the end of the day there's been so many more failures. You work with a hundred kids and the five success stories might get written about, but I never forget the others. The kids that die that other people maybe don't hear about. They stay with you. And at the end of the day you have to be able to go back and realize that God loves the people more than I do, that he cares more than I do, and it's his responsibility. So you go through a lot of pain and go with the failures, but at the end of the day I know that he's the one that's responsible, not me. And that's a good feeling.

Summary

From these discussions with agape artists using arts (primarily technology) in economic development, we again find a holistic and faith-integrated approach to ministry in communities. In each of these case studies, the emphasis was on the development of people and their skills, but more than that, on their attitudes and readiness for work. They try to expand people's aspirations along with their skills. The nature of their methods develops relational skills and the ability to work in community. They encourage people to return to their communities as leaders, to avoid a "brain drain" of the community. Place-based economic development using the arts has been used primarily in more affluent city centers in a macroeconomic approach. The places described in this and the previous chapter, for example, had significant microeconomic place-based development in order to create an environment for new business. But above all, in these case studies we can see the incarnational lifestyle of the agape artists who not only live in the community but who are "redistributing" their own human capital.

10

The Arts in Human Relationships

And Saul's servants said to him, "Surely, a distressing spirit from God is troubling you. Let our master now command your servants, who are before you, to seek out a man who is a skillful player on the harp. And it shall be that he will play it with his hand when the distressing spirit from God is upon you, and you shall be well."

1 Samuel 16:15–16 NKJV

At the very heart of community development is human development. The well-being of the residents of the community determines to a great degree the overall health of a community and a society. According to the 2001 UNDP (United Nations Development Programme) Human Development Report, much of this development aims to enlarge people's choices. Basic life goals have to do with the "capabilities to lead a long and healthy life, to be knowledgeable, to have access to resources needed for a decent standard of living and to be able to participate in the life of a community. Human development and human rights are mutually reinforcing. In order to develop, one must be able to live a life of dignity and respect."[1]

The UNDP report looks at a number of outcomes to see the progress toward global human development: Are people living longer and healthier lives? Are they more literate and better educated, and do they have higher incomes? Is there progress toward gender equality, environmental sustainability, and democracy? The indicators used to answer these questions are infant mortality rates, life expectancy, adult literacy, and more.

Increasingly, researchers are recognizing that spirituality is an important part of human development and well-being, a fact that Christians and people of other faiths have long known. From the Christian viewpoint, it is not until a person finds a new life in Christ that one has the spiritual power to meet the demands of the physical world. Faith development is part of human development. Faith provides a moral compass, a motivational fire, a living energy, and an inner peace that truly passes all understanding and that is externalized in serving others. Yet that faith cannot be known without human connection. It is the relationships in human development that bring about transformation. As missionaries, pastors, and ministers have long known, development without incarnational love and a long-term mature and mentoring relationship leaves people and communities without a transforming direction.

In this chapter we will examine how the arts, through relationships, help to bring about transformation of people's emotional and psychological health.

As you read this chapter, consider the following questions:

1. How do you define human development, from both a secular and a faith-integrated perspective?
2. What effects can and do the arts have on physical, emotional, psychological, relational, and spiritual development?
3. What is the significant role of relationships in using the arts in human development?
4. What is the role of the Christian as a citizen artist?
5. What is the role of the non-Christian in human development?

Arts and Health

His head was bowed over the ivory keys in silence. His mother, standing next to him ready to sing, was sadly still. I could hear every member of the congregation holding their breath, a breath that hitched the moment the wrong note was played. Our only question now was, What would he do next?

Thirteen-year-old Diego (not his real name) was playing in his first piano recital, before a neighborhood church crowd. He walked to the piano with pride and anticipation. He was to play the first verse of the piece by himself. He did it—perfect! He began the second verse, this time with his mother singing—Oh, no! A wrong note. Silence. His mother leaned over to whisper in his ear. We all waited and prayed that he would begin again. "Keep going," we wished to ourselves. "Or start over. But just don't quit!" The mother whispered again, and yet again, to the frozen boy. We hoped. The keys sounded softly, then a bit stronger. Mother began to sing again. The whole congregation joined in to sing the third verse. Now and again Diego faltered, but each time the voice of the piano eventually came in again. Everyone stood and applauded, attempting to convey that he should feel triumph. He did not. Emotional beyond consolation, Diego left the piano bench with a lowered head, a defeated heart, and tears in his eyes. He took his seat and hid his head between his knees.

After the recital ended, Diego walked quickly to leave the sanctuary. I caught him as he rounded the aisle with his mother and teacher close behind, who were also trying to catch up with him. Standing in his path, I lowered my face to see his. Cupping his chin in my hand, I raised his head so that his eyes could see mine.

"Diego, don't you dare be embarrassed or walk with your head down. You were the best of everyone tonight because of what you learned. You were very courageous. When you made a mistake, you learned how to continue on afterwards. What a wonderful success."

I repeated all these words again to make sure he heard me. His ever-so-slight smile and the now loosening muscles in his face let me know that it was not necessary to repeat my words a third time. Nodding heads from teacher and mother reinforced this truth.

I could see Diego from a distance now, a hop in his step, engaging with the other kids, his esteem restored. His mother found me and waited by my side while I ended a conversation with another acquaintance.

"I wanted to thank you for what you said to Diego just now. It's always better when it comes from someone other than me. He would not have been able to do that three months ago. He would have just crumbled. He's been working in therapy on this very thing. He's a perfectionist, and when he makes a mistake, he falls apart. This is the first time he's recovered like that."[2]

Diego and King Saul share a common remedy—music. The Scripture passage cited at the beginning of this chapter implies that in Saul's case, it was the inherent properties of the music that would bring healing to his recurring depression; the medium itself acts on the person, the brain, and the heart to bring about health. In Diego's case, it is his own engagement in the process of playing that allows the overcoming of psychological and personality issues.

"How do we know that it's the music that makes the difference in your clients' healing?" we asked Janelle, a licensed music therapist practicing in Philadelphia and the coordinator of BI's community arts programs.

"We don't always know," she replied. "But it's the relationship. That's what I tell the volunteer teachers. The music and the art are the vehicles to reach kids and their families—the vehicle to establish the healing relationship, particularly with those clients who are nonverbal."[3]

Most branches of psychology and psychotherapy would agree: the relationship is the primary instrument through which healing and therapeutic work takes place. There is no question that the concepts of transference and countertransference, critical tools in analytic therapy, are concepts bound in the relationship between client and therapist. So are concepts of basic trust and empathy. Perhaps with the exception of strict behavior-modification techniques, the healer's primary tool for healing is his or her ability to establish and maintain (through conflict and projection, anger and resistance) a balanced and healthy relationship with the client.

While perhaps not at first glance, in both Diego's and Saul's cases there was more involved than just the music. David was not just any harp player. First, David was excellent at his craft: "Look, I have seen a son of Jesse the Bethlehemite, who is skillful in playing" (1 Sam. 16:18 NKJV). The quality of the art must always be excellent if it is to be effective, owned, and taken as legitimate by those who are engaged by it. Second, David possessed other personal characteristics that allowed for an appropriate context for the healing through music: he was a man of valor and courage and was prudent, discrete, and handsome. In other terms, he possessed the qualities of any good therapist—he was confident in his craft, had strength of person, and was sure of himself, yet was able to provide a conflict-free, noncompetitive, safe space for the other. Third, and the strongest statement made about David, God's spirit was upon him. That is, David was able to love Saul without motive and, in David's low-profile position as the king's harpist and armor bearer, to humbly observe and learn from the king (v. 21). Saul, a miserable and depressed person because of feelings of rejection, inner guilt, and failed attempts to deflect blame for his disobedience (sin), was able to feel and express love as a result of David's spirit. Following the description of Saul finding favor with the agape artist David and the development of this relationship, we read, "And so it was, whenever the [distressing] spirit from God was upon Saul, that David would take a harp and play it with his hand. Then Saul would become refreshed and well, and the distressing spirit would depart from him" (v. 23 NKJV).

The patience, care, and excellent instruction of Diego's accomplished piano teacher, the soft encouraging whispers of a loving mother, and the silent support of his church congregation of family and friends all figure significantly in his ability to attain small restorative moments. Diego's music will give him many more chances to practice an important developmental life skill—how to recover from failure. Fact is, Diego is a good piano player, one of the more advanced students attending the Sabbath Arts School at the Ayuda Community Center. His piano lessons will therefore also afford him opportunities to succeed. His arts involvement serves for him, as for many others in mounting anecdotal literature regarding the impact of the arts, as a significant vehicle for emotional and psychological progress.

Transforming Art

Do the arts play a unique role in human development—in healing the wounds of life? Or can other vehicles be used in their place? Are the visual arts used in child therapy for particular reasons?[4]

One of the Temptations' hit songs of the seventies, "I Wish It Would Rain," was played in University of Pennsylvania dormitory rooms of African-American students many a night, not just because of its popularity but because of its ability to reflect and express the lovesick, heartbroken spirits of those going through the usual young adult dating woes. The music not only reflected their internal mood and state but it also provided an outlet and an expression that was itself indulgent and healing. The song was a signal to friends of one's state and brought empathetic and supportive responses. Playing music to fit our moods is a common practice and is a good self-healing technique that encourages catharsis and expression of life's hurts and pains without aggravating complaints or unhealthy repressions.

Music and the other arts tap memories along with the feelings and emotions that are connected to them, raising them to the conscious surface, where we can work with them if necessary. A recent ad in an AARP magazine (we are telling our age here) was offering "A Goldmine of 45 Musical Memories"—a set of songs inspired by the war years of World War II and thought to be the music that helped mend broken hearts, songs that touched peoples' deepest feelings about the life experiences of that era.

Annette Foglino titled an article she wrote for *Spa Finder* magazine "Everyone from Rock Stars to Spa Directors Is Recognizing . . . the Healing Power of Music."[5] The article features a story about Mickey Hart, former drummer for the Grateful Dead, and his playing and singing with Alzheimer's patients at a New York City health center after having observed the effect his drum playing had on his grandmother—she had spoken his name for the first time in almost a year. The benefits of music have been instinctively known and used for millennia by Native American and African drummers, Sufis, and Tibetan monks to achieve harmony, spiritual enlightenment, and physical well-being. Music has been used for decades by dentists, elevator maintenance people, and now spa directors and the most conservative of oncologists. Scientific research regarding the physical and emotional benefits of engaging with music is now plentiful:

- Listening to music can lower blood pressure by as much as 10 points.
- Stroke victims who exercise to music are more likely to experience improved coordination.
- Surgery patients who listen to comforting music feel less pain and recover more quickly than those who don't.

- Music can reduce stress hormones and raise levels of disease-fighting immune cells.
- Music counteracts the growing confusion associated with neurological disorders in ways that other treatments cannot.[6]

Dr. Oliver Saks, author of *Awakenings* (the novel and well-known movie), "has observed patients with Parkinson's disease 'who can't talk but can sing, can't walk but can dance.'"[7]

The Music Institute of Chicago has programs to serve the elderly based on the premise that involvement in learning and making music helps maintain both physical and mental health. A report on the outcomes of these programs goes on to say that playing a musical instrument (and wind instruments in particular, we imagine) is a gentle form of aerobic exercise and can help reduce stress. Nathan and Vivian being trumpet and flute players respectively, can attest to the need for continued practice if one is to maintain lung, breathing, and wind agility, an increasingly difficult task as one ages. The institute's programs are also based on "findings of neurobiologists that treating the brain to new experiences and stimuli contributes to keeping the mind agile; thus adults who preserve and enhance their mental functions can cushion the brain against early symptoms of aging. Music also provides a way of experiencing life: playing music keeps people in touch with their feelings, daily practice keeps them active in the present, and striving for new goals attaches them to the future. Group music making provides important social interaction, contributing to a sense of connection. [Integrated arts programs] strengthen speech, self-image, communication, problem-solving, and socialization skills . . . and reduce physical dysfunction."[8]

Researchers tell us that one of the ways music works within our minds and bodies is by producing alpha and theta brain waves. Drumming sounds are often quite effective at producing theta waves, which are associated with trancelike states similar to the stage just prior to sleep. Many types of music produce alpha waves, which are linked with deep relaxation states. Relaxing music (that which one finds comforting) has also been found to slow down the nervous system and induce muscle relaxation.

So the next time you are faced with anxiety from within or without, stress or fear, depression or irritation, sing (aloud or silently in your head—it doesn't matter) and be grateful for that last melody you heard that keeps ringing in your head. It could be providing good "sound" medicine.

While the Greek philosopher and mathematician Pythagoras is considered by some to be the spiritual godfather of sound medicine, God, David, and God's other ancient agape artists knew of the healing power of the arts when in the hands of people who love.

Our discussion has focused on music and its beneficial effects on health and well-being. But many other art forms also bring significant healing power. Visual arts and other arts have been effective with victims of the September 11 tragedy. The Villiage of Arts and Humanities in Philadelphia, through their Conquering Cancer Creatively program, uses life-size puppets to educate seniors about cancer screening. Working in partnership with the city's Department of Public Health and the Temple University School of Nursing, the program also employs photography, silk screening, rap, and painting to teach people about nutrition, exercise, HIV/AIDS, heart disease, diabetes, and so on.

Because the nature of the visual arts often make them a more accessible art form, we will focus on the visual arts as we now turn to discuss the impact of the arts on personal and social development.

Arts and Relationships

The power of any creative or expressive art lies in its ability to assist in extending the inner person toward external communication and toward connection. Vivian has often noticed that when she is singing, "Jesus, you're the center of my joy," she is more moved and engaged in relationship (to God, in this case) than when she is just listening to someone else sing it. She is involved in not only the words or message being recited but the whole kinesthetic experience of feeling the instrument (the body) fill with air, which is then forced out and released (along with any tension) over vocal chords that create a full, round sound of passion. Involvement in creating art is more powerful than being a mere spectator of art.

Joint art—within school or therapeutic contexts, one-on-one, or in groups—requires human connection. Visual art in human and community development is art whose meaning is shared and explained; it is not art that is just exhibited. Jürgen Moltmann's theology of play, discussed earlier, is especially relevant to these functional uses of the arts. No judgment is made regarding the value or the quality of the art piece, because the emphasis is on its connection to and between the people involved.

Janelle's use of improvisation techniques with a single child or with a group of children illustrates this point. She explains, "I'm not so concerned about how good the improvisation is as I am about how well the students can attend to and coordinate their 'creations' with each other. Improvisation teaches patience, self-control, making room for and attending to others. The 'call-and-response' variety of improvisation using drums, piano, or voice mimics conversation and requires that the second person wait until the first person has completed their phrase before starting. They are also encouraged to attend and listen to the creations in order to play something in sync with the rest."

MAXINE

Maxine Hull is an art therapist in her sixties who has been practicing in Atlanta for ten years. We interviewed Maxine and toured her home-based art therapy studios. Using a number of art pieces produced by her clients, she received with us the process and outcomes of therapy sessions. As well, she shared with us the foundational principles of her art therapy practice, which are consistent with the power of the visual arts illustrated in the preceding case studies. We describe these processes and principles here as a summary of the relationship building that is necessary in the healing process using the visual arts. Digital images of the drawings mentioned here can be viewed at www.urbanprophets.org.[9]

The soul and what it feels and needs is initially and most easily expressed through images (including form and symbols). The body never lies, Max believes. So we must listen to the body. Doing so is how we make art. "What does your body feel like it wants to do?" is often the opening question Max asks her clients at the beginning of a session. Stand up at the Sheetrock-covered board for more freedom of body movement? Or remain seated at the table, which has a more limited range of body expression? What textures and mediums does the body want to work from today? The strong but pliable wire or the smoothness of silk ribbon? The messiness of finger paints? The texture of fabric? Paint, chalk, collage, styrofoam, clay, paper, felt, string, wood?

Maxine watches the construction of the art. All of the information for the client's healing is in the piece, including (most importantly) how the piece was constructed. Watching Client 2 build the strips of paper in a path leading directly to the therapist or, as in the client's preceding piece, watching her construct an overlay of several strips is the only way to gain insight into the client's dynamics. While Maxine might interpret pieces of art that a client brings in, the most therapeutically productive pieces are those made "in relationship" with the therapist. Unlike verbal therapies that can use only words and perhaps touch, Max can join in the work when she senses the client needs support, by sharing the piece of paper and drawing with the client. Maxine drew the foundation (brown at bottom) and then some lightness (yellow) at the top. The client scribbled right over the yellow and didn't notice the foundation extending toward her. This was a ripe subject for Maxine to discuss with the client.

A person can gain perspective on a piece of work by hanging it up on the Sheetrock and standing back from it—the self externalized. (Max always brings the client back to the art piece and what it is saying and telling us—"Remember," she says, "all that we need to know is in the work.") It is more difficult to get distance and perspective from our situation and emotion. We don't always want to know all there is to know about ourselves, particularly if we fear negative sides or shadow sides that if externalized become evil and dangerous. The art allows this externalization in better ways. Max does not overanalyze or allow too much free association that leads away from the piece of work. She engages the client in what is there—what has been produced—and what it tells us.

Unlike our cognitive and verbal functions, which are controlled by our left brain, images are uncensored, and lots of subconscious, nonconscious, or unintentional material sneaks through. Much of our internal life is held in images (dreams, for instance) as opposed to language.

The art or agape therapist is an organizing force. Healing comes in the relationship that allows Client 2 to construct a piece of art that moves toward the therapist. The client was in effect moving toward Maxine in an effort to gain the support and structure usually given by parents, who, like agape artists, can bring organization out of chaos. The client hadn't noticed this movement until Max pointed it out. The orange triangles the client had used to stop or block green paper paths in a previous creation were dissolving.

The therapist's (and agape artist's) job is to act as midwife in bringing about new birth in the client by examining and exploring the artwork as a door to the client's internal world.

The psyche often moves ahead of our conscious knowledge of self. So clients often feel they are not making progress and get discouraged. Looking back over the artwork of past sessions provides vivid and tangible proof of change.

Transformation and encouragement come when we realize we can change. Hope is knowing you have self-control and can change what you don't like. If we can imagine the change, we can do it.

The therapist has to be aware of materials and their properties and what the use of each material will evoke from the body. The task then becomes to encourage the client to move beyond using the same media over and over.

While Maxine is not a Christian, she draws on her Jewish heritage and is concerned for the spiritual well-being of her clients. Similarly, the following examples of reports and research from a variety of arts programs, though not "faith-based" or Christian programs, are part of the good works of common grace that are moving people toward and into the NU JERUZ.

Art and Transformation

The Gallery 37 project in Chicago offers job training in the arts, opportunities for arts-related employment, and mentoring relationships with professional artists. This federal youth employment/apprenticeship program sponsors year-round programs in partnership with city offices, the mayor's Office of Workforce Development, public schools, city colleges, and the city's leading arts and cultural organizations. Listed as a 1997 Top Ten Innovation in American Government by the Ford Foundation and Harvard University's Kennedy School of Government, the program is designed mainly to boost job skills and work habits in growing arts career fields such as graphic design and video production. Through its downtown, neighborhood, and schools programs, the project employs approximately twenty-six hundred youth a year and creates work for one hundred professional artists.

While the program is not faith integrated, some of its students have strong ties to religious institutions. One of Gallery 37's former students, a young man who in 2001 was a BFA candidate, returned to see his former teachers a day before the tenth anniversary celebration of the program. Rachel Webster, Gallery 37's public relations coordinator, said about the student, "He is a pretty shy boy, quite religious, from a pretty dangerous neighborhood. His church had sold candy, taffy, and apples to raise money to send him on a Gallery 37 trip to study art and art history in Paris; he had graduated from our programs and started college. He wanted to express how our programs had affected his life, so that day, wearing a three-piece suit, he came into the summer tent carrying several large three-foot-by-three-foot pieces of wood under his arms and on his back. Put together, they formed a life-sized self-portrait of his crucifixion. 'My old life died here,' he told them. 'As I sat in church so many Sundays and watched my cousins disappear to violence and jail and dead-end jobs, art resurrected me as a new person. It's frightening, too, in a way, but that is who I am now.'"[10]

The outcomes reported by programs like Gallery 37 include increased self-discipline and employability and improved collaboration and communication skills. A similar program is TeenStreet Theater, a gang-prevention and jobs program of Chicago's FreeStreet Theater. TeenStreet, whose major goal is discovery of self through the arts, claims the following outcomes: markedly improved academic performance; commitment and an increased desire to pursue advanced studies in related arts disciplines; increased awareness of the complexity of issues impacting their lives and a new sense of empowerment to do something about them; significantly improved social interaction skills, problem-solving abilities, leadership qualities, and self-discipline; and employment for performances and rehearsals, leading to increased self-esteem and sense of responsibility.[11]

The visual arts are a popular medium for working with senior citizens and populations with disabilities. While GRACE (Grass Roots Art for Community Efforts, in Vermont) targets a rural population, they too have a goal of transformation through art. Aimed at seniors, their visual arts program minimizes the boundaries between the professional artist and the nonartist senior citizen, believing that "all people, of whatever age, physical capacity, or education have creative potential. . . . If one can't be cured of physical limitation, one can learn to transcend them. The arts provide a vehicle through which to learn this, consciously or unconsciously."[12] The outcomes of GRACE's visual arts (painting and drawing) work with elderly and special populations include overcoming isolation, expression of feelings associated with trauma and loss, and provision of an alternative to speech for communication.

Elders Share the Arts (ESTA) in Brooklyn has as its core process the Living History Theater, which speaks directly to seniors' needs to be heard, to have fun, and to be taken seriously. ESTA's techniques apply the research and writings of Eric Erikson (stages of the life cycle) and Robert Butler (work on life review) and employ some of the theater exercises of Augusto Boal. The Music Institute of Chicago, mentioned earlier, also uses drama to help seniors deal with life changes, loss of spouse, and feelings of isolation.

Arts and Prisons

The prophet Isaiah long ago proclaimed "freedom for the captives and release from darkness for the prisoners" (Isa. 61:1). Jesus talks of a final judgment and the blessings that await those to whom he can declare, "I was in prison and you came to visit me" (Matt. 25:36). According to many accounts, we are building more prisons in our country than educational institutions. As tough as we should be on crime, as terrible the acts of violence against society, Christians are called to minister to the "least of these." There is a role for the agape arts here as well, in the working out of transformation.

From the available research, England and Canada appear to be taking the lead in institutional and governmental commitment to the arts in prisons. The debate about arts in criminal justice is somewhat polarized. Some consider the arts too "soft" for prisoners, while others think the functional use of art negates its aesthetic value. But there is no question of value of the arts in delivering criminal justice agendas and aims while also maintaining the high quality of the art. In fact, the latter (excellence in the art technique) is found to be a critical requirement for realizing the former. Studies undertaken in the late seventies and eighties, supported by similar results in more recent studies, indicate that participation in the arts benefits not only the prisoner but also the prison staff.

An extremely wide variety of arts strategies are being used in prisons. A few examples (including StoryBook Dad, Bruce Wall's London Shakespeare Workout project, music and band programs, Dance United, and Clean Break Theater Company)[13] are producing the following outcomes, some with beginning empirical evidence, but most with strong case study and qualitative data. Through arts, the incarcerated

- Make more constructive use of time, with energy channeled in positive ways
- Express themselves effectively and in an acceptable manner
- Develop self-awareness and understanding and achieve a sense of self-worth

- Work collaboratively and respect the work of others
- Develop real skills in which they can take pride (reading, writing, and mathematics literacy; arts skills) and which may benefit them and others long term
- Find a route back into education if they have poor literacy skills
- Come more deeply in touch with themselves and their behaviors (including anger and violence, their roots, and the impact of their criminal behavior on others, as well as the development of alternative responses), especially when using the art therapies
- Maintain and strengthen links with family and friends
- Make choices and take on responsibility
- Find a way into employment
- Relate more effectively to prison staff and others through a shared interest
- Decrease in repeat offenses[14]

Arts programs are attributed with having reduced infractions of prison rules by 75–81 percent; are reducing recidivism (return to prison within two years) to 31 percent, compared to 58 percent for all parolees; and are leading to a 20 percent reduction in the propensity to violent and/or hostile feelings and expressions.[15] Many prisoners attribute the positive results of their involvement with the arts to having the support of an arts mentor and professional.

The positive responses of prison staff focused on slightly different outcomes, especially on outcomes related to security and control. From their perspective, arts programs for the incarcerated

- Increases positive relationships between prisoners and staff
- Makes prison run more smoothly and/or efficiently
- Improves the environment
- Releases frustration
- Controls aggression
- "Softens" hard character
- Has a calming effect
- Provides constructive use of time[16]

Professor Roger Graef is a filmmaker and criminologist who writes of the value of the arts in prisons. He believes art is an appropriate medium for working with prisoners in that "the motivations that drive artists are often similar: anger, frustration, and intense longing to make an impact, the need to be noticed, and demand for attention." Violence, he says, is a form of expression, of communication. "Art can encompass those feelings in a way that does not harm other people but transforms the experience of both the giver and the receiver and enhances their lives instead of damaging them."[17] While this may not be the primary motivation for agape artists working with others, the statement may nevertheless have some validity.

Some years ago Graef commissioned a film on art in prisons. He relates the story of a man he met during the project, a former carpenter who became a serial killer. The man had not spoken for fourteen years. Somehow he had ended up in an art class and discovered that he could draw. His work was not violent. Instead, he made rather good likenesses of his fellow inmates. They asked him if they could have the drawings to send to their wives and partners as Christmas presents. He agreed and was soon responding to more and more requests. He began to speak and in due course began taking part in prison activities in a constructive way. This was a gain for him, for the prison, and ultimately, for society.

This is only one such story. Graef also reports that theater in prisons, such as the Clean Break program, "gives voice to anguish, pain and confusion that each inmate felt was only their own private hell. . . . On themes like the awkwardness of prison visits, and the whole predicament of sustaining and rebuilding links with one's partners and families, such theater is invaluable. The drama also speaks to prisoners' own denial and inability to take responsibility for their actions. There is no therapy or counseling to speak of in prisons. . . . Theatre, music and art are directly therapeutic as well as educational in all senses of that word."[18]

An Anchor in Their Lives

Scott Parker is the founder and executive director of Starfish Studios, located in the Howard community north of Chicago, a ministry that makes movies with kids in the inner city. From the moment of finding his *eschaton* in college, Scott has wanted to work with the poor and reach fellow artists who are not Christians to give them work and bring them into the NU JERUZ.[19] His goal is to do feature films with kids of emerging talent.

Wanting to use his gifts more to serve than to preach and wanting to meet the needs of the community, Scott started "the film thing" five years ago as part of the after-school program at the Starfish Learning Center. Scott then wrote a feature film that the center wanted to produce in the neighborhood and use to raise money. Starfish Studios, Scott's production company, was started eighteen months ago in order to accomplish that goal, and he has been living cross-culturally and incarnationally in the low-income area of Chicago where the studio is located.

His apartment was open to the homeless (who slept on his couch many nights), and he ministered to the youth on the streets. Eventually, he developed a vision to work with young children through his new, mostly one-person, production company.

Since we met Scott, he has been keeping a journal of vignettes about the reactions and changes taking place within the students he is working with. Scott takes a straightforward, reflective, storytelling approach and sends us periodic updates, which not only tell us of his work but serve as impact documentation of his work. Scott's journal says much about him, his call, his ministry, and his impact. In the following excerpt Scott shares how the vision for his ministry changed from working primarily with the teens of the street to working with the children of his neighborhood. Having lived in the neighborhood for ten years, he is recommitting himself to raise up children who will become leaders in the community. It will be interesting for us to talk with him in future years and learn how his ministry has impacted the lives of these children.

Manassehs and Josiahs. When we first came, we were going after the youth. Calling them to repentance. There's a handful out there now. Living a somewhat Christian life. But my eye is on the next generation. The little Josiahs. The majority of my movie class students are in the third and fourth grade. God sees them as kings. D. L. Moody once said that a child was worth two adults. He has twice a lifetime to serve the Lord.

I think of the four kids I worked with in this last year's movie project. I think of Tim, who, because he told me he wasn't going to get in trouble at school, did a Jesus on a friend that had started to bully him. "You want to hit me, go ahead." He presents the kid his chin and puts his hands behind his back. "I'm not going to fight you, but if you want to hit me go ahead." The two of them are friends now.

I think of another kid who I drop off on a regular basis. I have to wait because he doesn't always know if his mom is going to be home. I remember him talking about Starfish, the after-school program he goes to: "It was Jerry really got me thinking about God and stuff. I really changed since I been there."

I think of the boy sharing that his mother had died in a car accident. I think of the girl who tells the group of kids who are there when he shares it, "That just stays between us. No one else gets to know about this." Because she didn't want the boy to get teased by anyone else.

I see the two sisters dancing with the two Dutch girls, learning new moves that aren't dirty. Just fun. I think about the Dutch girls explaining the meaning of the song "Not Guilty" to the oldest one. We're not guilty because of the blood of Jesus.

I think the tide is turning north of Howard. There's a Josiah generation about to be birthed. How did Josiah learn about the Lord? He didn't learn it from his dad. Someone must have taught him. His mother is mentioned very specifically right alongside of him. I could handle that. That'd be crown enough for me. To be one of the people who stood by this next generation. Who taught them the word of the Lord. It is a glorious thing God has given us to do. I appreciate all the prayers and all the support.[20]

This kind of reporting is, in the long run, an excellent way to document faith development through actions, as opposed to biblical knowledge. For example, in this report we can see indicators of changed spiritual lives: self-control, concern for the feelings of others, an awareness of God, and the awareness of appropriate behavior in dance.

Speaking Unconscious Blessings

Isaac said, "I am now an old man and don't know the day of my death. Now then, get your weapons—your quiver and bow—and go out to the open country to hunt some wild game for me. Prepare me the kind of tasty food I like and bring it to me to eat, so that I may give you my blessing before I die."

Genesis 27:2–4

Donna Barber has a simple explanation for why she does what she does: "I love God." She repeats her belief that God has a heart for the poor and that being a follower of Christ means tending to the needs of the "least of these." But the reason Donna lives a meager (though rich and fulfilling) life is also because she believes that what parents unconsciously give their kids is the blessing of speaking their future—affirming them and moving them toward that future.[21] Donna says that like Esau, Isaac's eldest son, many kids don't have anyone to speak that blessing into their lives. "I want to do that for them. Each child was created with a purpose. They just don't know what it is yet. I help them to find it out."[22]

Donna is convinced that the traditional church is off track because it is too much into itself. God is building his kingdom on earth, and Donna wants to raise up kids who are actively involved in building that kingdom in line with God's purpose for each of their lives; and to her, that means that the church has to go to them.

She doesn't use traditional evangelistic methods to accomplish her grooming of little kingdom architects and masons. She may not ever mention Jesus; she may never give an altar call. Donna Barber's evangelistic method is to share Christ by loving and accepting children unconditionally through the arts. Certainly she cares about their spiritual salvation, but she realizes that some of us are planters, others are waterers, and still others are gatherers—those who are there for the harvest, for the "increase." And you never know which one of those roles you are playing in someone's life, she says, "but only God can save souls."

Donna and her staff love the children they work with and hope for opportunities to share the reason they do what they do with the kids. When Miguel (not his real name) continues to be a troublemaker, instead of yelling at him, scolding, or criticizing him, Donna confronts him with a vision, a dream, a revelation, a blessing for his life: "Don't you know that God loves you and has something for you, and who you're pretending to be is not who you are?"

Donna explains to us, "That's the way God responds to me—unconditional acceptance, whether I behave or not. God operates at maximum love all the time, and nothing you do will change that."

So Donna attempts to operate at maximum love too, speaking blessings into kids' futures. Donna came upon Millie (not her real name) fighting with another girl in school. She'd seen Millie starting to attend the Spanish church service in the same building as her own worship service and decided to confront Millie with how to apply what she might be learning in church.

"Millie, do you think God is pleased with this behavior?" The little girl, shocked at the reminder that God is in school too, stopped fighting and went her way.

As a child Donna Barber received dance, drama, and piano lessons. She became a consummate vocalist and artist but wanted the security of a family and a home for her kids. She could not therefore see herself spending life on the road. She majored in communications and theater and was headed, she thought, to a job in TV production or public relations. It didn't turn out that way, but Donna is nevertheless still working in her field, intentionally employing the arts—dance, drama, and visual arts—as a vehicle for building character, esteem, and vision in young people. However, this came about accidentally.

In 1996 Donna, her husband, and their two children moved from Philadelphia to Decatur, Georgia, right on the Atlanta border. They joined a large church (a thousand members) and quickly learned that most of the people were "commuters." It was not a community-based church as they had hoped, and not surprising to them, most of the community didn't even know the church was there. It was, however, a surprise to the members, who, in what Donna terms their arrogance, couldn't imagine the community residents not knowing them.

Propelled by a strong commitment to incarnational service, Donna and her family began to plant what they hoped would be a true community church in the East Lake neighborhood of Atlanta, but not in the usual way. It would be four years before the first worship service ever took place. Worship services were established after all of the during-the-week programs. Their "church" consisted of summer camps, teen Bible study, Kid's Club, and community dinners held at the Barbers' house for the many homeless people in the community who were displaced by the tide of gentrification. Through these activities Donna and her husband saw needs and began responding. They believe that what goes on in between Sundays is the real work of the church. The Atlanta Youth Academy, a Christian grade school, grew out of their efforts and is still thriving. It was at the academy that Donna began to take note of the power of the arts to impact people. Because the academy served mostly children with working parents, an after-school program was needed. Donna started a "labs" program that brought scientists and architects to the students to share what they loved about their work. The goal was to motivate the children toward their future—more of speaking the blessing. Donna also added dance and mime sessions to the labs. The students' interest in the arts sessions was immediately obvious.

Donna's role models for using the arts were the teachers, parents, and staff she met while working at another Christian school, Cornerstone Christian Academy, founded by Tony Campolo in west Philadelphia. Having moved to west Philadelphia just as her youngest child was ready for school, Donna enrolled her daughter at Cornerstone. The school was just around the corner and was a neighborhood alternative to secular, public school. The Barbers were making very little money at the time, so in order to afford the tuition, Donna took a teaching job at the school. It was their chapel tradition that convinced her. She'd never seen a school care about and love her child the way this school did. These people were different. To Donna, these people were urban "missionaries," with the city as their mission field rather than a foreign country. Many of them had left lucrative professions to work at Cornerstone. The Friday chapel service was where faculty, staff, students, and parents came together to sing, pray, praise, and give thanks in celebration. The warmth of these services gave the students a sense of security and acceptance, and they saw the school as "their church." The year-end chapel service incorporated dance, drama, and music. It was more powerful than any motivational speech or sermon, and Donna witnessed its impact across all age groups.

So when the year-end assembly for the Atlanta Youth Academy rolled around, Donna intuitively knew to include performances by the kids from the after-school arts labs.

"There were people hugging and crying," Donna observed, "and after the performances, parents vocalized how they couldn't believe it was their kid."

Not only had the children's involvement in the arts created new esteem, behaviors, and confidence for the students, but it garnered them new parental respect. Parents had new respect, new imaginations, new images of their children. Transformation. That kind of thing leads to new hope as well.

Donna had replicated at the Atlanta Youth Academy what had been most meaningful to her and her child at Cornerstone. And now, in 2002, having moved to another, more needy section of Atlanta a year ago—thanks to a benefactor concerned about the kids in that community and to Bob Lupton's interest in revitalizing that community—Donna is being more intentional than ever in building an after-school program with a deliberate arts emphasis.

South Atlanta was supposed to be one of the worst sections of this progressive city, but as we approached, it looked nothing like the 'hoods we were used to. The houses were old and worn, mere ghosts of grander days when the area was a thriving college town. But the grass was plentiful and green, and the houses had yards and space around them—not like the row house hyperghettos in Philadelphia. It felt like a small, rural country town in the South. South Atlanta is home to many struggling families and a great number of kids living in poverty and being raised by grandparents. It has the worst high school in the state of Georgia, and the prostitution problem with young girls is growing. There is not a lot of beauty here.

We climbed the big concrete steps leading to the front porch of Community Fellowships—Donna's house. We should not have been surprised. After all, their first ministry had begun this same way, in their home. Donna had warned us that she would be rushing around packing and preparing for a trip to the West Coast to be with a friend who has just lost a loved one. She took a few minutes to fix up her hair a bit for the camera and to give the kids further instructions. She settled in to talk with us about her passion: the arts-based after-school program at John Hope Elementary School, which was serving as the educational home for the primarily Latino and Spanish-speaking children who were being bused in because their school in another section of Atlanta was being rehabilitated. These children were in their first year of a dance program. Donna had brought in Movin' in the Spirit, a faith-integrated, community-based dance organization, to deliver the dance program at John Hope. Using music appropriate to the Latino culture and tying activities to Latino history, the program was effective—but only after a cross-cultural discovery that gender separation was important to especially the boys' ability to participate. The program also includes visual arts and will hold its first arts day camps this summer (2002). Donna had hoped to include creative writing to support language arts improvement, but the language barrier (most students and families speak only Spanish) was a formidable barrier during this first year.

"So why the arts?" we asked.

"God gave us the arts to bring beauty into our lives," Donna replied. "There is not a lot of beauty in some of these kids' lives. God gave us arts to just make us feel good about ourselves and to discover things about ourselves that we never knew."

One of the keys to the program's success in helping students feel good about themselves is that Donna and the program teachers push hard and expect a lot. They also give a lot of praise in return for accomplishment. The kids know that what they've produced is quality.

"This sense of accomplishment crosses over into the classroom. Now they have the confidence to do math, as well as to dance." Donna goes on to explain a critical point: "We believe in holistic approaches—working with the whole child. The arts feed the spirit of the child."

Educators have known for the last twenty years that the affective dimensions of a learning situation are very important to children's learning. The degree to which learning takes place is mediated by our feelings related to the learning. The image we have of ourselves as learners is established early in the education process, but it is alterable according to our subsequent experiences with learning. Arts experiences can therefore be powerful learner-image enhancers.

Donna's arts program, just like the after-school labs she began in East Lake, plans activities that take students out to events to begin *en vivo* arts etiquette and social decorum. It also brings artists to the school.

"We help," Donna says, "by exposing them to as many people and as many choices as possible." Donna feels it's a matter of social justice. But rather than taking on primarily an advocacy role (as many other programs do—and should), Donna's goal is to give people the choices and skills to claim justice for themselves. She emphasizes this with a story of two boys who wanted to be involved with the other kids in a drama program, but everyone, including them, knew that they were terrible at acting. Wanting to affirm and encourage them honestly, Donna suggested involvement in the technical end of the drama production. The boys became very good at their task and subsequently pursued it as a career—a career they probably would never have considered otherwise.

Donna and others involved with Community Fellowships do advocate for a child by going to his or her school and speaking to the teachers. But in doing so, Donna's real hope is to have an impact on the school. "I want to influence the teachers in that school. I want to influence the administration of that school." She also wants to influence the system and policies that work against student achievement of success.

Evaluating the impact of the after-school program is becoming a more formal undertaking as its first year nears a close. At midyear each teacher at John Hope was asked to fill out a questionnaire on the changes they had observed in each child involved in the program, including observations about behavior, academics, and self-esteem. (They should probably get data on all children, involved or not, for a control group.) The midyear evaluation indicated favorable results. "The kids are still struggling academically, but the esteem issues are promising," Donna reports.

Donna's story illustrates the critical characteristics of arts-based programs that can aid in spiritual development. Successful programs do so by:

- Providing unconditional acceptance and love whether the child is good or bad
- Presenting God's expectations as the guide for kids' everyday behavior
- Empowering children with the choices and skills to claim justice for themselves
- Revealing God's purpose for the children's lives

- Influencing parents, teachers, administrators, and judges to view kids the way God views them
- Aiming to increase respect for all—kids and parents

Summary

Throughout this chapter we have seen that art, when used in loving relationships with others, helps to bring about personal transformation and in turn moves us toward social transformation. Research is scant in this area, and it would be difficult to say that the agape arts in human development provide a panacea for the world's problems. But the important thing for the many gifted artists who have yet to find their *eschaton* in bringing about the NU JERUZ is that there are places in the deepest parts of our society that have been untouched because of our failure to deal with the creative aspects of people's lives.

We as Christians must recognize that there is much to learn from those who do not call themselves Christians but who have the gifting and desire to do good in the world. To dismiss their work because they are not in the "fold" is to dismiss the common grace of God and his ability to use those outside our boundaries to accomplish his work in the world. We must also recognize that there are many people of the Christian faith already working in these fields who, for whatever reason, remain the quiet ones of God.

Principles

From this chapter we draw several principles for using the arts in human development and for building relationships of transformation:

1. The arts help to initiate and establish relationships.
2. Artists who are effective in bringing about transformation in the lives of others develop relationships in which their roles extend beyond the artist role.
3. The arts are effective in the spiritual, emotional, and psychological development of the person and help to externalize inner realities. They are a catalyst in releasing people from inner captivity.
4. God is at work in the world through the arts and through artists who may not call themselves Christians but who have been gifted for compassionate service to the "least of these."
5. There are many places of service for artists who have yet to find their *eschaton* in the NU JERUZ.

11

Arts as Education

In this chapter we will look at the arts as a powerful tool for teaching and learning. Traditionally, the church has used the arts in children's Bible schools, and hymns have been used to teach doctrine and theology. Some Christians in public education have taken the rhythm and rhyme of gospel music and have adapted it to teach students difficult subjects such as geometry, algebra, and biology. When test scores remain such an important, albeit debated, method of entrance to academic success, the arts provide an effective method of improving academic performance, through the holistic transformation of children and youth.

As you read this chapter, consider the following questions:

1. What characterizes a biblical model of education? How does this model support the use of the arts in teaching?
2. What are some of the various learning styles? What effect do they have in the learning process, and how are they connected to the arts?
3. What barriers might traditional teachers and educational systems face when introducing the arts in education?
4. What are the varying impacts on students and teachers when the arts are used to teach?

Therefore you shall lay up these words of mine in your heart and in your soul, and bind them as a sign on your hand, and they shall be as frontlets between your eyes. You shall teach them to your children, speaking of them when you sit in your house, when you walk by the way, when you lie down, and when you rise up. And you shall write them on the doorposts of your house and on your gates, that your days and the days of your children may be multiplied in the land of which the LORD swore to your fathers to give them, like the days of the heaven above the earth.

Deuteronomy 11:18–21 NKJV

And Moses said to the children of Israel, "See, the LORD has called by name Bezalel . . . and has filled him with the Spirit of God, in wisdom and understanding, in knowledge and all manner of workmanship, to design artistic works. . . . And he has put in his heart the ability to teach."

Exodus 35:30–34 NKJV

The Arts, Creativity, and Learning

Like asset-based community development (discussed in chapter 8), education over the last several decades has moved from a deficit-model of "remediation" for inner-city youth and underprepared college students to one emphasizing developmental, strengths-based frameworks. These strategies utilize curriculum, policies, lessons, and activities that start from the capacities, skills, and assets of these students. Recently, we were discussing the growing writing needs of our graduate students at Eastern University. We recognized the connection between writing and thinking and were considering one of the most recent mantras on the subject: "Students who don't write well don't think well." Such thinking has led some educators to attempt to improve the way students write by improving the way they think. But our own experiences with students in the classroom and in evaluation settings caused us to take pause.

Some of our students who write poorly think just fine, and that thinking is evident in their oral communication. This is particularly true for students from people groups whose cultural cognitive styles emphasize oral, aural, and relational methods for communicating and learning. Deficit models of teaching writing might begin with grammatical rules and linear processes, but strengths-based and developmental models might begin by instructing students to write as if they were conversing about their ideas on a particular topic, followed by discussion and revision of their thoughts, audience, tone, message, and so on, which is again followed by more conversational writing and further revision. Teaching rules of form and punctuation might come much later in the process.

Biblical models of education (which are almost always couched in terms of acquiring wisdom and truth) are akin to the education styles mentioned in the Scripture passages above. The first passage tells us that education was not bound to a particular time and place but was integrated with the rest of daily life. Education was mostly oral, therefore highly relational, and comprised a significant part of family life. The second passage, which recognizes artistic intelligence or "wisdom," connects artistic skill with teaching and with faith. The craft of teaching has been recognized as an art form in many ways. Other relevant biblical concepts of education include the idea that the goal of education is to prepare one to engage in good works (2 Tim. 3:16–17; James 3:17), that education should be practical in application, and that wisdom involves gaining knowledge of one's purpose—God's will and dream for one's life (Col. 1:9–10). It is likely that artisans were engaged in teaching their craft through apprenticeship, and thus, they were likely to teach apprentices many other things through their shared art.

The creative process for most students is a natural one, as is our need to experience joy and laughter and to have our souls touched. Amy Scheer believes that "children who do not laugh become disillusioned old men and women; those whose hearts are not touched become men and women with hearts of stone."[1] The arts not only meet these natural yearnings but also provide vehicles for learning that tap the creative and artistic strengths present in all of us. For example, the annual youth retreats of the Star of Hope Baptist Church (which we will describe below) are geared toward learning about God and the application of faith in our lives but also incorporate the arts to build a variety of writing and communication skills in the process.

This year (2002) at the youth retreat, students will be required to write scripts about events in their lives that have taught them a lesson. The writing process will follow a strengths-based format that begins with an oral telling of the story, followed by critical thinking and analysis of the events in the story. Students will need to describe the event well enough for a reenactment, build some depth into the characters, and write conversation in a sequence that conveys meaning. The intermittent practice of scenes and rewriting based on the "effectiveness" of their communication of ideas gives opportunity for more substantive but project-based learning regarding the rules of writing and communicating.

Courtrooms and Cuffs

The Ballad of Amos

Composed and written by the Star of Hope retreat kids
October 2001

Amos, the Prophet, mouthpiece from God
Came from Tekoa; Tiller of the Sod
God called him North to spread the news
"Come seek the Lord and you shall live"

Stop selling slaves for clothes and shoes
Don't worship idols you sinful Jews
Do good not evil or you will burn
"Come seek the Lord and you shall live"

Stop taking bribes you evil tribe
Sitting in your mansions so satisfied
While the poor still cry and babies die
"Come seek the Lord and you shall live"

Do not seek Bethel. Go to God's arms
Stop killing women for land and farms
He will restore you Israel
"Come seek the Lord and you shall live"

God sent a vision of a ball of fire
To burn the earth due to God's ire
But Amos prayed, "Forgive them Lord"
"Come seek the Lord and you shall live"

God kept the faithful and burned the rest
He fried them up like a chicken breast
Hot, hot, hot, hot. Hot, hot, hot, hot
"Come seek the Lord and you shall live"

God will rebuild His fallen kingdom
Build up the ruins, set them up again
But it's not over 'cause sin still lives
It happens over and over again
It happens over and over again
It happens over and over again

Several years ago Vivian administered a Bible "achievement test" to the youth in her Sunday school class. The results were disappointing and raised concern that even longtime Sunday school students were not learning or retaining what they had learned about basic Bible characters, their stories, and the lessons those stories conveyed. This led Vivian to focus that year's annual three-day youth retreat on teaching stories from the lives of Bible characters. She felt that the teaching, however, would have to be different from the typical Sunday school classroom because that approach was obviously not working. She decided to be intentional about participatory learning, which had been used in the Star of Hope church school for more than twenty years, but only intermittently and depending on the initiative and creativity of the particular teacher. It was difficult to get teachers to try a new teaching approach, one in which they weren't doing most of the talking.

Vivian developed a retreat curriculum format that was based on intentional and planned integration of the arts to teach biblical truths, character stories, and life-application lessons. The youth would be participating in a holistic experiment that engaged all of their senses in learning. The results were exciting but not unexpected by Vivian. A 90 percent gain (based on pre/post testing) in biblical knowledge and understanding was registered by students who participated fully and consistently in the in- and out-of-class activities, as opposed to a much lower gain for students who chose to remain passive learners.

The project started with vigorous training and preparation of the staff, who were unafraid to use their creativity and imagination to become *God's Street People: The Minor Prophets,* as Vivian had titled her retreat format.[2] The staff and older teen students prepared huge paper murals depicting scenes from the lives of each of the featured Bible characters. These murals served as backdrop scenery and environmental context for the learning space. Teachers gathered other artifacts to simulate a scene that would be as historically realistic as possible. Staff members had each been assigned a Bible character to portray and had studied their characters to learn how they would behave. During the retreat they donned costumes, to be worn during the entire retreat, and behaved in a manner that would assist the students in guessing the identity of each character, although the main characters were announced in class.

On the first day of the retreat, Vivian entered the classroom as "Amos, the Prophet," a southern (Judea) farmer turned prophetic judge of the people of Israel. Other teachers portrayed Habakkuk, Micah, and Zechariah. Through observation of costumes, actions, murals, and artifacts, and through iterative questioning and dialogue, students learned of each character's demographics, occupation, family background, and so on. Having Amos as a main character lent itself handily to a courtroom drama, which commenced immediately. With the assistance of a court bailiff (one of the staff), the students were immediately thrown into roles of various communities of people neighboring Israel that had been indicted by the prophet. They were handcuffed, arrested, and charged. Other students were pressed into service as defense or prosecution attorneys. Now the real work began. The students flew to their Bibles, trying to figure out what they had been charged with, what appeals could be made, and what sentences could be meted out. They needed to prepare for the playing out of the courtroom scene.

Visual and handcraft arts sessions focused on subject-relevant artifacts and messages. Dance sessions taught additional general biblical truths. Each of the four class groups was asked to compose a song (to a common melody) about their subjects as a capstone activity that would demonstrate all that they had learned. Classes were free to choose the art format of other culminating activities, including story scrolls, cartoon boards, dramas, web site pages, documentaries, crossword puzzles, and so on. Life application of story lessons was often made using appropriate song lyrics from rap, rhythm and blues, or rock songs and from current film clips and news stories chosen by students and teachers.

Months after the retreat the students still retained a significant portion of their learning. They were still singing their "capstone" songs. "The Ballad of Amos" had helped. Why? And what are the replicable principles incorporated in this arts-based retreat format?

1. Require students to do the learning through discovery and search and research, both individually and in small groups.
2. Use arts and artifacts to create an authentic environment and learning context that reflect the time periods being studied or modern-day equivalents.
3. Organize learning around specific projects and project materials (project-based learning).
4. Allow students choices regarding the art forms used.
5. Require students to engage in creation (not just recreation).
6. Use art forms to assess learning as well as to teach.
7. Require students to teach a portion of their learning to someone else.

Music Aiding Memory

How many times as a child, or even as an adult, have you recited the alphabet song—"A-B-C-D-E-F-G"—in order to remember which letter comes after another? I do it all the time when I'm looking up something in the phone book or the dictionary as a quick way to know if I need to turn the pages forward or backward. Is S before or after R?

A ritual of our weekly Sunday school opening period is to have everyone, teachers and students alike, recite a Bible verse. Increasingly, our young students come from homes where their parents are not Christians or do not attend church or Bible study regularly and therefore do not assist their sons and daughters in learning verses or completing homework for the next class. Consequently, we have several students each week who say they don't know any Bible verses. Many of these same students, however, participate in the children's choir, where many of the songs they learn are based on Bible verses. One Sunday we insisted with one young student that he in fact did know a Bible verse. He persisted that he didn't. But when we asked him to repeat the words of the children's song (based on Phil. 4:8) they'd sung in church the week before, he recited it perfectly, beaming at the realization that he had something to offer the group.

The young people around us are always singing. It is not hard to notice that while they have great trouble learning the words to their Easter poems or to dramatic parts they were asked to learn for the Christmas play, they know every line, phrase, and nuance of their favorite rap and hip-hop songs. Why? Three reasons. First, repetition. They heard the words and songs over and over each day. Second, the rhythm, phrasing, and musical notes aided memory, even when they were not sure of the meaning of the words or phrases. And third, and perhaps most important, learning with music is aural, that is, learning comes by hearing and doing rather than by reading.

Most of us have a preferred mode of learning. When teaching, we must remember that *how* we ask students to learn cannot be separated from the tools and methods we use to deliver our lessons. Not all of us are aural learners, but when coupled with repetition and music, it is an effective mode of learning for just about all of us. It is the method of choice for teaching gifted and average students as well as those with learning disabilities or difficulties.

We took note of how our young people were learning the words to lengthy rap songs and decided to copy the technique when producing the year's Christmas play. We had given up on handing out poems and recitations for holiday Sunday school programs. Unlike in our days as youths, students were not memorizing their pieces, and more and more students were acting their parts with papers in their hands.

With the aid of a few teachers and older students, we made an audiotape of our selected Christmas musical. We read the parts into the tape and dubbed in the music from the song tape that accompanied the script. This was in contrast to our previous and mostly unsuccessful methods of teaching plays: written script, written words, and lengthy rehearsals with a choir director teaching the music. We purchased a carton of inexpensive audiotapes, borrowed the church's cassette dubbing machine, made fifty copies of the tape, and handed them out to the students with the instruction to listen to it on their Sony Walkman for two weeks.

When we later held auditions for the musical, we were stunned to find that many of the students could recite the dialogue to all the parts, and even though they didn't have all the notes quite right, they also knew the songs. Needless to say, this made the audition ten times easier and held many unanticipated advantages:

1. We quickly heard different students recite a variety of parts to determine the best character combinations.
2. The students, able to hear their peers recite parts, were also better able to understand our decision about who should play what part, without the usual jealousy and disappointment. They were also able to experience how different it was to play a particular part opposite several different people.

3. The students participated more fully in the decision making, indicating their choices without shyness. And because many of them knew more than one character's part, they served as prompters for those who forgot a line.

4. The group was less dependent on students who accepted a part but didn't show up regularly for rehearsals. This aural audiotape learning method produced natural understudies.

5. We didn't have to focus so much of the rehearsal time on parts and words, which meant that we could spend more time on interpretation and meaning, dynamics, vocal projection, and staging of musical numbers. We also had time for the students to make the language "their own" by "on-the-spot" rewriting of the script. Some of these things were aided by the fact that the students had heard us on the tape giving expression to the words.

6. We could also spend more time on interpersonal issues—the self-confidence and growth issues related to students performing in front of others.

7. Students with talent in dance and choreography had more time to work on steps and dance routines.

8. Best of all, the time from start to production was much shorter, the quality greater, and the fun more plentiful.

Key to the success of this experiment was the selection of an interesting, culturally relevant play whose music and plot would interest our students.

Our hypothesis was proven: Asking students to learn by repetitiously *hearing* the play was a quick and successful way for them to learn lengthy and complicated dialogue. Not only that, but the vehicle of drama allowed them to experience the application of biblical lessons to their lives. There is a caveat, however. Experiential learning may not always be the most effective in every situation. Choosing the right method depends on age, gender, ethnicity, content and context, as demonstrated in our next example.

Nathan, who has participated in the Star of Hope retreats, used the experiential arts method in two different contexts: one with primarily African-American and Latino teachers who were part of the Pennsylvania Association of Christian Schools and the other with primarily Anglo teachers and artists in an urban church setting. In the first context, a teacher-development workshop for the African-American and Latino teachers on using the arts to teach disciplinary subjects, the teachers laughed, moved, and made sounds for ninety minutes through two exercises. The first exercise was on teaching about the environment, and they sang (and danced) a song about a hippo to learn about the environment in Africa. When it was all over, the informal post-test (the teachers were learning about pre/post testing of discipline subjects using the arts) revealed in addition to learning a new song, they had also learned new information about the geography and language of Africa, new African terminology and their meanings, the importance of environment and ecosystems, and how African parents teach their children about safety.

In a second exercise, informal pre/post testing was also applied to learning about the human digestive system. Nathan drew from a drama exercise borrowed from master teacher Jackie Samuels, a Chicago artist and educator, who demonstrates her techniques in BI's Institute for the Church and Community Arts. The class dramatizes the human digestive system. One teacher commented that she and many of her colleagues had forgotten how much fun teaching could be and said, "I now have something to take back to my class." She and many other teachers have become rejuvenated teachers who are facilitators and coaches of the learning process—a process that allows their own creativity and gifts to come alive in the midst of rote and unimaginative curricula and stimulates their desire for lifelong learning. Learning new material in new ways allows educators to maintain empathy for the tasks of younger learners in their classrooms.

In the second context, however, our lesson on informal pre/post testing did not receive the same reception. While the primarily Anglo audience participated, they were not nearly as animated and active or as relational. (One person even commented, "I hate these kinds of things.") The context was different. In the first context, the teachers were motivated to improve their teaching, while in the second context, the group was more motivated to learn about the arts themselves. But there was another important factor. Different people and different cultures often have very different learning styles. The first group found participatory learning to be exciting, active, and relational. The linear cultural tradition of the second group calls for more discussion of the subject matter. They were not as interested in revealing or expressing their personalities as was the first group.

As we will see (in chapter 12) from the example of a children-focused church, using puppets as an educational tool or as a worship expression may work better for audiences who are used to watching television or other mediated activity. They may not be as relational. When using the experiential arts as a mode of learning, one must consider the personality, culture, and learning style of the intended audience.

Rap, Rhythm, and Rhyme

Dale's cone of experience is a well-known and standard concept taught to every education major. While Dale apparently never placed percentages on learning modes, other theorists have postulated that people remember 10 percent of what they read, 20 percent of what they hear, 30 percent of what they see, 50 percent of what they hear and see, 70 percent of what they say or

write, and 90 percent of what they say as they perform an activity. Harriett Ball
is exquisite in her ability to create fast-paced, high-energy learning that has
students constantly on their feet shouting and reciting and singing (drill), while
pointing and moving (reinforcing) and "doing" fractions, measures, geometry,
grammar, and just about anything else that can be taught.

"I don't know what you come to do . . ." Harriett begins to sing an old
familiar gospel tune. But the next line isn't "but I come to praise the Lord"; it's
the beginning of a series of call-and-response lines about coming to school to
learn. Harriet doesn't allow anyone (her students or those attending her training
sessions) to take notes. "The body is your legal cheat sheet," she continually
reminds us.

Harriett Ball is wrapping up a typical training workshop for teachers. Her
strong contralto voice belies her gospel training as she belts out her lyrics set
to a familiar Kenny Rogers tune.

> You got to know when to hold 'em,
> Know when to fold 'em.
> Know when to walk away,
> Know when to run.
> You don't mouth your anger
> While sittin' in front of children.
> 'Cause it'll come back to haunt you
> 'Fore the day is done.[3]

She is delivering the last message of the day, as she would in the classroom,
using the arts. She's spent most of the time involving the packed audience of the
2002 Black Alliance for Educational Options symposium in using rap, rhythm,
movement, singing, and rhyming to teach geography, science, language arts,
grammar, and math; but she doesn't leave without also conveying something
else about teaching: how to love students.

But it's in love, and they know this. Because one little girl came up to me. She
reached up and grabbed my arms. She said, "I never"—tears flowed—"I never
knew I could learn. Thank you."

[I] let them know that I care about you and anything that you care about.
And that's when you teach. . . . Teachers are like ministers. You do more than
what you're paid for. Longer hours. You go into your pocketbook sometimes,
you buyin' clothes, you buyin' mattresses, you buyin' alarm clocks cuz Mamma
can't get up, cuz she's on drugs, or what have you—you know, she didn't come
in. If you really love those kids, you're gonna go far beyond. If anybody else tries
to cut that child, you're there. You're his friend. You're his advocate.

And love them she does. So much so that she has allowed her pioneering work
to be used without royalty (sometimes without her permission and without

due credit). She freely gives away her techniques if it will benefit the children who have lost hope and the teachers who are fatigued from trying. Harriett Ball tells us that she sees school as "a time for imagination, to enjoy, because I know when I was growing up, it was always come and sit down and be still. And I saw things in another way. It was like a world to explore, and I wanted the kids to enjoy school." Then, she is off teaching again.

"You wanna do fractions, you gotta talk to Bubba. He the man who knows fractions. You gotta know how to talk to Bubba: Haaaaeee-yah! Haaaeee-yah!" She makes the motions of two karate moves along with the sounds, one with her arms crossed in an *X,* and the other with each arm at right angles like an *L.* "Write the numbers in the bubble. The largest number floats over the largest what? Biggest fraction! Bubba says 'Eat me.' Put your hand on it"—she lays her right hand on the blackboard and traces the > space between her thumb and index finger—"the *greater than* sign, which is the *mouth, eating the larger fraction.* Whoop, there it is!" Ahas are heard from the members of the teacher audience as they get it. Some of their own confusion about the greater-than and less-than math signs has just been cleared up. Harriett has just acted out the calculation motion and direction that the kids will go through to find common denominators and do cross multiplication. But these terms, intimidating to kids who have decided they "can't do math," are not used. She then takes us through the whole instructional lesson, making us talk back to her in rhythmic shouts and rap, reciting what we're doing, moving our hands in the air as we cross multiply—all of which reinforces the learning. She concludes, "And I can *see* what they're doing without grading papers. I am assessing my class."

Harriett knows what math intimidation feels like.

> It still does not come through, and the reason is—and I didn't know until recent years—that I was a different type of learner. I was tactile-kinesthetic. They didn't even talk about that during those days. You were slow or fast. Something was wrong with you. The elevator didn't go all the way up, ya know? Something's wrong.

Creating Pride

We walked into a classroom at an Atlanta elementary school with Jennifer Moyer. The class was in the middle of a history lesson on slavery. The students and their teacher had traced themselves, cut out the paper replicas, and hung them around the room to create a context for the lesson. At the moment we stepped in, the students had all wrapped themselves in chains and leg irons (constructed with paper). At the teacher's signal, they broke free of their chains with a great shout followed by laughter and dancing and joy. And as we walked out of the teacher's classroom, Jennifer put a big star on her door.

Jennifer Moyer is the full-time manager of teacher development for Creating Pride, a faith-integrated, nonprofit Atlanta organization founded by Ann Olstholthoft and dedicated to fostering creativity and pride in young people and teachers through art making. Jennifer had been spiritually mentored by Ann and felt called to Creating Pride (CP) as a way to "give back" and to fulfill her own godly purpose. A graduate of the Chicago Art Institute, Jennifer expresses her faith in her work by sharing God's love and his character. "We [the staff at CP] are Christlike in our behavior, actions, and relations. We pray together as a staff, and a number of the teachers have a faith and appreciate a blessing at the end of teacher workshops."[4] Jennifer believes that teacher development is the most critical step in igniting teachers' creativity. Then the key is to make sure they have access to supplies and, even more important, to let them own the projects and art-based lessons they use to teach their disciplinary subjects. She does *not* tell the teachers what to do.

Teachers must vote to invite Creating Pride into their school and must pledge to meet the challenge of "being more creative" in the classroom in order to ignite the talent of their students and must pledge to use art and creativity to teach. Each CP school selects one or two people to attend a three-day summer institute focused on "Leading Your Peers" and finding art resources in Atlanta. Their job is to implement "art hour" teaching—one hour in each class, every week. Jennifer along with the "peer leader" teachers visit all the teachers each week to do three things: compliment something the teacher is doing, provide support (help with resources and art or craft techniques), and help connect art projects to the school's curriculum (for example, a poem using vocabulary words). All of the teachers we observed displayed "authentic creativity in learning" (no Xeroxing, no models, no tracing allowed), and the students displayed imagination and original thinking. CP holds teacher-mentor workshops twice a year for teachers focused on providing other teachers with easy, practical solutions for using the arts in the classroom and on working with them to develop their innate creativity. These workshops also teach new techniques, have a team guild for collaborative work, and offer a watercolor painting session for relaxation! Creating Pride nurtures the transformation of teachers so that they can assist in the transformation of their students.

Community-Based Arts Education

In his excellent book on using the visual arts in education, *Step Outside: Community-Based Art Education,* Peter London advocates the use of visual arts in experiential education. He integrates academic learning with the environment. This kind of learning enables students to experience and to see the world in a new way. While most teachers see time spent in the environment as a field trip, Peter sees the outdoors as a classroom.

> Community-based arts programs differ from field-trips in the same way that encounters with tigers in jungles differ from encounters with tigers in zoos. In community-based art education, the child's encounter with a real but focused aspect of the environment provides the initiating context for a genuine meeting between the inherently curious mind of the child and the even more curious world.[5]

Experiences in the community outside the classroom are more than casual field trips. They are real opportunities for field research in which students conduct interviews, take samples, map, document, measure, compare, draw, and record hard facts. Upon returning to the classroom, teachers have "teachable" moments to discuss learning. London advocates community-based learning because

1. It is inherently artistic.
2. It begins with students' knowledge and curiosity.
3. It is relevant.
4. It is contemporary.
5. It is accessible.
6. It acknowledges concern about safety.
7. It is inexpensive.
8. It is multisensory.
9. It is a natural and easy way to learn.
10. It is interdisciplinary.
11. It enhances the transferability of learning.
12. It nurtures self-identity.
13. It nurtures self-esteem.
14. It encompasses at-risk children.
15. It reveals hidden dimensions of the community.
16. It builds community cohesion.
17. It builds closer relationships between school and community.
18. It contributes to advocacy on behalf of the arts.[6]

From a faith perspective, we can add that community-based education teaches the truth by giving children firsthand experience of the world, allowing them to experience both the glory of God's creation and the fallenness of humankind and the evils of society. The artist-teacher has every opportunity to help the student by training their eyes to see both the power of creation and the need for the redemption found in the NU JERUZ—the transformation of our environment, God's creation, and of those who have been given the opportunity to live, work, and re-create in it.

Arts give kids the desire to learn

Championing Art and Learning

We've all observed the tragic cuts in arts programs in public schools, as such programs are the first to go in a budget crisis. This is particularly the case in inner-city, rural, and low socioeconomic status (SES) areas of our country. If education policymakers were reading the research literature on the impact of the arts, they would do just the opposite. G. Thomas Houlihan, executive director of the Council of Chief State School Officers, acknowledged in a *USA Today* article that "many school superintendents, principals and teachers are unaware of the value of arts education." In a letter that prefaces the Champions report, an in-depth study of the impact of the arts in education, former U.S. Department of Education secretary Richard Riley recognizes that "arts teach young people how to learn by giving them the first step: the desire to learn. . . . And a key factor in changing American education for the better is to increase high quality arts learning in the lives of young Americans." He concludes that the Champions study "also shows that the arts can play a vital role in learning how to learn . . . [and that] learning in the arts can not only impact how young people learn to think, but also how they feel and behave."[8]

James Catterall has conducted studies over the last eight years demonstrating the powerful effects of arts involvement with secondary and high school students on a variety of school performance indicators and accompanying behaviors and attitudes. Similar results have been seen in the studies of other education and arts researchers. Catterall's analysis of data from a 1988 National Education Longitudinal Survey is one of the first studies to demonstrate comprehensively that students involved in the arts do significantly better than their noninvolved counterparts on academic performance (based on grades and composite standardized test scores in reading, writing, math, geography, and history) and have lower school dropout rates, exhibit better attitudes toward school and toward community service, and watch less television.[9] One of the more important findings is that the academic performance advantages of arts-involved students increase over time (a 36 percent advantage in eighth grade, growing to a 46 percent advantage in twelfth grade).[10] These advantages are evidenced not only for high socioeconomic status kids but also for students of low socioeconomic status backgrounds.

Shirley Brice Heath's research compared after-school programs categorized as "sports/academic," "community involvement," or "arts" programs. Not surprisingly, the youth in all the programs (which were all aimed at disadvantaged youth) were doing better in school and in their personal lives than were youth from the same SES categories not in after-school programs. What was surprising is that students in the arts programs were doing the best, even though they were more "at risk" than those in the other programs. Characteristics unique to the arts cause arts programs to be more effective and are believed to be a combination of "roles, risks, and rules."[11]

In the hands of well-prepared, skillful teachers, the arts provide learning experiences and environments that engage the whole student: their minds, their bodies, and their hearts. But Christian teachers like Harriett Ball and Jennifer Moyer also engage the souls and deeper yearnings of both the students and the other teachers they train. Their work is motivated by the faith imperative of pure agape love. It is their concern for kids in need of hope, rather than their love of art or teaching, that reaches and touches the heart of every student. It is the power of the art itself to stir the soul. It is their lack of fear and willingness to engage fully in their students' lives that allows the passion of the arts to touch the students and to cause them to believe in their own potential. Certainly, a passion for art and teaching are also significant and necessary in having effective and well-taught classes.

Summary

The arts reach students who might otherwise be left behind. The arts respond to the variety of learning styles and intelligences explored and written about by Howard Gardner. Even before Gardner formalized his seminal work on multiple intelligences, teachers have for decades known and responded to those who learn through tactile-kinesthetic, visual, auditory, or experiential methods.

The studies contained within the Champions report summarize additional factors unique to the arts that lead to enhanced educational achievement, school behavior, and attitudinal change. The quoted material in the list below is from the report's summary stating the benefits of arts-based learning.[12]

1. The arts, unlike the learning style generally used in other disciplines, "engages and nurtures not just one, but the development of several skills and competencies": personal, social (or interpersonal), and cognitive.

2. The arts "provide a motivation (sometimes the only motivation) for otherwise disengaged youth" to remain connected with school and after-school programs and reaches students that might otherwise not be reached.

3. "Often, underachieving and problem students excel in arts learning environments." For example, Randall, a Philadelphia high school teen, was failing most of his ninth grade subjects. But Randall was the best student in a structural design course, in which he built a boat and received an A. It was a course that required skill in geometry, physics, history, and English. In this class Randall was an "overachiever," which gave him an alternative-learner identity and gave teachers a new view of him as being gifted. Randall was also practicing future workplace behaviors, afforded him by this opportunity to work in a studio setting.

4. The arts are central in "transforming learning environments into places of discovery and accomplishment, ownership and pride." Creating Pride in

Atlanta transformed the learning environment of a number of elementary and middle school classrooms. The halls of the school became a veritable gallery of student work related to disciplinary learning. The second-floor foyer at the Sandtown Community Learning Center held the three-dimensional construction of a portion of the town that served as the students' "laboratory" for a physics lesson on electricity.

5. "Use of the arts involves significant staff development," as illustrated in the examples of experiential arts methods used by Vivian and Nathan for the Star of Hope youth retreats.

6. "Direct involvement in relationship with the artist broadens career options that students might not have considered." Dan Curry is an artist who for over twenty years has developed an art program with a Job Corp Training Center in Pennsylvania. His easygoing personality and patience have helped him in his work with youth who are struggling to get their lives on track. He has helped his students to produce excellent art—and clear visions. His open studio hours, space to create, and friendly conversation with his students are the result of a loving acceptance and a nurturing personality in God's service. Several of his students have been successful in pursuing sustained work in the arts, including art restoration and art therapy. Others have simply enjoyed the opportunity to create.

The work of Duane and Stacey with Messiah Dance Works over the past ten years has produced excellent dancers and demonstrates the "value of extended participation and practice to obtain excellence." Their holistic involvement with the arts teaches students self-discipline and encourages self-directed learning, a quality that is necessary for later success in learning.

Engaging in arts-based learning allows for the possibility of multiple outcomes (as opposed to right and wrong answers), thereby encouraging complex, multidimensional, and critical thinking. Each of the arts has particular strengths:

Drama: Helps with understanding social relationships, complex issues and emotions; improves concentrated thought and story comprehension.

Music: Improves math achievement and proficiency, reading and cognitive development; boosts SAT verbal scores and skills for second-language learners.

Dance: Helps with creative thinking, originality, elaborations and flexibility; improves expressive skills, social tolerance, self-confidence and persistence.

Visual arts: Improves content and organization of writing; promotes sophisticated reading skills and interpretation of text, reasoning about scientific images and reading readiness.

Multi-arts (combination of art forms): Helps with reading, verbal and math skills; improves the ability to collaborate and higher-order thinking skills.[13]

Part 4

Renewal in the NU JERUZ
Celebration

12

Celebration of Renewal
Dancin' in the Streets

> You turned my wailing into dancing;
>> you removed my sackcloth and clothed me with joy,
> that my heart may sing to you and not be silent.
>> O LORD my God, I will give you thanks forever.

Psalm 30:11–12

The final stage of the A.R.T. model is that of celebration. Celebration is important in publicly recognizing goal accomplishments, thanking those involved in bringing about the NU JERUZ, rejoicing amidst our labor, and propelling us into a new state—that of renewal. Christians understand this concept in their regular worship, where they celebrate the victories of life through the cross of Christ and the liberating power of the resurrection and give honor, praise, and thanksgiving to a loving, creative, and playful God, the author and finisher of the faith.

In personal and community development, the celebration of projects and programs is an essential part of the process. Celebrations are often spontaneous, with dancing in the streets, but more often they are carefully planned and carried out with formality and decorum.[1]

For the church, the celebration of spiritual renewal should demonstrate the joy, the message, and the essence of the NU JERUZ while yet looking with hope for the kingdom to come. That celebration often comes in the form of the worship experience, and it can be either a shining witness or a tarnished promise to those outside the church. We have met some shining witnesses who are in our midst creating a renaissance for the church and its celebration. In the stories to follow, we will first experience celebration in the street and then look at celebration within the sanctuary.

This chapter should answer the following questions: What kind of churches are experiencing renewal in the NU JERUZ? What critical indicators or signs give evidence of renewal in the NU JERUZ? What principles can guide a faith community in crossing the barriers of race, class, and ethnicity?

Celebration

> Meanwhile, the older son was in the field. When he came near the house, he heard music and dancing.
>
> Luke 15:25

> As the ark of the LORD was entering the City of David, Michal daughter of Saul watched from a window. . . . She saw King David leaping and dancing before the LORD.
>
> 2 Samuel 6:16

> You turned my wailing into dancing; you removed my sackcloth and clothed me with joy.
>
> Psalm 30:11

Topless Church

It was a church without a top, a building without a congregation, a community without hope. In the early 1980s the local congregation that had resided in the church building migrated to northeast Philadelphia. One can only surmise the reason, but the neighborhood east of Allegheny Avenue had begun to look more like Puerto Rico than an Irish Catholic neighborhood. So the congregation left, but not without first enlisting one of Philadelphia's most courageous and artistic evangelists, Luis Centeno, to preach to the drug addicts and street people and start a new church in the building. Centeno cut his "street preaching" teeth among the homeless and down-and-out, a population from which he had come.

Around the time that the original congregation vacated the church building, Luis Centeno was deputizing his new church, Bethel Temple, at a conference held in Wayne, Pennsylvania, at the Church of the Savior—a conservative nondenominational church in the upper-middle to upper-class area of town eighteen miles west of Philadelphia. It was there that Luis met sculptor David Day. David remembers the moment Luis approached him, saying, "I had a vision from the Spirit about you the other night. I'm not sure what it means, but when it is clear, I'll let you know."

David had been looking for a vision. At an early age he had apprenticed with his father, a jeweler on Philadelphia's Jeweler's Row on Eighth and Market Streets. David says, "God gave me good hands and my father taught me how to use them."[2] After a stint in the military for several years, David landed a job with the Container Corporation of America. He had been prepared to pack boxes, but when executives saw the arts experience listed on David's resume, they sent him to the structural design department, where he was put in charge of a project the design department had been working on for some time. The department managers instructed him to do the best he could, telling him, "We don't have the time to train you, so play around with it and see if you can come up with a solution." A mere two weeks later, David had completed the project and was immediately put in charge of all the new products for the company.

While working for the Container Corporation, David met another artist who was good at graphic design and took itinerant projects to support his painting. The artist encouraged David to enter the Academy of Fine Arts, which he did. One day as David was carving stone alone in the basement of the art building, a professor, sculptor Alan Harris, sternly approached him, saying, "Don't you know you are supposed to be in drawing classes?"

David replied, "I don't want to draw; I want to carve stone."

Harris, taken with David's skill and spunky attitude, instructed him to begin lessons at Harris's home studio. There, David learned the art of bronze casting and other sculpting skills. Harris advised him to seek skills from those who have them: stone cutters, welders, and the like, and then open his own studio. He did, with success.

Raised a Roman Catholic, David has always enjoyed the aesthetic religious experience—the mystical pageantry and the liturgy—but he was disenchanted with other aspects of the church life. He soon met his wife, Marion, at a New Year's Eve party. Marion had recently been born again. Shortly after their marriage, a friend invited them to an evangelistic revival meeting.

David remembers the service well. "It was a revival meeting with a Bible thumpin', goin' to hell type of Southern Baptist preacher. In the service the preacher asked the question 'Where would you go if you died tonight?' I thought to myself, 'I don't know.' And the preacher started a dialogue with the congregation. 'Would you like to know?' 'Yes,' I replied silently, and at the end of the service me and my thirteen-year-old son walked down the aisle."

The family gravitated to Church of the Savior, which had just initiated an artist affinity group that explored the biblical and theological idea of art. And then one day Luis Centeno approached him and invited him to Allegheny Avenue.

Luis showed David the graffiti murals of the neighborhood Latino gang. The murals contained strong satanic symbols. No one ever touched the murals; they were sacred. Luis said, "I want a symbol that is equally as strong and good from a creative standpoint, with lots of color that can represent the multiethnicity of our neighborhood."

Taking David by the church, Luis said, "We are a church without a top. I want you to put a top on it. Something visible, to stand out like a lighthouse to draw those who wander in the city in despair and hopelessness to find healing and hope. Put a top on the church."

David and Luis organized the church to pray and plan for this "church top," to work out the project, and to wait for the Holy Spirit to inspire the art. As in most good creative projects, David was learning much about the subject matter and the community. He began to see "an immediate cycle of intellectual process, prayer, the power of Holy Spirit, and the manifestation in my hands." The church began to define what made the body of Christ unique at Bethel Temple.

The body life of Bethel demonstrated the interconnectedness of all the people. "There was a realization of the brokenness of their humanity and a humbleness that bonded them together," David Day said. "They recognized the need for Christ in their lives."

David took that theme and began to construct a cross, the most unique cross to top any church in Philadelphia. Using found objects—junk steel and rejected farm implements—he began to construct a cross that was integrally connected, with each piece holding up the other.

Six months later—on Saturday, September 30, 1995—a sixty-foot crane lifted the one-ton, fourteen-foot abstract cross of Jesus into place above the church. The abstracted form of Jesus, in which the clear face of Jesus looks down on Allegheny Avenue and merges into a colorful mix of shapes and forms, now stands as a lighthouse of hope and encouragement and community. It is a covenant of the church congregation to serve the community in need. It is a celebration of the NU JERUZ on Allegheny Avenue.

Today David and Marion are members of Bethel Temple, working alongside Luis in the community.

What do we mean by celebration in the NU JERUZ? It is not so much a celebration of the fall of our enemies (Prov. 24:17 tells us not to gloat) but a celebration of renewed spirits, minds, bodies, and communities.[3] The milestones in our lives bring joy out of sadness and should be celebrated.

To celebrate can mean to perform publicly a solemn ceremony, to honor an occasion by refraining from ordinary activities, to mark an anniversary by festivities, or to observe a special day with festivities. To celebrate is both to rejoice at the victories of liberation, healing, and wholeness—the renewing of life—and to praise the Giver of that renewal of mind, body, spirit, and relationship. To celebrate is to recognize an important milestone.

In the A.R.T model, celebration is the point in the transformation process in which people, communities, and societies come to a place of renewal. It is the celebration of their arrival at a new point in their transformation. We emphasize that "arrival" is not a definitive or finite word but one of recognition that a task is complete, a project accomplished, a vision realized.

All community development workers would agree that marking an accomplishment with celebration is critical in the life of an organization. Celebration can be spontaneous and intentional, as we saw in the response of the mothers in Norris Square, when the spontaneous celebration of freedom resulted in an impromptu mural. Celebration can also be a carefully planned event. The mothers of Norris Square (chapters 5 and 8) also held this kind of celebration, when they intentionally planned a celebration for the creation of a formal mural that honored the heroes of the community so that their children would not forget.

Celebration Leading to Renewal

> Consequently, you are no longer foreigners and aliens, but fellow citizens with God's people and members of God's household. . . . In him the whole building is joined together and rises to become a holy temple in the Lord.
>
> Ephesians 2:19–21

As powerful as celebration is to a person, community, and society, when the celebrants enter a new level of transformation, they must once again assess their present state and become aware of their place in society. Because the arts carry symbolic power, art may become an icon of culture and represent the status quo. Such icons of culture may then become barriers to social transformation. At times cultural symbols add to the stability and history of a community. At other times, however, they are barriers to change.

This phenomenon has been particularly noticeable within the church. The church sometimes celebrates its traditions to the point that those celebrations become in-group icons that inhibit the very mission of the church. However, we have observed what some are calling a "renaissance" within the church taking place all around the country (and the world). Through our travels we have been privileged to worship with some of these congregations, and we are privileged now to share some of their stories.

The Reformers

We wondered where the reformers were, reformers who had a vision for inviting people into the church as a way of welcome and reconciliation. Several years ago we had the pleasure of meeting one of the most remarkable Christians we have ever met. Gentle, full of humor, creative, incisive, courageous, intelligent, and devout, Malkhaz Songulashvili is serious about reforming the church through the arts in a way that welcomes all people into the presence of God. In 1992 Malkhaz and Father Petere Martin, a Catholic, cofounded the Ecumenical Publishing House in order to publish Christian literature. In 1993 Malkhaz assisted in founding the first Protestant theological seminary in the Republic of Georgia. In 1994 he was elected head of the Union of the Evangelical Christian Baptist Churches in Georgia and was ordained to the ministry. And in 1997 he was bestowed the title of Presiding Bishop, which is an office elected every four years. If this is not impressive enough, he is also the director of the United Bible Society in Georgia. And in 1997 Malkhaz became the senior minister at the Central Baptist Church in Tbilisi, Republic of Georgia. The congregation authorized him to carry out reforms in the areas of worship and social ministries. Malkhaz Songulashvili is a prophet, a mediator, and a celebrant of the NU JERUZ. What is he like? One must experience worship in his congregation to know. His story serves as a model of what leaders can do when they understand the power of the arts.

On a Hill Far Away

It is 3 A.M. and there is a stillness so quiet, so powerful, that were it not for the occasional sobbing, one would feel frozen in a masterpiece of time and breadth so grand that only Michelangelo could do it justice. One thousand people are crammed into a small building, sitting on wooden benches, squatting on the floor, standing by the walls, peering into the windows from the outside, all leaning forward in anticipation as they corporately witness their own execution.

Slowly, very slowly, and accompanied by the solo voice of an operatic soprano, a procession of men bear a huge wooden cross down the aisle, stepping carefully so as not to trample the children under their feet. The cross is laid flat with a heavy thud on the floor in front of the people, a group of men and women painfully raise crude hammers and begin to nail the sins of the people into the wood. Within minutes the cross is crimson from the red slips of paper on which each person has written the confessions of their lives. As the cross is lifted and planted upright, a team of black dancers garbed in flowing red chiffon express the tears and sadness of the silent worshipers who are transfixed by the cross, many of whom now begin to weep. Others are trying to control their overflowing emotions, which would likely burst into shouts were it not inappropriate for this somber moment.

Throughout nearly three days and nights of an unending passion of color, sound and sight, taste and touch, we were truly in the middle of a feast of the faithful, prepared by a master liturgist, in celebration and honor of the Savior. This celebration was not technical. It was not loud. It was not plastic or commercial. It was real. It breathed.

Quietly, we filed out of the room and boarded ten waiting buses for a journey to the mountain. Riding through the dark city streets to the edge of civilization, we entered an open plain where the stars glistened, glimmered, and danced, shining on our journey of transformation. Still in the dark, and now on the mountain, we processed by candlelight to each stage of the cross, where we heard readings of Scripture, watched dances, and sang songs, all in preparation for the Lord's Supper. As the sun began to illuminate the landscape, we journeyed onward to a temporary wooden platform that had been decorated with flowing ribbons of cloth that were now unfurling in the early morning breeze. After partaking in communal bread and wine, a dozen white doves were released into the morning sun, now breaking in the distance over the city of Tbilisi. Our silence broken, we rejoiced and shared another feast of bread, wine, fruit, and delicacies prepared by the women of the church. It was glorious! The journey we had all traveled to get there added to the glory.

Bishop Malkhaz Songulashvili, the leader of this worship experience, is a minister with a mission—to reform the worship of the church. One cannot miss him in a crowd. Unmistakable. Ever in a purple robe, black socks, and sandals, a cross around his neck, bearded and balding, Malkhaz walks slowly, as if in eternal contemplation. One should not mistake his mild demeanor to be void of humor or anger. At the event we described, a college professor of the local university was standing near the communion table and lit up a cigarette and smoked during the communion service as if he were at a ball game. Malkhaz didn't seem to notice and later laughed it off, saying, "He is a little strange, but we invite him to participate in the feast of our Lord anyway." On the other hand, Malkhaz has faced off armed patrols on behalf of Chechen refugees, whose rights he defends. More recently he traveled to the United States to testify before a House committee on religious persecution in Georgia. And following an attack by a rogue Orthodox priest who instigated the burning of 150,000 Bibles in the United Bible Society, where Malkhaz is director, he angrily demanded government control from the president of Georgia, threatening a mass demonstration in front of the palace. Bishop Malkhaz Songulashvili is a prophetic voice in his society.

Several years ago Malkhaz began what his church members call "the Reform," a reformation of worship through the arts. Three basic concerns of the congregation had prompted the reforms. One, Baptists had a sectarian (cultic) image in the culture. Two, members wanted the worship environment to be, and the culture expected it to be, aesthetically pleasing: "We are in a church, not a garage." Third, beginning in the fourth century the country had developed a rich Christian heritage and members felt that "Christians should not be ignorant of their heritage."

Empowering the many gifted people in his congregation, Bishop Malkhaz commissioned a series of frescoes depicting the life of Christ. The frescoes are displayed on special days in a church building shared by Russian Baptists who do not appreciate his reforms. Throughout the year, the members of the congregation composed music and wrote a special drama for vigils like the one described above. This has drawn criticism from a number of local pastors. In the past the vigil was a night of preaching and singing. In the minds of many Baptist pastors, preaching is exclusively synonymous with the Word of God. But when the Reform started five years ago, the Bishop, along with a planning committee, decided to eliminate most of the preaching and focus on more participatory forms of worship. The reason for this decision was that attendance at the vigil had dwindled over the past years until there was a question as to the viability of the program. Malkhaz and the committee felt that the Word of God could be preached in drama and music in a way that attracted people to the vigil.

During the vigils Bishop Malkhaz invites youth to share experiences from their personal ministries outside the church. One young woman wrote a play about two homeless people who find themselves in a local church. The theme of the play is giving to others as Christ gave to us. Following the drama, Malkhaz invited three young people to give testimony to the congregation about their vision for ministry in the city of Tbilisi. Two young women now visit the homeless on the streets and assist in providing food and care for them. A young man with a heart for the disabled has volunteered his time to repair wheelchairs and other devices needed in an institution for the disabled.

Probably Bishop Malkhaz's most controversial reform has been the use of symbols in the church sanctuary. We mentioned the controversy of the cross in our chapter on the power of the arts. In 2001 Malkhaz commissioned the making of a six-foot brass menorah. Involving leaders from the Jewish, Orthodox, Catholic, and Lutheran faiths, the menorah was dedicated in a worship service as a reminder of the Jewish roots of the Christian faith. While the Jewish rabbi and the Catholic bishop politely declined to participate in the communion that culminated the service, the congregation attending the service proved an unprecedented interfaith cooperation.

The reform is not a one-man show, however. With the mandate of the twelve-hundred-member congregation, a worship reform council of fifty people began to work on change. Meeting as often as seven times a year, and dividing into subcommittees, long discussions were held about the incorporation of folklore, iconography, music, drama, and dance. The result is that the reforms at Central Baptist Church are expected to lead to change in the other sixty-six Georgian Baptist churches of the country. Young people are now thoroughly involved in the church, and there is a sense of expectation and joy in worship services.

The Reform is not without its critics. In 2001 a few European Baptist leaders wrote letters to the Baptist World Alliance, of which the Georgian group is a member, and demanded that Central Baptist be removed from the organization because the church was no longer Baptist. "If the church had dwindled and died, no one would have said a thing," Malkhaz responded. "We had a church void of young people. There are always critics when one is doing something. And we want to be a church known for what we are doing, and *not* what we are not supposed to do. It is entirely possible that the critics are also responding out of fear of change and loss of control." Much of their criticism was born from the Georgian church's historical context.

Russian Baptists entered the Republic of Georgia in 1867. A Georgian-speaking Baptist congregation was founded in 1919 by Ilia Kandelaki, a Georgian home missionary who was assassinated by Communists in 1928. During the occupation of the country by the Soviet military and through the oppressive political and religious constraints of Communism by the Soviet Union until 1990, many Georgian Baptists viewed the influence of Russian Baptists as Russian culture with the gospel.

With the breakup of the Soviet Union and the independence of the Republic of Georgia, the ground was fallow for Georgian Baptists to develop a sense of identity, and they yearned for a gospel and worship relevant to their own culture. Enter Malkhaz Songulashvili.

In 1997 Malkhaz became the senior minister at the Central Baptist Church in Tbilisi, and the congregation authorized him to carry out reforms in the areas of worship and social ministries. Their concern is the contextualization of the gospel in the Georgian culture, drawing from the spiritual heritage of the country and utilizing their iconography, liturgy, and music.

It was through Bishop Malkhaz's concern for reform and renewal that we led two special groups of African-American artists to participate in the Easter celebration described at the beginning of this book. Malkhaz wanted to open the world—other than white America, which Georgians have seen through television and American missionaries—to his congregation and requested BuildaBridge to enlist the African-American groups Messiah Dance Works of Philadelphia and Anointed Generation of the Holy Temple from Penns Grove, New Jersey. Intentionally, both Georgians and Americans—separate in language, culture, and worship tradition—were included in every phase of the worship service to relive and dramatize the gospel narrative, our common faith. While both cultures became critically aware of their differences, and we had to work out misunderstandings along the way, we celebrated and rejoiced at the renewal of our faith and the expansion of our understanding of the kingdom of God.

The most important lesson we learned from Malkhaz is the important role the pastor plays in leading the congregation to renewal. It is the pastor's role to nurture artists and to provide opportunities for their inclusion in creating the aesthetic experience as leaders of worship. In this case, Malkhaz's academic study of his culture's traditions and art has led not only to an appreciation of their meaning but to a relevant worship for his congregation.

As strongly as Malkhaz wants a relevant worship that includes the traditions of the past, Pastor Tommy wants a relevant worship based upon the present.

Crossing Over: Rap and the Reality of the NU JERUZ

To the Jews I became like a Jew, to win the Jews.

1 Corinthians 9:20

Who?
"Urban D," "Z," "Spec," "Nice," "Fat Daddy."
What are they sayin'? *props, representin'?*
"Show your neighbor some love and say wuz up!"
"Yo, hook us up. Get us off" (the two thieves speaking to Jesus on the cross).

These were the unfamiliar words and to some very familiar worship traditions and Scriptures that Pastor Tommy was explaining in the style and lingo of the hip-hop crowd sitting in front of him for the now regular, standing-room-only, hip-hop youth service held every Thursday night at Crossover Church in Tampa, Florida. With the sound turned down, you might have thought you'd walked into a concert by NAS. The typical "wave your hands in the air" and "jumpin' straight up" movements of hip-hop artists and fans was goin' on. But with the sound turned up, it was just a different kind of praise.

An hour earlier Pastor Tommy had held his first new-members class for this growing church that is responding to and reaching unchurched and Christian young people growing up in the MTV-BET world. Pastor Tommy is educating a spiritually uneducated audience by contextualizing the gospel. He's keepin' it simple and keepin' it "real."

> Grammy winners thank God for helping them write a song about shakin' your bootie and filled with curse words. Naw, that ain't it. You gotta do what the Word says. Don't just say it. Live it. Then it's real. James 1:22.[4]

Pastor Tommy receives letters and E-mail every month from traditional churches. Their pastors tell him and the other leaders of Crossover to stop what they're doing. But he was letting the newest recruits know, "We are a real church, not a club! We follow the Bible." And everything that followed—the Thursday service, the communion observance, our interviews with his staff and congregation—proved it. At Crossover the gospel is expressed and taught through the music, dance, and art forms of the city, all without compromising the message of truth or the walk of the leaders.

Urban D is Tommy Kyllonyn's nationally known recording name. At concerts, fans flock to his CD sales tables and clamor for autographs, which he gives freely, staying as long as it takes to serve everyone. But at Crossover and in the neighborhood, the young people and their parents hug him and know him as Pastor Tommy. At either place, though, his message is the same. Tommy is no lightweight. He's authentic and comes not only with the credibility of knowing and living the hip-hop culture but also with a solid biblical and theological background. Tommy is a college graduate with a concentration in youth ministry. But much of Tommy's preparation for his unconventional church and pastoring came as a white boy growing up in a rough Philadelphia environment. He was busy playing basketball, rapping, and sneaking out to go on "graffiti tagging" jaunts with his buddies, when his father, a pastor himself, moved the family to a rural setting in Chambersburg, Pennsylvania. Tommy suffered severe culture shock and constantly looked for ways to return to the city.

After a stint at Valley Forge Christian College, Tommy was asked by a friend to run a subway ministry to the homeless in Philly. This proved to be a critical turning point in Tommy's path at a time when he was struggling to decide his own commitment to God. The ministry put him back in the city and confirmed what would later be a clear priority for him: counseling, discipling, and seeing people grow.

That is Tommy's description of his current pastoral role, a role he considers far more important than his recording and concert career, which is doing well enough, except that Tommy does a lot of stuff for free.

"Evangelism and ministry by way of my music is for a season. When I'm fifty years old, I probably won't be doing as much hip-hop. But it's great now to be used to save people. But the thing about concerts is there's no follow-up with the people."

Being a pastor to his congregation is where Tommy sees the reward and the transformation. And it's not just teens that are being drawn to Crossover. Rebecca, age twenty-two, heard of the Thursday night service by word of mouth. It's not her culture, but she loves the kind of down-to-earth fellowship that is happening there. Kevin, age twenty-three, comes because "It's me. I'll still be here when I'm thirty-three." Lucy brings her three kids here on Thursday nights. She has her own church that she attends on Sunday but enjoys this service too.

Crossover's target population is unchurched urban people. In Florida this means a multiethnic congregation of people that cross lines of class and race. It means people that live in the "inner city" as well as those from less densely populated sections of Tampa that might pass for "suburban." But Tommy explains that both "urban" and "hip-hop" are more than code words for poor, black, and Hispanic people.

"The number one music all over the world is hip-hop. R & B is number two. DJing, fashion, hair, attitude, dance, art are all elements of the hip-hop culture, and we use them all to reach people." Tommy is passionate about letting his young crowd know that Christ is real and relevant to them and that they are in need of a relationship with him. Many but not all of those who flock to his Thursday services and the once-a-month "Soul Sessions" are fatherless, abused, poor, school dropouts. They have lots of other problems according to Tommy and other Crossover leaders, and that's why Crossover is trying to build a more holistic ministry. Soul Sessions are held on the first Thursday of each month and use a "living-room-talk-show format" in place of the sermon. Cohosted by Tommy and an African-American church leader, four panelists address real issues such as suicide, abortion, and abuse.

Tommy and his multiethnic leadership crew were surprised at the response of many of the young people, who started revealing their own painful experiences with these things. Through confessions that brought relief, as well as through the rap lyrics and poetry composed by the kids following the session, the church has become ever so aware of the need for the church to address the whole needs of the young people coming through their doors.

So in addition to relevant worship, the church is responding through other services as well as through the physical environment of the church. They are creating an outdoor patio area with graffiti spray-painted picnic tables where kids can come to hang out. The area currently serves as the space for their rap concerts and as an after-service Thursday night gathering. Tommy's vision is to expand the patio area (it's getting crowded), add an awning (the night we were there, all the young folk were being invited to show up Saturday to install it), and convert an unused space into a café. This might add a small stream of revenue for the church, already begun by the hip-hop shop in the small foyer of the building, where faith-centered magazines and a variety of Christian rap and hip-hop CDs and paraphernalia are available.

The front of the church "stage" is a full-wall graffiti mural with a contextualized salvation theme, and if you don't look closely, you'll miss the rejoicing angel in heaven that's break-dancing with a head-spin move. The back center of the stage has a polished hardwood square specifically for break-dance rejoicing. And two graffiti-painted vans sit outside in the gravel parking area, ready for runs through the community to transport the young worshipers to and fro in style.

We learned from Tommy that hip-hop is spiritual. It is a spiritual language infused with the language of the street but also the meaning of the gospel. Like Malkhaz, Tommy is making worship relevant to an audience—youth—who before had found no meaning in the church. And like Malkhaz, Tommy has a leadership style that incorporates the arts and artists in every possible medium to celebrate renewal.

And while Tommy is hip-hopping, children are playing in Chicago.

Playing with God: Kid's Church

"God tricked me into it," chuckles Tom Sullivan, the enthusiastic director of Kid's Church at Spirit of God Fellowship in South Holland, Illinois. Kid's Church is a unique puppet theater that plays on Sunday morning to an audience of over five hundred kids and their parents in place of Sunday morning worship. Tom and his assistant John Russell, a former band director and now a lawyer, are a bit radical for two conservatives. Combining conservative theology and liberal social action, they are more than a Kid's Church that uses puppets for worship. They are part of a movement to change their communities.

In the 1970s Tom's parents, Dr. and Mrs. Sullivan, started a Bible study in their living room as part of their local Catholic church in South Holland, Illinois. When weekly attendance grew to one hundred people, the Sullivans decided to start their own church, a nondenominational church, which continued to grow. South Holland, Illinois, has been a changing community over the past ten or twenty years. Once primarily a white middle-class community, the Sullivans have watched their community change to be 60 percent African-American and Latino. As part of their new church they felt called to a vision of a diverse community. While other folks moved out, the Sullivans stayed and developed an outreach into the neighboring town of Harvey. Restoration Ministries ministers to former drug addicts and alcoholics, helping them readjust to society, and also ministers to children. Kid's Church began as a response to the many parents who had nothing for their kids to do on Sunday and for whom church did not seem to be an option since they were not attending any of the twenty-three churches in the area.

It was almost by accident that Kid's Church started in the fall of 1988. According to Tom, who had just returned from a mission trip to Mexico in which he did children's theater, "I came back to my home church and started complaining that there was nothing interesting for the kids, so I complained enough that they challenged me and said, 'Why don't you do something about it?'"[5] He started a program with six people who had no experience, and before long it had turned into a full-blown Kid's Church ministry using puppets.

With a master's in education and experience in theater, Tom decided to try an innovative idea and have Kid's Church on Sundays, when parents could bring their kids for the theater/puppet productions. Regular worship for adults would be held on Wednesdays. There are now over forty people involved in the Kid's Church program, from camera operators and sound technicians to actors. They are all volunteers. The church has never had paid staff. The pastor, Dr. Sullivan, works as a dentist. And only recently did the church hire a full-time maintenance person to attend to the large, convertible sanctuary/theater.

> It has been the most successful outreach our church has had over the past fourteen years. A lot of unchurched families attend who want their kids to come to something. They don't attend the church on their own. They're hearing the gospel, and seeds are being planted in their life. It's a very nonthreatening, safe environment for people to come and hear about God.

Why doesn't the church hold a worship service on Sunday? Spirit of God Fellowship is not a small church congregation. The church has no debt, counts on volunteerism, and has a sanctuary-theater that seats fifteen hundred people and is equipped with state-of-the-art lighting, sound, and theater props, much of which is donated. Carrying on the tradition of their original Bible study, the church worships on Wednesday. Continuing that tradition led to innovation.

> We have an outreach to a facility in Mantino, Illinois, called Brandon House. It's a residential drug rehabilitation facility, and we've been running a Bible study there on Monday nights for twenty years. We bus them in to our service on Wednesday night, and if we met on Sunday they wouldn't be able to come. We've developed this culture in our own church that Wednesday night is the night to meet. And Kid's Church started on Sunday. Bringing the family to church on Sunday can be such a nerve-racking, tumultuous affair that we wanted to simplify all that.

Kid's Church has been a place in the church where misfits feel comfortable. "There are creative types who are not the most socially adept. And so getting involved in Kid's Church ministry, where they can be creative and have an outlet for it . . . even become a minor star . . . gives them a confidence in their gifts and their abilities, and in themselves, which translates into their life."

Tom refuses to recruit workers for Kid's Church but instead waits for people to join. The staff believe that God places people in their ministry for a purpose, not a performance, and do not turn away anyone who has a heart for it. They teach and walk with the volunteers and watch them mature. It is part of their theology.

> We believe Christianity is fun. We believe God can be a very serious topic, but that God likes to laugh too. We saw the church so solemn and serious so much of the time. Our theology from the beginning was "Let's take the basic principles

and build foundations in children's lives." And we knew that if Kid's Church was successful, we would see thousands of children come through over the years. And for most of them, we would never know the impact it would have in their lives, because we would plant seeds. Jesus said in order to see the kingdom of God you have to be like a little child. And the concept: Little children have fun. They goof off. They have a totally different way of looking at the world. And that's kind of the way we've approached Kid's Church.

The kids' program was not an afterthought. Children are so important in their eyes that something special had to be created for them. "For most mainline churches, the kids program is an afterthought. The kids get dismissed. They go off, and it's something that somebody else runs. The pastor has nothing to do with it. And our philosophy has always been that the service should be just for the kids. The adults are there as well to show the kids that the service is also important for the parents."

Are they making an impact and reaching their community? While they do not have a formal evaluation, a commonality with many of the artists we interviewed, they can witness to a growth in multicultural attendance of the Sunday theater. "The Hispanic [community] is a little trickier, because it's a split community. Half are bilingual and half speak only Spanish. But the Hispanic church that is affiliated with Spirit of God has a children's outreach that is a version of Kid's Church that they do that'll reach out to the Hispanic kids, especially the ones who don't speak English."

Kid's Church is on local cable television, and those who have graduated from college are now working in their communities or have returned to continue in Kid's Church. They have summer road shows and often build a float for the community parade, for which they have won an award. Many people ask for permission to use the theater scripts, which they also give freely.

The sweetest victory may be their leadership role in the community. For many years they were considered a cult by most of the twenty-two churches in the area because they had regular worship on Wednesday instead of Sunday.

Through Restoration Ministries and urban outreach, the other churches in town started coming to us and saying, "We need to learn. We've never had an African-American member in our church. We don't know what to do." And they would actually ask if we would have people from our church come and sit in on Bible studies with them or if they could join different things at our church so that they could be exposed and start learning how to reach out to the community. Consequently, my father, who's the pastor of our church, eventually became the president of the South Holland Ministerial Association. Being a dentist, he was the first one without a doctoral theological degree to ever sit in that position, which was a huge deal for South Holland and for the religious community here. So we've changed 180 degrees from being cult status to being the cutting-edge church that everyone wants to learn from.

Improvising with God

Several years ago Eric Elnes was on a spiritual retreat when he received a vision from a bass—a fish, that is. While Eric was praying by a beautiful lake, a large bass jumped out of the lake in front of him. Through this experience, God spoke to him about leading his congregation—the Scottsdale United Church of Christ in Scottsdale, Arizona—to experience "a second of the awe of God."[6] Eric was virtually a Luddite (one opposed to technological change) when it came to the worship service. He credits his father with encouraging him to discover technology as a worship medium. Reluctantly, Eric began to think of ways this could happen in his church. The innovative fifty-year-old Scottsdale church is nestled in the quiet suburbs of this small city outside of Phoenix and is surrounded in the desert by the Paiute Indian population and the Tonto National Forest.

It took what one church board member called the "Oh My God! grant," given by a popular Christian musician who wanted to encourage innovation, for the church to set off in a new direction. The Studio, as they call it, is a jazz worship service. The service is a mixture of "sanctuary" jazz, dance, readings, and live painting synchronized to sermon and technology—digital clips of movies that enhance the topic and flash biblical and famous quotes throughout the scripted service. It is a service that invites others to participate in the awe of Holy Creativity and in what God is doing. One feels this invitation like the comfort of a favorite chair but doesn't get too comfortable and fall asleep. Participation is planned, with singing and creative activities that often culminate in a group work of art.

Some of the artists, whom the church pays to participate in the service, are agnostic at best but have grown in their understanding of God and commitment through the worship ministry. "At first this was a job, but now I want to be here every week," one artist confessed. A visual artist who has painted images of Jesus during the service reflected on his learning, "My father told me to get bar mitzvahed and that was it. I've learned so much about this guy Jesus I didn't know." He has been at the Studio for a series of worship services and has painted portraits of members during the week. Eric welcomes these artists, saying, "He wants to offer his art in worship to God. I can't deny him the opportunity to do that."[7]

The worship service is an invitation for "outsiders" to find a place, a creative place, to worship and serve. Each week the church publishes a list of ministries for participants who want to become involved—everything from flower arranging to service in transitional homes. Though controversial for many churches, and initially for many of its members, the church has taken a strong stance of openness for homosexuals. One elderly grandmother commented, "We have relatives and friends with children that are gay, and we have known and loved them all their life. We cannot deny them a place of worship." Elnes believes "Gays want a place where they can be human and where 'gay' is only one aspect of their life. Not where they are members of gay churches and that is the center of who they are."

Rob, a local police detective and a member of the worship planning committee who has an understanding of diverse learning styles and its importance in presenting information, comments, "This is what our worship does. It is highly experiential. We use the term *Studio* to differentiate from *contemporary* that tends to be message based. The Studio worship is more experiential based." Rob became involved in the planning team after bringing his children to experience the Studio and now enthusiastically participates in the services.

Eric has assembled a worship team of seven people who assist in writing the service each week. He comes to the group each Wednesday with what he calls "the 1.0 version," which includes Scripture and a theme. The team then brainstorms and takes two weeks to build a 3.0 version. Eric, once opposed to technology in worship, now prepares the technology for the Studio. Rehearsal is minimal, but the professional jazz musicians have little trouble improvising the theme.

The Studio is growing. By some standards it is a small service, with about fifty adults in attendance, but the intimacy of the sanctuary enhances the feeling of the Studio. On most Sundays the sanctuary bustles with children who participate in processionals and dances.

This worship form works well in environments where there is an openness to creativity and a desire for the spiritual atmosphere and ambience created by the arts. Replicating the Studio might be difficult for many urban congregations without the resources of artists, technicians, or the vision of a pastor and trust of a congregation. And church congregations reliant on the spoken word (preaching is an art form in our view) might feel uncomfortable in the Studio.

One cannot deny that the Studio celebrates life through the arts in a technologically and creative culture. Jazz is a medium comparable to traditional sacred music, having the ability to demonstrate nuances of emotion not possible with rock, rap, and other contemporary music. All members are treated as artists. The Studio, through jazz and other art forms, allows for prayer and contemplation and uses diverse learning styles in an age where traditional worship has lost its relevance as a communicative and celebrative event. In the Studio the members of the congregation are collaborators in and creators of the worship experience, and that idea can be replicated regardless of technological skill and access to professional artists.

Signs of Renewal

Celebrating renewal in the NU JERUZ is a creative act. It is an art. It also requires working out a plan that uses the celebration itself to welcome others, across all barriers, into the heart of the kingdom of God, the church community. Based on our research, we can suggest basic principles used by multicultural congregations in both the working out and the celebration.[8]

The Hug

Congregations must "create a friendly space" for diversity and include those outside the sanctuary. The best example of this comes from A Place Called Hope in Miami, Florida, a worship center in a local strip mall. Here the visitor is met with hugs and cheek kisses as they enter the expansive converted worship center. This is more than a "greeter gauntlet" where one feels pulled in by the assigned greeter of the week, whose grab-and-pull technique muscles you into the door. No, at A Place Called Hope, the four greeters' varying ethnic and faith persuasions are cultural and spiritual huggers, more like your favorite aunt who, with an extroverted personality and open arms, invites you into the house for milk and cookies. Yet the friendly space is more than a greeting; it is an environment where the clothes you wear and the condition of your hair (or nails) don't matter. It is indeed like going to a large family reunion.

The Rap

As you read in the examples above, each congregation created a worship celebration that met the spiritual needs of the worshipers and the social needs of the community. For Bishop Malkhaz, it was a celebration that included the rich Georgian culture. For Urban D (Tommy Kyllonen) it was the inclusion of hip-hop for an urban youth culture. For Tom Sullivan, it was a celebration to meet the needs of children more used to video games and television cartoons than an ancient liturgy. These churches find ways to change neighborhoods and to incarnationally celebrate renewal in the language(s) of the community. They have chosen not to move out but to move on with the kingdom in their neighborhoods. Diversity of ethnicity is not an option for these churches; it is a necessity, a natural expression of an already diverse population that has primarily worked through the matter of race and must now struggle with more pressing social issues. One finds within these churches a common faith with different languages of expression. Diversity and finding a common language of expression are more a result of the sociological and geographical proximities of people than the forced design of a godly talk.

The Power and the Politic

Creative renewal begins with leadership. Unless the pastor and other church leaders have a vision, creativity, trust, and a willingness to share power, creative worship cannot and will not take place. Part of this formula includes sharing ethnic power with a diverse group of ministers. As an example of this principle, we again cite A Place Called Hope in Miami, Florida. Located in a changing community with large Catholic and Jewish populations, this charismatic Pentecostal congregation has enlisted ministers from these populations. Among the greeters were a priest and a Messianic rabbi. Churches with diverse leadership model the kingdom in ways words, statements, and policies cannot. Pastors who share their sermon time with other communicative art forms and congregations that are willing to adjust to a new ritual may find true renewal in their worship experience.

In our research we found leadership that is more egalitarian than authoritarian. Leaders of many of these worship experiences share their power by seeking involvement and delegating responsibility throughout the participating congregation.

The Creative

Congregations that seek to celebrate and experience renewal value the arts and artists as a gift of God in their midst. Encouraging and nurturing artists requires a flexibility and openness often outside the bounds of traditional culture. While there are many artists who will give of their time freely, and we support volunteerism, many artists earn their living by playing gigs and often live without health insurance and retirement policies. Congregations who may not have the benefit of an "Oh My God! grant" can still take care not only to provide a creative space for the artists but to support them in other ways. One possible way of supporting artists would be to barter for their time. Providing church space for a studio or enrolling an artist in the staff health-care plan may speak more than a weekly paycheck. And as we saw from the Scottsdale example, inviting even non-Christian artists to experience worship is a way to witness and demonstrate the love of an inclusive God.

Outward Bound

The majority of artists in our examples are involved in strong ministry outside the worship context; most are involved in social action. The church's focus should not be inward but should be outward work, which in turn brings inward renewal to the church. A cycle is completed as the celebration of renewal propels participants back out into the world again. As we saw in the worship of Bishop Malkhaz, in the cross atop Bethel Temple, and in the Kid's Church in Illinois, worship was intimately connected to strong social and community action. Diverse and creative worship as celebration is more than a performance; it is a remembrance and catalyst for sending the faithful out into the world to live their faith.

The Bible, More than a Book

Within the United States we witnessed a strong reliance on the Word of God but little use of the printed word. Books are down (but not out), hands are free, and technology has become the medium of transmission. Demonstrated most clearly in the Scottsdale example, the worship planners understood the nature of experiential learning and the culture of a media-driven society in which a generation has become used to synthesizing the point from a participatory process. Multiple processes are used within a stimulating environment to tell a story and celebrate a time.

The Spaces, the Names, the Rituals

Celebration for many has moved out of the church sanctuary and into the mall, the office park, and the warehouse. Congregational space is convertible, and the congregation has the option to grow, move, and transform. Whether for a worship service, a concert, a play, a business incubator, or a youth retreat, space is treated as a servant. This does not mean that a church has to meet in a garage. As in the example of Malkhaz, portable art can be stored during the week and then strategically placed before services to beautify and transform the space into a place of beauty and awe. Architecture can be transformed from within, much like the lives of those who come from a mobile and increasingly unpredictable society.

The names of these congregations with convertible spaces often sound more reflective of the consumerism of our society rather than the traditional sectarian denominationalism of our past. Whether from the tradition of Baptist, Methodist, Anglican, or Catholic, the younger generation is finding a church home in the Studio, Art Spirit, Tribe, or Circle of Hope. Shopping for a faith community that meets one's lifestyle and spiritual needs, a community of likeness, has critics worried about the potential danger of propelling faith into cyberspace, disconnecting it from the concrete reality of daily living. But it may be the daily living that calls and beckons the need for renewing the values of faith in a world where religion failed to bring peace.

It is in the rituals of the celebration that we return to an aesthetic expression that includes the sounds, sights, movement, and smells that have been part of Orthodox worship since ancient times, an aesthetic expression that leads celebrants to a sacramental experience of the Spirit of God in their midst. The thirst for this wonder and awe of the Spirit come from an honest desire to connect with God and his kingdom amidst the violence and uncertainty of our times. We need a time, a space, a ritual, that allows us to weep, to shout, to dance, and to feel.

The Arts of the Community

In any church we attend, the first signs of a diverse congregation and the first things we look for are the art on the wall and the songs listed in the bulletin. Truly diverse congregations have incorporated the aesthetic expressions of their diversity. The paintings, pictures, banners, songs, dramas, and dances (even worship styles) are symbols of culture. The ability of the congregation to "blend" these into a patchwork of worship, a garden of culture, requires a major shift in its culture. The ability to release other symbols of church culture that could be a barrier to inclusion is a major sign of openness. But we have yet to arrive at true celebration of the NU JERUZ in many of our churches in a very diverse United States.

New Art for a NU JERUZ

We are waiting with anticipation for the emergence of truly authentic arts that are representative of a NU JERUZ.

Summary

Manny Ortiz is affectionately called "Matchmaker" by the members of Spirit and Truth Church in north Philadelphia, where he has pastored for many years. This nickname was given to him by the young members who have found their life mates at the church; most of these matches culminated in interracial marriages. Ortiz has worked, first in Chicago and then in Philadelphia, to bring about the NU JERUZ in the present through racially and ethnically reconciled churches. His church is involved in the arts through a dynamic and contemporary worship. A substantial number of the church's artists partnered with BuildaBridge International to establish the Sabbath Arts School as an outreach of the Ayuda Community Center, the church's CDC.

Ortiz believes the multiethnic church has both a qualitative and quantitative dimension. The quantitative dimension involves having a significant number of people from different ethnicities, not a "smattering of one culture or another."[9] The qualitative dimension has to do not only with the life and organization of the church but also with its commitment to matters of reconciliation and justice. Ortiz offers some basic principles for what he calls "Building a New Humanity." Quoting anthropologist Paul Heibert, Ortiz states, "The church's task is neither to destroy nor to maintain ethnic identities but to replace them with a new identity in Christ that is more foundational than earthly identities."[10] This is a reflection of the Great Commission—African-Americans are reaching out to Asians, Hispanics are sharing the gospel with African-Americans, and each ethnic group is reaching out to the others and working with them in building the kingdom of God. And, we might add, crossing socioeconomic barriers in the process. The ultimate goal of a multicultural church is not multiculturalism for its own sake (quantitative) but a genuine community in which all seek justice, peace, and reconciliation in structure, ministry, and worship toward the common goal of the NU JERUZ.

Ortiz lists six important principles for developing the New Humanity, referred to in 1 Corinthians 12:13.

1. Declare in written form the biblical position of the church on this matter of unity in diversity.
2. Develop a mission statement that will assist the church in its focus to do ministry that is effectual in the context of a multiethnic community.
3. Develop a philosophy of ministry that will put the mission statement into action.
4. Involve multiethnic leaders in the process.
5. The church must be deliberate in determining how to resolve conflicts.[11]
6. Multiethnic small groups should be established. [Arts groups are an excellent way to do this.]

There is a direct link between the worship of the church and its mission in the community. Like Isaiah, who received his call through a holy and aesthetic worship experience and moved into the world to do justice and walk humbly with God,[12] the church, through the celebration of the cross and the victory it represents, sends the congregation to be in the world, calling people to God, ministering to them, and being the presence of Christ in the public square. But like the New Testament ingathering of the faithful when their voices communicated in every known language, so the church's worship is renewed to celebrate the fruits of its labor in a diverse world. Without the call there is no sending, without the sending there is no labor, without the labor there is no harvest, and without the harvest there is no celebration and renewal—only tradition bound by culture.[13]

Postlude

Lessons Learned

Throughout *Taking It to the Streets* we have provided theories, models, and reports of how others are taking the gospel to the streets. In chapter 1 we described two experiences in the city, both of which were frightening. They were only two among our many experiences in the city, most of which were not that dramatic and were, in fact, quite pleasant. But these two frightening experiences left us wondering what we could do, how we could respond to the needs that presented themselves to us in violence, and what changes we would have to make to become a part of the redemptive process.

In 1995, beginning with several international arts travel and ministry projects, we developed the concept for a nonprofit arts program that could serve as a facilitator and mediator for arts ministry, between artists of the Christian faith and the needs in local communities both in America and abroad. We had lived incarnationally in different worlds and had used our artistic gifts in the church and in educational and community contexts for many years. It was time to formalize our experiences and become catalysts, encouragers, and mentors to artists, churches, and communities that recognize the power of art to serve others as they seek redemptive transformation. It was our *eschaton*.

In 1999 we formed BuildaBridge International (BI), a nonprofit arts education organization whose motto is "Crossing cultural boundaries and bringing faith to life through the arts in the tough places of the world." Through our Institute for the Church and Community Arts, our Community Arts Program, and our Educational Safaris (the educational and overseas service/mission program of BI), we are growing and developing what we hope is our effort to put one's faith into action through the arts. It has not been easy. Our desire to learn and create an avenue for arts in ministry led to the research that eventually led to this book. We wanted to find out what others were learning in their work, and what valuable lessons could be gleaned and applied to our own ministry. Here is what the artists we interviewed said.

Lessons for Artists Who Want to Make a Difference

What lessons have successful urban prophets, agape artists, and celebrative artists learned that they would share with others? What should an artist interested in being a catalyst in the kingdom know before getting started? What qualities do we look for when we seek to collaborate and work with others in mission? Below we list the top eleven lessons suggested by our research.

Accept the Call

We found that nearly every successful artist involved in ministry outside and inside the institutional church operated out of commitment to a higher calling. Some, like Mark Sandiford, had "Jonah" experiences and discovered their call after hitting the wall in the secular world. Others, like Duane Wilkins, felt so strongly about what God was calling them to do that after finding little support in the traditional church, they began their own organization. For some, like Pastor Aaron Penton (whose outdoor concert was described in chapter 1), the calling was to a traditional evangelism and a strong commitment to the local church. Twenty-two-year-old Penton works as the Associate Music and Youth Pastor at Trinity Church in Miami and coordinates the band and youth choir.

For other artists, like Phillip Brown, Donna Barber, and Scott Parker, the call was to be salt and light in the world. But all the artists had a commitment to a higher calling that was received from God, affirmed by others, and for which they developed their craft. For most of the artists, the art was not the focus, although each strived for excellence in what they did. All of the artists viewed their work in the streets as a ministry. That ministry was to transform both people and communities into the kingdom of God. Art was a vehicle for impacting the lives of those who live in the streets of society. This art was freely shared with others.

Stick to the Mission   unchurched

Urban D sat in a meeting of the leaders of Crossover, discussing the Thursday night youth service. "Aren't we spending too much energy on the hip-hop people? What about the suburban youth and others in our community?" a leader asked. "That is not our mission!" Urban D retorted. "There are churches on every corner, and not one of them is concerned with the urban youth culture. This is our mission. If you cannot commit to it, then I suggest you find another church!" It is not uncommon nowadays to hear the phrase "What is your personal mission statement?" Artists who have a goal for their life and a focus or mission for their art can stay on track.

Sell Out

The majority of artists we interviewed "go for their dream" wholeheartedly, some at the risk of alienation from other Christians, and others at the risk of going bankrupt. They often find themselves betwixt and between the Christian world and the secular world, which is a very lonely and isolated place to be. They are at times misunderstood or criticized by churches that offer little prayer or financial support and may be equally misunderstood and ridiculed by the church's secular counterparts. Fortunately, artists like Brian Joyce are beginning to speak out and to do great work in bringing credit to the faith and their art.

In the face of a lack of support, many artists give of their own resources. We found this among recording musicians and community missions alike. They work odd jobs outside of their profession in order to make money to support their vision and dream. All were artists who act and don't just talk. This leads to the next, and the most important, quality we look for when working with artists.

We asked each of our interviewees, "Have you suffered because of your artistic work and ministry in the street?" Almost unanimously the response was, "I would not say that I have suffered, but I have sacrificed." We heard of exhausting ninety-hour workweeks and time away from family. Others gave up the idea of fame, fortune, and family. Many artists work two or three jobs to make ends meet in order to use their art to serve others through volunteer ministry. Duane Wilkins works full-time as a social worker in Philadelphia's Department of Human Resources, serves as a minister in his church, leads Messiah Dance Works, and even volunteers with BuildaBridge as a resident artist.

Show Up

Vivian has an expression, which we both use, and it is one of the few offensive words we use in this book and in our speech, but it captures the importance of this quality: "You can't do s**t if you don't show up." Many artists have good intentions to be involved in their community and in arts mission activities. They volunteer and then don't show up. In our experience, there are a number of reasons for this. Some have very poor time management and forget to write dates and times in their calendars (if they keep one). Many artists just have too much to do and are overwhelmed by their many activities; this is especially true of those who work several jobs to make ends meet. Poor communication between the church or community organization and the volunteer is another reason. But in the end, it often comes down to a lack of commitment. Serving in the community is just not a top priority to those who don't show up. The result is that leaders of community arts activities must scramble for substitutes, so that students who are badly in need of lasting and meaningful relationships are not disappointed once again in their lives. We often tell our volunteer teachers, "This program is not about you; it is about our kids. If you can't show up, don't get involved in the first place."

Make the Lemonade

Long before and after the classes, productions, and performances we attended, we found committed artist-servants taking care of the nonart details. When volunteers—and even paid staff on occasion—do not show up, "the show must go on," as the theater expression goes. Mark Hallen said it best: "Someone has to make the lemonade." Mark knows. Mark is the director of the Eastern University theater program, is developing the Germantown Theater Guild in his own community, and operates a summer theater camp that brings suburban and urban kids to experience art and develop relationships for five weeks. Mark's role in these programs is not only one of planning, organizing, and managing; it is also one of attending to the details, the small mundane matters that require a servant attitude and motivation. He does it well.

Be Incarnational

As we've mentioned throughout the book, perhaps the greatest quality of urban prophets and agape artists is their ability to live incarnationally. Referring again to the theology of play, true agape artists are able to *be*, to be with others, and to be there for others in their ministry. The greatest transformation and impact of arts organizations does not come from the art but from the relationships that are built through the arts. These incarnational artists know their audiences intimately through similar experiences and can empathize with them and relate to them on a common level of understanding. Like Duane and Stacy of Messiah Dance Works, Dana Velps of Moving in the Spirit, and Scott Parker of Starfish Studios, many of the artists we met have become parents to a parentless generation of children who are often tired of living.

Get a Real Job

We had to chuckle at the honesty of Scott Parker when he told us that the greatest lesson he had learned was to "get a real job." Scott takes a small salary—about a thousand dollars a month—out of the donations he receives. And with a little help from his friends along the way, he follows his call. "If you get a career job, you'll never work on your craft. You'll do it for somebody else. And so I took this route." Scott substitute teaches in a local school, which ended up being a ministry and a blessing. "Every kid at the local elementary school knows me, the teachers know me, and the principal knows me." Scott has earned a level of trust at the school, and everyone there is glad to work with him.

In the down times of financial support, Scott worked odd jobs to make ends meet. He admits that his film background could have been enhanced by further professional preparation in advertising and marketing. Having a professional degree and qualifications provides opportunities for professional relationship building and brings personal credibility to any artistic ministry. While Mark Sandiford was half joking, he was serious when he said, "Get a wife who supports your work!" Many artists' spouses work full-time jobs so that a ministry can be fulfilled.

Find a Support Group

Perhaps the greatest need of artists of the Christian faith who work in community ministry is that of personal support and comradeship. We found that many artists work in isolation, even when others are doing similar work in the same city. They do not know that the others exist. We have observed a growing movement among artists to join together for common support. There are several national organizations, such as CITA (Christians in the Theater Arts) and CIVA (Christians in the Visual Arts), that seek to support theater artists and visual artists. Some denominations, such as Southern Baptist, have a long tradition of church music organizations, but community artists, either because of the nature of their work or the newness of the field, are not afforded this opportunity. In New York, Dallas, Chicago, and Los Angeles, we found a number of formal and informal artist groups that meet together for prayer, Bible study, and support.

Support groups offer more than the chance to develop professional relationships, however. Many of the agape artists we interviewed were a part of a vital congregation and had strong ties to the communities in which they lived. While some of the artists' families may not understand the artist's life of ministry, many families were highly encouraging. Professional support groups, families, church involvement, and community participation are a solid base for the urban prophet and agape artist who would find a life in arts ministry.

It Is Always Cross-Cultural

The majority of the organizations we observed and the people who lead them are cross-culturally competent. Cross-cultural competence includes being bilingual, understanding the nuances of variances of the English language, understanding cultural differences, and living with the pain of the racism and class prejudice that still exist within our country. We discovered Asians working in African-American neighborhoods, African-Americans working in Latino and white neighborhoods, Latinos working in mixed neighborhoods, and Anglos doing the same. Most of them worked across socioeconomic barriers as well, living much below what they could have earned elsewhere.

Avoid Burnout

As our friend Judith Mayes used to say, "When you get tired sit down, and if that doesn't do it, lay down and take a nap." Artists involved in ministry must learn how to *be*, to be in joy. Making art can be rejuvenating for artists. Support groups that pray together, network, and collaborate can help artists avoid burnout. And the development of one's craft through further training is as critical as rest and fellowship.

Let Go

Finally, a unique lesson for artists is learning to let go. Many artists, especially public performance artists, have a need to control their own work. There are two basic reasons for this: (1) Artists are often perfectionists and want to control both the process and the product. This is understandable, because the artist often has the unique ability to see a picture of the finished product and wants to produce the best for his or her own integrity as an artist and for the glory of God, the giver of the gift. (2) Many artists have felt abused and taken advantage of when they have seen their work copied, sold for profit, and outright stolen without any compensation. So there is a real concern for ownership and justice within our society driven by a free-market economy and private enterprise. But if the giver of the gift can give so freely, so the artist can give and expect the return from God to be "pressed down, measured, and overflowing." This kind of giving of one's gift takes both faith and trust.

The Quiet Ones of God

As we were finishing the final pages of our manuscript, we discussed how to end the book. We have been overwhelmed at the experience of meeting such wonderful people and reviewing their work in the process of researching and writing about the impact of the arts and faith. We decided to share what the lives of these quiet ones of God have said to us.

They are quiet and humble folk. They live out their lives without concern for fame or fortune as they seek the will of God in their lives every day.

They struggle, but they are joyous with a good sense of humor. They appear to live in the present and focus on people and the communities in which they live.

They sacrifice. They give up more than most people will ever give up, and their lives convict you and cause you to wonder if you could ever give up as much. That's been the real challenge to our faith. Do you really have the guts and the courage to get in the middle of people's lives and live without comfort and security? Their lives convict you to examine how much you put your money where your mouth is.

They are gifted people. We met so many gifted people, people who used their artistic talents and incarnational lifestyles to teach people about Jesus.

They are deep people. They've thought through what they are doing, and they are theologically clear—though they may not be theologically trained.

They are unafraid. They are unafraid of the uncertainty of their lives, their livelihoods, and their survival.

They have glorious visions. They have wonderful visions of what can be done with people in community.

They act. They act and God blesses it. It is absolute proof that people who together take their lives and neighborhoods into their own hands can do any- thing—can defeat any power, because "if God be for us, who can be against us?"

These quiet ones are living their *eschaton*. Will you live yours?

As you have read this book, you may have been inspired to become involved in the agape arts to help bring about the NU JERUZ in the tough places of the world. Buildabridge International was founded in 1999 to assist artists of the Christian faith in crossing cultural boundaries, bringing their faith to life through the arts in the tough places of the world. BI currently offers three programs that are opportunities for learning and service.

The Institute for the Church and Community Arts (ICCA), through East- ern University and Eastern Baptist Theological Seminary, provides nondegree training and degree credit courses and experiences on the undergraduate and graduate levels in faith-integrated use of the arts in community service and mission. In process are a master's degree program and a doctor of ministry in church and community renewal through the arts.

BI's Community Arts Program facilitates local church and community cen- ters in establishing after-school and Saturday community arts schools. We call on volunteer and resident artists to assist us in developing programs with street children, homeless kids, and refugee children in Philadelphia and abroad.

Educational Safaris is the educational and overseas service/mission program of BI. Each year we provide artists with the opportunity to travel to other regions of the world to learn about the faith and art of other cultures and to share our faith through arts missions. BI invites resident artists, performing groups, and students to embark on the adventure of faith and art in action.

With over twenty years in cross-cultural and arts education experience, Nathan and Vivian are available for training and consultation in the following areas: orientation to overseas living, cross-cultural communication, organizational culture analysis, intercultural (NU JERUZ) worship, and arts pedagogy and curriculum writing for general and Bible education.

Children, families, and communities are being touched and encouraged through BuildaBridge International and through the artists and ministries mentioned in this book. These agape artists welcome your prayers and support. Contact information for the artists featured in this book can be found on the web site www.urbanprophets.org.

Contributions to BuildaBridge are used to support our programs described above, our ministry to at-risk children in the transitional homes of Philadelphia and in the tough places of America and abroad, and our programs for the education and training of agape artists.

Give a Child the Gift of Joy
BuildaBridge International
P.O. Box 34550
Philadelphia, PA 19101
Email: ncorbitt@buildabridge.org
www.buildabridge.org

Notes

Foreword

1. Herbert Marcuse, *One-Dimensional Man: Studies in the Ideology of Advanced Industrial Society* (Boston: Beacon, 1992).

Introduction

1. We make a clear distinction between Christian artists and artists of the Christian faith. We define *Christian artists* as artists who use specific Christian images and whose ministry is focused on the Christian community. *Artists of the Christian faith* are artists who live and work in the "secular" world outside the church, although they may be part of a faith community and may minister there as well. These artists integrate their faith in their artistic expressions in ways that communicate to the broader world; they seek to be salt and light to the many who are not aware of or not accepting of the Christian faith.

2. The notable exception is in the city of Chicago, where a support and prayer group for artists of the Christian faith was started by Brian Bakke in the 1990s. The group continues to meet today, though Bakke has now moved away to work with the Mustard Seed Foundation in Washington, D.C.

3. C. S. Lewis, *Mere Christianity* (New York: Macmillan, 1952), 175.

4. The term *NU JERUZ* comes from the hip-hop world of rappers and gangs. While we use the term to refer to the kingdom of God in the present, the term seems to have several meanings in hip-hop culture. In searching the Web, we came across several web sites that used the term NU JERUZ. We also talked to many people about this term; most said it meant New Jersey. Lauryn Hill refers to the New Jerusalem in her song "Every Ghetto, Every City" *(The Miseducation of Lauryn Hill),* which describes her childhood in New Jersey. We infer from Lauryn Hill's music that New Jerusalem is a nostalgic term for a wonderful childhood, when things were safe and life was full. Others use NU JERUZ as a "shout out" (a rapper term) at parties and are referring to the future when black brothers and sisters will live in a new world. While particular ethnic enclaves may not see or believe in Dr. Martin Luther King's "beloved community" that reaches across class, race, and religion, the NU JERUZ, as we use the term, is a foretaste of the New Jerusalem and offers an urban hope for a new heaven and a new earth, with new systems—the kingdom of God on earth.

5. Jürgen Moltmann, *The Theology of Play,* trans. Reinhard Ulrich (New York: Harper & Row, 1972), 31, 43.

6. http://www.ccda.org is the web site for the Christian Community Development Association, started by John Perkins.

7. This definition of the NU JERUZ was influenced by conversations with Tony Campolo in a series of faculty discussions at the Campolo School for Social Change at Eastern University regarding evangelism in the pluralistic urban context, and by Albert Nolan's thinking in *Jesus Before Christianity* (1976; Maryknoll, N.Y.: Orbis, 2001).

8. Nolan, *Jesus Before Christianity,* 62–88.

9. Silvio Waidbord, "Family Tree of Theories, Methodologies and Strategies in Development Communication: Convergences and Differences," *The Communication Initiative,* http://www.comminit.com/stsilviocomm/sld–2881.html (May 2001).

10. S. R. Melkote, *Communication for Development in the Third World* (Newbury Park, Calif.: Sage, 1991), in Waidbord, "Family Tree of Theories."

11. See Marshall McLuhan, *Understanding Media: The Extensions of Man* (New York: New American Library, 1964), in Waidbord, "Family Tree of Theories."

12. A. Singhal and E. M. Rogers, *Entertainment Education: A Communication for Social Change,* 2d ed. (Mahwah, N.J.: Lawrence Erlbaum, 1999), xii.

13. Conversation with Dr. Gwen White, faculty, Department of Counseling, Campolo School for Social Change at Eastern University, Philadelphia, 29 August 2002. Behavioral scientists believe that if you change the behavior of the individual, you can change society. There is actually strong evidence to the contrary. Earlier we said that there was an ecology of change. The individual and community are critical in this concept. The so-called change back theory states that an individual who does not have a support group or community is very likely to revert to the original behavior. This indicates an important role for the church and is possibly the reason for the rise in emerging faith communities that are not bound to tradition and seek a more participatory relationship in church life and worship that deals with the many social and personal issues of those seeking faith as an answer to their problems.

14. William Cleveland, "Mapping the Field: Arts-Based Community Development," http://www.communityarts.net/readingroom/archive/intro-develop.php.

15. Ibid.

16. Ibid.

17. http://www.community arts.net/reading room/archive/25creativecommunity.php

18. Ibid.

19. Ibid.

20. Don Adams and Arlene Goldbard, *Creative Community: The Art of Cultural Development* (New York: The Rockefeller Foundation, 2001), 14.

21. American settlement houses had their roots in a British academic effort to encourage university students to move into depressed communities and work to improve the living conditions of the poor.

22. Adams and Goldbard, *Creative Community,* 43.

23. At the height of the program, $200 million was invested in CETA arts jobs in 1979, when the unemployment rates of the time were at their highest. Ibid., 53.

24. At the writing of this manuscript, the Working Group on Human Needs and Faith-Based Community Initiatives coordinated by Search for Common Ground USA has released an initial report, "Harnessing Civic and Faith-Based Power to Fight Poverty." See http://www.working-group.org.

Chapter 1: Taking the Gospel to the Streets

1. Elijah Anderson, *Code of the Streets* (New York: W. W. Norton & Company, 1999), 50.

2. Chestnut Hill is an outer-city section of Philadelphia noted for its wealthy residents and historic homes.

3. Ron Sider, *Good News and Good Works* (Grand Rapids: Baker, 1993), 28–29.

4. Jung Young Lee, *Marginality: The Key to Multicultural Theology* (Minneapolis: Fortress, 1995).

Chapter 2: The Language of the NU JERUZ

1. Robert Linthicum, *City of God, City of Satan* (Grand Rapids: Zondervan, 1991), 64–79.

2. Though this was a class project and we cannot verify the students' sample, we should note that such negative comments came primarily from a white fringe culture. Blacks tended to have a more positive response.

3. Ron Sider, *One-Sided Christianity? Uniting the Church to Heal a Lost and Broken World* (Grand Rapids: Zondervan, 1993), 61.

4. Steve Turner, *Imagine: A Vision for Christians in the Arts* (Downers Grove, Ill.: InterVarsity Press, 2001), 80.

5. John Perkins, http://www.ccda.org.

6. Ibid.

7. Ibid.

Chapter 3: The Arts in Redemptive Transformation

1. *Standing Out in a Drive-by World*, in "A Study of Model Community Arts Programs, Phase II Case Studies and Recommendations," (2001), 16. This document, which we will hereafter cite as the Howard County Report, was developed and published by the Center for the Study of Art and Community (http://www.artandcommunity.com/) and the Center for Cultural Assessment. It was prepared for the Howard County (Maryland) Arts Council and the Horizon Foundation.

2. John W. de Gruchy, *Christianity, Art and Transformation: Theological Aesthetics in the Struggle for Justice* (Cambridge: Cambridge University Press, 2001), 253.

3. Lee Spitzer, *Endless Possibilities: Exploring the Journeys of Your Life* (Lincoln, Nebr.: Spiritual Journey Press, 1997), 40–42.

4. Ibid., 3.

5. Ibid., 9–25.

6. Thanks to Ben Bryant for an excellent discussion of this model.

7. These ideas are drawn from de Gruchy, *Christianity, Art and Transformation*.

8. Ibid., 200.

9. Paulo Freire, *Pedagogy of the Oppressed* (New York: Continuum, 2002), 12.

10. Mark Mattern, *Acting in Concert: Music, Community, and Political Action* (Brunswick, N.J.: Rutgers University Press, 1998), 33.

11. Ibid., 142.

12. For more information on the Community Bridge project, see the Howard County Report, 58–60.

13. Denise Wilson, "Movement in the Arab Culture" (student paper, Eastern University, July 2000).

14. de Gruchy, *Christianity, Art and Transformation*, 229–32.

15. Albert Nolan, *Jesus Before Christianity*, 171.

Chapter 4: The Transforming Power of Art

1. Peter London, *Step Outside: Community-Based Art Education* (Portsmouth, N.H.: Heinemann, 1994), 14.

2. Augusto Boal, *Theater of the Oppressed* (New York: Theater Communications Group, 1985), viii.

3. Ibid.

4. "The Informal Arts: Finding Cohesion, Capacity and Other Cultural Benefits in Unexpected Places" (research brief, Chicago Center for Arts Policy, Columbia College, Chicago, 2002).

5. Roger Graef, "The Impact of the Arts in Criminal Justice Settings," http://www.a4offenders.org.uk/pdfs/Impact_arts_settings.pdf.

6. Amy Scheer, *The Youth Drama Program for Churches and Communities*, http://www.buildabridge.org/Webmag/ONLINE_BOOKS/Drama/Drama%201.htm (2002).

7. Moltmann, *Theology of Play*, 112–13.

8. Richard Florida, *The Rise of the Creative Class: And How It's Transforming Work, Leisure, Community and Everyday Life* (New York: Basic, 2002), 323.

9. Moltmann, *Theology of Play*, 72.

10. "Tom's" Declaration of Independence can be found in Scheer, *Youth Drama Program.*

11. Boal, *Theater of the Oppressed*, 171.

12. See Barry Liesch, "Creativity in the Bible," http://www.artsreformation.com/a001/bl-creativity.html (1999).

13. Scheer, *Youth Drama Program.*

14. See Kathleen Hiyake Chuman, "The Arts as a Catalyst for Community Development" (student paper, University of California, June 1998).

15. Maria Panaritis, "He Looked Up, and It Changed His Life," *Philadelphia Inquirer*, 18 August 2002.

16. Freire, *Pedagogy of the Oppressed*, 12.

17. Ibid., 44, 47.

18. Ibid., translator's note, 35.

19. Boal, *Theater of the Oppressed*, 141.

20. Mattern, *Acting in Concert*, 36.

21. Ibid., 141–44.

22. Turner, *Imagine*, 80.

23. Eloise Meneses, telephone conversation with J. Nathan Corbitt, 15 July 2002.

24. See a discussion of this in J. Nathan Corbitt, *The Sound of the Harvest: Music's Mission in Church and Culture* (Grand Rapids: Baker, 1998), 151–56.

25. Turner, *Imagine*, 20.

26. Ibid., 80–92.

27. G. H. Hovagimyan, "Barbie vs. Piss Christ: Battle of the Icons," http://old.thing.net/wwwboard1/messages/534.html (10 November 1997).

Chapter 5: The Artists of Redemptive Transformation

1. University of Michigan architecture professor David Scobey created the Arts of Citizenship program, in which the arts are part of a society. He visited Broadway Park in New York, saw only homeless men, and wondered how to make it a place for children, visiting classes, and homeless men, making it a classroom in the street.

2. Quotes in this chapter from William Cleveland are from a telephone interview with J. Nathan Corbitt, 25 September 2002.

3. All quotations in this paragraph are taken from the Adbusters Media Foundation's web site: http://www.adbusters.com.

4. Orlando Costas, *Christ Outside the Gate* (Maryknoll, N.Y.: Orbis, 1982), 26.

5. One of the more recent examples of rap speaking prophetically of injustice in the United States that was brought to our attention is the song "My Country" by the rapper NAS. The chorus goes, "My country sh*tted on me, they want to get rid of me." His raps depict the evil of the ghetto and lay the blame on a white elite society.

6. D. J. Haynes, *The Vocation of the Artist* (Cambridge: Cambridge University Press, 1997), 185.

7. Christopher Small, *Music of the Common Tongue* (Hanover, N.H.: Wesleyan/New England Press, 1998).

Chapter 6: Arts as a Voice of Justice

1. Turner, *Imagine*, 21.

2. Corbitt, *The Sound of the Harvest*, 82, 86.

3. http://www.ucc.org/news/r083002g.htm.

4. Nolan, *Jesus Before Christianity*, 58.

5. Ibid., 75.

6. Ibid., 101–2.

7. The homeless person is Hans Nelson, a.k.a. HansSoul. "I Feel Your Pain" is from his CD, *The New Jerusalem.*

8. From an essay by Meghen Duggins, "Personal Reflection," Department of Urban Economic Development, Campolo School for Social Change, Eastern University, 10 September 2002.

9. For a complete description of invisible theater, see Boal, *Theater of the Oppressed,* 120–55.

10. Duggins, "Personal Reflection," n. 4.

11. George Lakey, *Powerful Peacemaking: A Strategy for a Living Revolution* (Gabriola Island, Canada: New Society, 1987), 49.

12. All quotes from Barbara Nicolosi are from an interview with the authors, tape recording, Los Angeles, Calif., 19 April 2002.

13. All quotes from Anthony Motley are from an interview with the authors, tape recording, Washington, D.C., 29 July 2002.

14. All quotes from Todd Farley are from an interview with the authors, tape recording, Pasadena, Calif., 15 April 2002.

15. All quotes from John Bjerklie are from an interview with the authors, tape recording, New York, 17 February 2002.

16. All quotes from Sister Helen David Brancato are from an interview with the authors, tape recording, Philadelphia, 31 May 2002.

17. For more information on Training for Change, see http://www.trainingforchange.org.

18. All quotes from Brian Joyce are from an interview with the authors, tape recording, Philadelphia, 15 November 2001.

19. Turner, *Imagine,* 43.

Chapter 7: Arts as a Call to Redemption

1. See Haynes, *Vocation of the Artist,* 201.

2. All quotes from Phillip Brown are from an interview with the authors, tape recording, Philadelphia, 18 February 2002.

3. Mark Sandiford, "Must Come Correct," *Emancipation,* Safehouse, 2002. Used by permission of Mark Sandiford.

4. All quotes from Mark Sandiford are from an interview with the authors, tape recording, Atlanta, 23 February 2002.

5. All quotes from Hans Nelson are from an interview with the authors, tape recording, Philadelphia, 17 June 2002.

Chapter 8: Arts as a Community Builder

1. Ed Schwartz, "Building Community in a Neighborhood," *Institute for the Study of Civic Values,* http://www.libertynet.org/nol/buildingcommunityinneighborhood.html.

2. Augustine, *City of God,* trans. Gerald G. Walsh et al. (New York: Image, 1958).

3. Carol Anne Ogdin, "Community Defined: What We Know," http://www.smithweaversmith.com/WhatWeKnow.htm. Although Ogdin adds a fifth element to the definition of community—self-determination—we do not include it in our list since it is evident to us that many true communities in all the other senses feel disempowered and oppressed by poverty.

4. John Kretzmann and John McKnight, *Building Communities from the Inside Out: A Path toward Finding and Mobilizing a Community's Assets* (Chicago: ACTA Publications, 1993), 5.

5. Ibid., 96.

6. Adams and Goldbard, *Creative Community,* 47. The New Deal also established the importance of oral history as a basis for cultural preservation. Most of the surviving slave narratives were, according to this source, collected during this era.

7. However, the responsibility for moving a generation of young people away from the passivity and media mind control of watching television (media controlled by the elite culture) is not the sole responsibility of arts programs and after-school cultural enrichment. It is also dependent on a family system that has hope and aspirations, conditions often not found in poor, oppressed communities, where the power of illegal drugs and gang action is also resilient. This sentiment is consistent with SIAP results, in that arts-engaged youth also tend to be more engaged civically in other ways. The important role of the artist is to clearly see the impact of the arts on youth development and to engage the family and broader community as part of this development.

8. CCD proclaims culture as a new human right, just like we have a right to education and work; this position has strong implications for public policy and funding paradigms for the arts that must change in order for this "right" to be realized. CCD practice has been to "demand public space, support and recognition for the right of excluded communities to assert their place in cultural life" (Adams and Goldbard, *Creative Community*, 20). "Community-based" art, especially that of urban nonwhite and rural communities, lacks evenhanded treatment and must continue to fight for legitimacy in repeated attempts to convince funders of their worth, while the conventional, elite or "high arts" garner billions from government and private funding just because they "are," with no requests to ever justify themselves with outcome studies. We are not advocating that they should. But an evenhanded approach would allow for the same credibility leeway for community art. What study has said that the Philadelphia Orchestra or Opera Company (passive, sanctuary art) have had as great or any greater impact on a child's self-esteem or academic performance? The SIAP study points out the critical role arts play in keeping communities diverse *and* in increasing their populations. "Cultural districts" significant enough to support artists are necessary for this to happen, and if the "Avenues of the Arts" are funded in only expensive, developed city centers and not in local communities, the right to culture, culture's positive benefits, and the community all die.

9. Community-building art cannot be described in terms of end products like concerts and ballets but instead crosses art-discipline boundaries with even larger implications for its social and developmental and spiritual goals as well. It lets us imagine how the world could be different, and in this imagination, it brings us closer to the NU JERUZ. Not to say that CCD art desires or accepts a lower-quality product and process-oriented work. Rather, it strives for a less intimidating, more approachable art that may seem more homemade than slick.

10. CCD practice willingly draws on "the entire cultural vocabulary of a community"—whatever resonates with community members' desire to achieve full expression—from the cooking of Las Motivas to comic books, from African-American step-dance groups to Asian flower arranging to Native American drumming circles. Pop, folk, ethnic, and local cultures are to be accessed and expressed with as much value as, and equal to, conventional art of the power elite. The symbolic nature of art makes it a useful political tool to both shore up the elite (power) culture and to lodge protest against it.

11. While CCD does not suggest using these principles as "measuring rods," their definitions and theoretical elements readily lend themselves for use in assessing the power of a project to address particularly community versus individual human development. Key theoretical elements in this section are taken from pages throughout Adams and Goldbard, *Creative Community*, primarily pages 59–69. We have expanded the points in this list to be more inclusive.

12. This report is available through the New England Foundation for the Arts web site at http://www.nefa.org.

13. "Social Impact of the Arts Project (SIAP)," *University of Pennsylvania School of Social Work*, http://www.ssw.upenn.edu/SIAP. This study is one of seven being conducted in seven different cities and is an affiliate of the Arts in Community Building Indicators Partnership (ACIP). ACIP's aim with the affiliate work is to create tools and methods that can be adopted or adapted by other practitioners in the community arts and community-building-related fields. SIAP was founded in 1994 with the purpose of gathering systematic data on the role of arts and cultural activity in the life of Philadelphia. The study utilized the census data of 2000.

14. All quotes from Sister Carol Keck are from our visit to the Norris Square community, Philadelphia, 28 August 2002.

15. These two teachers were Dr. Helen Loeb, an education faculty member at Eastern College (now Eastern University, where she is just retiring as chair of both undergraduate and graduate education programs) and Ms. Natalie Kempner, a sixth grade teacher at Miller School.

16. The after-school nature program was funded over three years for $30,000, by the American Baptist Churches (ABC-USA), Valley Forge, Pennsylvania.

17. From this project, funds were secured to send Iris to Cuba to study urban gardening and farming. Others will no doubt follow in this heretofore unlikely career path.

18. The construction of El Fogón was funded by the Horticultural Society of Philadelphia.

19. Mission Fuge, a Southern Baptist youth work group, came to Norris Square to build the huts. Independence Blue Cross will supply paint and labor for the stucco huts to receive their "mud" color.

20. Norris Square serves as a model for holistic community transformation. Students entering the masters degree programs at the Campolo School for Social Change spend time at this site in the field portion of their initial residency for their first core course.

21. All quotes from Steve Smallman are from an interview with the authors, Baltimore, 31 July 2002.

22. Ray Bakke, *A Theology as Big as the City* (Downers Grove, Ill.: InterVarsity, 1997).

Chapter 9: Arts as Economic Development

1. http://www.osec.doc.gov/eda/html/2a1_whatised.htm.

2. See http://www.ccda.org for a brief history and description of the activities of the Christian Community Development Organization.

3. John Perkins, "Message from the Chairman and the President," http://www.ccda.org (11 April 2003).

4. "The Principles of Christian Community Development," http://www.ccda.org (11 April 2003).

5. Ibid.

6. See especially Tony Campolo, *Revolution and Renewal: How Churches Are Saving Our Cities* (Louisville: Westminster John Knox, 2000).

7. Ibid., 160.

8. Ibid., 166. Campolo admits the somewhat ideal nature of such groups. But nevertheless he mentions examples that clearly illustrate the power of such groups to accomplish the outcomes discussed. Anyone experiencing the impact of any good group process, be it a therapy group, a cohort education class, or AA, can understand the group's potential for this kind of empowerment and support.

9. Viv Grigg, personal conversation with the authors, Philadelphia, 31 August 2002.

10. Paul A. Jargowsky, *Poverty and Place: Ghettos, Barrios, and the American City* (New York: Russell Sage Foundation, 1997), 5.

11. Ibid., 6.

12. Ibid., 213.

13. Ibid.

14. David Rusk, *Cities without Suburbs,* 2d ed (Washington, D.C.: Woodrow Wilson Center Press, 1995), 1. See also Rusk's *Inside Game/Outside Game: Winning Strategies for Saving Urban America* (Washington, D.C.: Brookings Institution Press, 1999), and *Baltimore Unbound: A Strategy for Regional Renewal* (Baltimore: Abell Foundation, 1996).

15. Rusk, *Cities without Suburbs,* 127.

16. Ibid.

17. Jargowsky, *Poverty and Place,* 211.

18. "The Role of the Arts in Economic Development," *National Governors Association,* http://www.nga.org (25 June 2001).

19. Florida, *The Rise of the Creative Class,* 231ff.

20. Tony Campolo, personal conversation with the authors, Philadelpha, September 2002.

21. All quotes from Mary Anne Degenhart are from an interview with Vivian Nix-Early, 25 September 2002.

22. All quotes from Rudy Carracso are from an interview with the authors, tape recording, Pasadena, Calif., 19 April 2002.

23. All quotes from Coz Crosscombe are from an interview with the authors, tape recording, Philadelphia, 2002.

Chapter 10: The Arts in Human Relationships

1. http://www.undp.org/hdr2001/chapterone.pdf.

2. This recital was held by the Ayuda Sabbath Arts School (SAS) at the end of the school's spring 2002 semester. The recitals, held twice a year, are an important part of the school's goals to celebrate incremental achievements of students, to give opportunities for public practice of social behaviors, and to affirm the students' gifts and self-worth. The Ayuda SAS is an affiliate of BuildaBridge International and serves a multiethnic population in north Philadelphia.

3. All quotes from Janelle Junkin are from conversations with the authors, 2002.

4. For additional background information from a Christian perspective, read Nathan Corbitt, *The Sound of the Harvest* (Grand Rapids: Baker, 1998), 141–72.

5. Annette Foglino, "The Healing Power of Music," *Spa Finder,* 38–42.

6. Ibid., 40.

7. Ibid., 42.

8. Howard County Report, 44. This study report identified model arts programs across the country to assist the council, the foundation, and their advisors to learn how the county's arts resources can contribute more directly to community health and wellness. The study summarizes research and provides profiles of exemplary arts-based programs focusing on three health and wellness issues identified as county priorities: youth development, issues regarding the elderly, and community cohesiveness. The report can be obtained by contacting the Arts Council of the Howard County Center for the Arts (http://www.hocoarts.org/).

9. Maxine Hull kindly granted us permission to use client artwork for educational purposes. Color illustrations of fifteen pieces of artwork by her clients can be viewed on this book's companion CD or, as stated, at http://www.urbanprophets.org.

10. Rachel Webster, Howard County Report, 10. Gallery 37, like most community-based programs, has not engaged in any documentation research or impact studies. However, this and other anecdotal evidence is available from Gallery 37 (for a resource manual and video see http://www.gallery37.org).

11. Howard County Report, 16–17.

12. Ibid., 30.

13. StoryBook Dad is a project in which prisoners create and tell stories orally, which are recorded onto tape and sent home to their families, thus maintaining a dialogue between prisoners and their children. Bruce Wall's London Shakespeare Workout project stages full productions of Shakespeare's plays. Dance United was formed in 2000 in England to promote dance development with excluded groups. They have worked with street children in Ethiopia and have staged projects in Tbilisi, Republic of Georgia; in Ulster, Ireland; and in women's prisons in England. Clean Break Theater Company uses a drama-based approach to assist women in anger management. During the period of March 1998–May 2000, forty women went through the program, whose aim was to develop emotional intelligence and literacy. The main outcomes of this program included understanding the roots of one's anger, using self-talk strategies to overcome anger, and understanding how to deal with other people's anger and how to walk away.

14. This list of outcomes, compiled by the Prison Service Working Party on the Arts in Prison (London), is a general summary of findings. This document is titled "The Impact of the Arts in Criminal Justice Systems" and is no longer listed on the Unit for the Arts and Offenders web site. For more information, see http://www.a4offenders.org.uk/. Also see Francois Matarasso's "Use or Ornament? The Social Impact of Participation in the Arts," http://www.creativenz.govt.nz/what/advocacy/benefits.html (1997).

15. "The Impact of the Arts on People Caught Up in the Cycle of Offending," http://www.a4offenders .org.uk (using the Strait-Trait Anger Expression Inventory or STAXI scale).

16. Ibid.

17. *Including the Arts: The Creative Arts—The Route to Basic and Key Skills in Prisons* (Manchester, England: Bar None Books, 2001; Standing Committee for Arts in Prisons, 2001), http://www.a4offenders.org.uk/new/sections/publications/pages/publicationsfr1.html (10 April 2003).

18. Ibid., 14. For further reading, see http://www.communityarts.net/readingroom/archive/hillman 71.php.

19. Scott Parker, interview with the authors, tape recording, Chicago, 13 April 2002.

20. Scott Parker, personal journal, 5 August 2002.

21. Donna Barber credits this concept to having read *The Blessing* by Gary Smalley and John Trent (New York: Simon & Schuster, 1990).

22. All quotes from Donna Barber are from an interview with the authors, tape recording, Atlanta, 8 March 2002.

Chapter 11: Arts as Education

1. Scheer, *Youth Drama Program.*

2. This and other arts-based retreat curricula are planned for publication sometime in 2004. Watch the BuildaBridge web site (http://www.buildabridge.org) for availability.

3. All quotes from Harriett Ball are from "Rap, Rhythm and Rhyme," a workshop presentation at the Black Alliance for Educational Options Annual Symposium, Philadelphia, February 28–March 2, 2002.

4. All quotes from Jennifer Moyer were made during our visit to Rainbow Elementary School, Atlanta, 22 February 2002.

5. London, *Step Outside,* 25.

6. Ibid., 28–53.

7. Tamara Henry, "Study: Arts Education Has Academic Effect," *USA Today,* http://www.usatoday.com/news/education/2002-05-20-arts.htm (19 May 2002).

8. Richard Riley, preface to *Champions of Change: The Impact of the Arts on Learning,* ed. Edward B. Fiske (Washington, D.C.: President's Committee on the Arts and the Humanities, 1999), iv. The Champions report is a compilation of studies conducted by seven teams of researchers referred to as the "Champions of Change." This report was an initiative developed in cooperation with the Arts Education Partnership (http://aep-arts.org) and the President's Committee on the Arts and the Humanities (http://www.pcah.gov) and was funded by the GE Fund and the John D. and Catherine T. MacArthur Foundation.

9. For more information on Catterall's studies, see James S. Catterall, *Involvement in the Arts and Success in Secondary School,* Americans for the Arts Monograph Series, no. 9 (Washington, D.C.: Americans for the Arts, 1998); and Jaye T. Darby and James S. Catterall, "The Fourth R: The Arts and Learning," *Teachers College Record* (1995). National Education Longitudinal Survey data is managed by the National Center for Education Statistics at the office of Education Research and Improvement, United States Department of Education. The 1988 data comes from a panel study that followed twenty-five thousand students in American secondary schools for ten years. It addresses development for children and adolescents over the period between eighth and twelfth grade.

10. James S. Catterall, Richard Chapleau, and John Iwanaga, "Involvement in the Arts and Human Development: General Involvement and Intensive Involvement in Music and Theater Arts," *The Imagination Project* (Los Angeles: UCLA Graduate School of Education and Information Studies, University of California at Los Angeles, September 1999), 7–8. This study was one of the seven studies included in the Champions report.

11. See http://www.shirleybriceheath.com/.

12. Quotations are from *Champions of Change.*

13. Henry, "Study: Arts Education Has Academic Effect." This article summarized the findings of the Champions report regarding the benefits of particular art forms.

Chapter 12: Celebration of Renewal

1. For information on a street dance group that celebrates, see http://www.dancinginthestreets.org.

2. All quotes from David Day are from a phone conversation with J. Nathan Corbitt, Phoenixville, Pennsylvania, 20 September 2002.

3. For an interesting antiwar discussion of the Middle East and celebration in war, see http://www.antiwar.com/hacohen/h092101.htm.

4. All quotes from Tommy Kyllonyn are from an interview with the authors, tape recording, Tampa, 21 June 2002.

5. All quotes from Tom Sullivan are from an interview with the authors, tape recording, South Holland, Ill., 14 April 2002.

6. http://www.pastoralexcellence.org.

7. All quotes from Eric Elnes are from an interview with the authors, tape recording, Scottsdale, Ariz., 25 March 2002.

8. For an understanding of the effects and processes of culture in worship, read J. Nathan Corbitt, "Music as Priest," in *The Sound of the Harvest*, 49–80.

9. Manuel Ortiz, *One New People: Models for Developing a Multiethnic Church* (Downers Grove, Ill.: InterVarsity, 1996), 88.

10. Ibid., 130.

11. Ibid., 135–38.

12. de Gruchy, *Christianity, Art and Transformation*, 253.

13. For a study of this, see Corbitt, *The Sound of the Harvest*, 25–48.

J. Nathan Corbitt is professor of cross-cultural studies at the Campolo School for Social Change, Eastern University, and is cofounder and president of BuildaBridge International, a nonprofit arts education organization serving the poor around the world. He is the author of *The Sound of the Harvest: Music's Mission in Church and Culture, The Global Awareness Profile,* and numerous articles on music, the arts, and cross-cultural issues.

Vivian Nix-Early is dean of the Campolo School for Social Change, Eastern University, and is cofounder and chief operations officer for BuildaBridge International. A clinical psychologist and published author, she is director of youth activities and the church school superintendent for Star of Hope Baptist Church, Philadelphia.